I Visited Heaven, But Lived In Hell

A Wounded Warrior, A Failed Life, The War Rages On

7/2/13

TO JANICE

Good Luck & Good Bless

Nelson

Nelson Peregoy

908 601 3770

Red Willow Publishing
www.redwillowpublishing.com

Authors note: I have made this autobiographical novel as accurate as possible to keep the storyline parallel to the way I remember it. All the names have been changed and no reference should be made or implied to any actual person or place.

Dedication

I dedicate this book to the men and soldiers who have, are now, and will in the future serve in harm's way to keep our great country free. The traumas of war produce psychological injuries. No soldier wants to be branded with being a psych case, so in many cases the illness goes untreated.

The incidence of alcohol and drug abuse, multiple marriages, incitation, domestic violence and suicide are many times higher for these veterans than is normal in our society.

Please visit my website and learn more.
www.sendasoldierabook.com

Thank you, good luck, and God bless,
Nelson

Acknowledgements

These are the people who helped me write this book. Importantly, each of them met me after the book was being formulated, and each has told me they choose to know me as I am now, not as the book describes my wretched life.

Marilys and Paul Colby, Cheryl Durbin, Nancy Pitcher, Virginia Coates, Dennis Sallomi, Bill Dawson, Bob Misak, who edited an earlier copy, and of course Muriel Brown my best friend and life partner. She tested my truths, corrected grammar, and helped formulate the flow. Most importantly though, Muriel encouraged me when I didn't want to go on. I can't count the hours we spent crying together as the acid poured out of me, trying to get this story on paper.

My most sincere thank you to each of you and please know this book would never have been published had it not been for your help.

Table of Contents

Chapter 1
Death Calls In Vietnam

It was raining straight down like a cow pissin' on a flat rock. I had no way of knowing if it was my night to die.

It was monsoon season and the rain was relentless.

"You're cleared for takeoff, Quiet Three. Go, Super Spook and protect us, y'all hear."

"Roger that, Phu Bai tower. Quiet Three's on the roll."

Pushing the throttles forward to full power, I felt the aircraft shudder, doing its takeoff dance like a wild animal straining against a harness. Then, releasing the brakes, the thrust plastered us back against the Martin Baker ejection seats as the giant propellers cut into the air and hurled us down the runway. My takeoff roll number three hundred and seven was underway.

"Quiet Three, Phu Bai tower. Contact north area departure on channel three, now."

I engaged the mike button on my control stick again and responded, "Quiet Three going to channel three. If we're lucky, we'll see you in a few, tower."

When the airspeed reached 140 knots, I eased the control stick back and after using 4,000 feet, I carefully finessed the aircraft off the runway. The Mohawk was a short takeoff and landing aircraft or STOL. When it was low on fuel and not very heavy, it would jump off the runway in less than 1,000 feet, climb 6,000 feet a minute straight up and land on a 600-foot strip. Load it with 3,000 pounds of jet fuel and it became a slug. Once off the runway, I had to quickly get the landing gear up to reduce the drag and then do a slow climb to altitude. I raised the flaps and pulled the power back a little to climb power. Eighteen-year-old Spec 4 Jerry Thompson, my infrared photography systems operator, commonly called a tech, was sitting in the cockpit beside me.

The OV1 Mohawk surveillance system was an ultra-high resolution infrared photographic system that was capable of looking through the jungle cover. The monitor in the cockpit showed a map of terrain directly below the aircraft. This helped us identify enemy troops, trucks, sampans, and storage areas even though they were covered by jungle growth. The one big-time disadvantage of this system was that its optimum efficiency was 50 feet above the ground. This, of course, was not conducive to pilot longevity.

"Systems coming on, L-T," Jerry said. Jerry sat a short six inches to my right.

"Shit, I hate that. If the system didn't work, we could abort this mission stay home and drink whiskey, Jerry."

Even though I had just been promoted to First Lieutenant three days earlier, I had already picked up the nickname, L-T, short for lieutenant. The Army graced me by promoting me three ranks after my three hundredth mission.

It was 2:33 in the morning, June 6, 1966. It would take 11 minutes to cross the DMZ into the North. The clouds were always so close to the ground our heads were in them when we walked.

"L-T, the rain may let up a little when we cross the Z."

"I goddamn hope so."

Jerry came back on the intercom and said, "By the way, L-T, any word on your rotation home?"

I pushed my mike button and said, "I've decided not to go home, Jerry. I'm gonna apply for citizenship. Think I'll just get me a little patch of jungle heaven and start a monkey farm when the war's over."

"That's too funny, LT. This is a nice place to visit, but I don't think I'd want to live here. Seriously, whatever happened to the hundred missions and you're out deal?"

I smirked and said, "Jerry, forever it's been 100 and you go home, right? Well, somewhere around the 170 mark

I got notified, just like we all did, that all the pilots in the unit are frozen in assignment. No available replacements, the orders said. I think the Gods are pissed at Mohawk jockeys. Doesn't matter, it's a nice warm feeling to realize you're needed. Know what I mean?" I laughed.

"How many you got, anyway?"

"Tonight is three zero seven and climbing. A few more and I can get fries with it." We both had a big laugh.

In a moment Jerry came on again. "Shit, sir, that sucks."

"Jerry, the official word now seems to be silence. I think everybody in the Department of the Army at the Pentagon is somewhere in a bathroom stall jacking off."

It didn't make any difference how many—after a hundred or so we were all numb with fear and the fear was all consuming. After long enough, it permeated every cell in the body. It was total. While we were in combat, we lived in a drug-like fog, moving like an endless wheel trying to find a way through a maze or hanging onto a fraying rope and watching it unravel.

Every 24 hours was like the 24 hours preceding it. Get out of bed at 2:00 in the afternoon, breakfast next, spend the next hour performing a preflight of the aircraft, flight briefing at 10:00 p.m., break for dinner then back to meticulous flight planning until launch time, usually around 2:00 a.m. If you were lucky enough to get back on the ground then it was flight debrief and head for the Johnnie Walker scotch. Drink until you passed out and then get up the next afternoon and do it all again.

I never had much use for alcohol. In fact I only drank it a few times and never anything stronger than beer or champagne. Unfortunately, that changed when I flew my first low-level night combat mission over North Vietnam. It must have been 5:00 a.m. when I finished debriefing and left the flight line; the sky was starting to lighten and the rain was still coming down in sheets. I crossed the mud street to my hooch, soaking wet and so cold and tired I couldn't stop trembling. When I opened the door to my hooch I heard, "Welcome, my man, how does it feel not being a virgin anymore?"

My hooch mate, Jimmy Bill Hale, a tall lanky Mississippi redneck, was soaking up his umpteenth shot of scotch. Breakfast, he called it. Jimmy Bill drank at least a quart of scotch every day, including before and after his mission. He always said, "I don't drink at all on takeoff or landing, I'm afraid I'll spill it."

I said, "Hey, man, how about I borrow some of that goon juice—just enough to calm my nerves, you know."

"See! You see!" he yelled, slapping his palm on his thigh. "I told you you'd come to love old Johnny. Get after it, boy."

He passed me a half full quart bottle of Johnny Walker Red. As I took the bottle I looked up and said, "Father, forgive me."

I took a long swig and said, "Shuee. Shit, Jimmy Bill that stuff burns like fire, all the way down to my fucking toes, man. Damn."

"Yeah, well, just trust old Jimmy Bill, you'll learn to love that pain. Just think of it as liquid sunshine. You remember what the sun is, don't you?"

"I don't know, man, that's some vile shit."

"Yeah? Well you can hate the taste, but you'll love the feelin'."

I turned up the bottle again. I couldn't get enough, fast enough. I don't remember the rest, but when I woke up the next morning two things had happened. First thing I knew about immediately; I had a headache bad enough to kill a large mule and a sick feeling in my gut accompanied by hot and cold sweats, like a female ape in high menopause.

The second thing that had happened I didn't find out about for several years—I was set out to be an instant alcoholic. From that moment on and for many years, I drank to pass out. It was a nightly escape—a guaranteed way to stop the demons from coming and a blessed release from the fear. Alcohol provided a protection from reality. I know the scotch numbed me to the insanity around me.

The insanity was everywhere. The United States government and its entire population—as well as the U.S. and foreign press—were all made insane by this unwanted war. The Vietnamese people and the U.S. soldiers who fought in Vietnam were also totally insane.

When it all started in the early '60s, it was a wonderful feeling to think we were liberating a population dominated and suppressed by Communism. That quickly changed. Those of us who were in Vietnam felt alone and abandoned. We were sent to Vietnam to do an honorable job, but the world branded us dishonorable for doing it. American soldiers felt lower than dung.

The U.S. government actually didn't know how to get loose from the problem. For over 10 years, the governments sacrificed over 54,000 lives to the false altar of South Vietnam.

Meanwhile, we were fed a generous daily dose of hate in the press; not just from the U.S. press, but our allies, too. They said our entire country hated the baby-killing soldiers who were serving in Vietnam. Hell, we knew firsthand the Vietnamese people hated us; all they wanted was to be left alone to eat their rice. The truth was that 99% of the Vietnamese population was illiterate; they didn't know or care who we were, or who ruled their country for that matter. How many times had I heard, "Go home, GI." It was the only English phrase most of them knew.

The only people who were happy that we were there were the smattering of the South Vietnamese hierarchy and the elite who were reaping great power and riches from the U.S. involvement. And, of course, the barmen and whores loved us for the green dollars we brought.

During my 19 months in the 116th Arial Surveillance Airplane Company we lost 13 of 31 pilots. Each time a pilot went down, of course, an observer went in with him. I learned in flight school there was a condition known as the

Invincible Syndrome. I believed that many pilots were lost in Vietnam as a result of this. When a combat pilot flew against anti-aircraft fire of any kind for an extended period without getting hit, he felt invincible. So he'd take greater and greater risks until he was finally shot down.

In Vietnam, it was not a matter of whether or not we would die, it was simply a matter of which night. Like I said—I had no way of knowing if this night was my night.

"Damn, LT, this is some shit weather. The friggin' gooks ought to be home making babies stead of blowin' SAMs at us poor bastards. After all, we're only here to win the hearts and minds of these people—right?"

"Yeah, well, you just keep your head in that scope between your legs. The clouds are so heavy I can't see shit out the front."

The OV1 Mohawk was a butt-ugly twin turbine aircraft that looked like a praying mantis and had three vertical stabilizers on its tail. The standing joke was that it took a strong pilot to handle three pieces of tail at one time. There were two ejection seats side-by-side in the cockpit; we never expected them to function properly. The Mohawk carried a two-man crew; the pilot sat in the left seat and the tech in the right one. There was a center console that held the throttles, flaps, gear, and the emergency release of the extra fuel tanks under the wings.

The Mohawk flew thousands of low-level night missions in North and South Vietnam. It was flown in support of fighter and bomber aircraft. Mohawk pilots were the dumb-ass numb-nuts who went in low, identified the target, and reported its exact location to the bombers. All of the missions of the 116th were low-level night missions and all were over North Vietnam. We mainly concentrated on the Ho Chi Minh Trail, the main supply route from China and North Vietnam.

There was no way to identify either the aircraft or the crew. There were no markings on the aircraft or our flight suits. There were no numbers on the aircraft's black boxes.

We even flew with no dog tags and no guns. Basically, we were not there.

Exactly 11 minutes after takeoff we crossed the DMZ into the North. Jerry said, "Feet wet." That meant we were over water.

"Okey dokey, my man," I said. "Let's get on the deck and out of these damn clouds."

"L-T, we gonna hug the beach until we get to our initial point, right?"

"Yeah, I plan to stay on the deck until we're due east of our target area then up and over the pass and down the valley quick. Shoot the picture, then up and out again. If we're lucky, they won't know we're coming until we been there."

"Yeah, well good luck on that, L-T."

"Jerry, you just find the target when I put us over the river. I want a perfect picture of that dock."

Flying at 280 knots, 50 feet above the jungle in the mountains in the dark, produced an instant pucker factor.

"Jerry, my ass is so tight you couldn't drive a greased flax seed up it with a sledge hammer."

I said a short prayer, pushed the stick forward and felt the aircraft accelerate as we descended out of the clouds. My radio altimeter was at 35 feet.

Jerry said, "Damn, sir, I sure hope the friggin weather is better up there where we're going."

I could see the spray from the white caps below us. As I approached the beach I turned north and delicately nursed the aircraft up to 50 feet so we were skimming the bottom of the clouds.

At the 10:00 p.m. target briefing we were told our target was a North Vietnamese Army convoy loading supplies from sampans along the Ue River. It was 90 kilometers southwest of Hanoi.

I said to Jerry, "My plan is to go north up the coast then turn west just before reaching the small hamlet of Thanh Hoa. That puts us 20 klicks northwest to the Lue Pass, right?"

"Okay, L-T, we going to stay on the deck all the way?"

"You bet we are. That keeps us below the SAMS. When we get to the pass we'll climb to 4,000 feet to cross through it."

Okay, L-T. Remember that pass is narrow as hell and there are 8,000 footers for 75 klicks either side of the pass."

The mountain range ran north and south and the only cut through it was the Lue Pass.

"Right. We'll stay tight on course and altitude. We damn sure don't want to bump into any granite clouds up there. Once through the pass, we'll immediately drop down to the valley floor and when we cross the river turn south two klicks to our target."

Although it had lightened a little where we were, we had been briefed that the entire target area was socked in with clouds that stretched all the way to the ground in the mountains.

The headphones in our helmets became very quiet while we both pondered where we were and what the hell we were doing there.

The silence lasted until I heard Jerry say, "Okay, L-T, we're just about to Than Hoa. Think we should pick up heading two-eight-zero for 14 minutes then climb like hell to get over the pass?"

"Roger that, coming left to two eight zero now," I said as I punched the stop clock on the dash and set it for 14 minutes. When it started flashing I knew we should be at the pass. As we left the coast behind, the clouds seemed to have a few light spots in them but the weather was still crappy. I held my altitude at 50 feet.

I heard my controller transmitting, "Quiet Three, this is High Flyer, we have you on radar. You are released from North Control at this time."

"Roger that, High Flyer. Thank you for your assistance." I knew that High Flyer was a command and control aircraft probably at 35,000 feet. Those aircraft flew out of Thailand and stayed on station circling for 12 or more hours at a time. There was always one over the South China Sea directing all the traffic below.

"Three's turning west for Lue Pass."

"Hey, good buddy, we got bad boy flight of two F4s for your cap cover tonight. They're over you now at angles fifteen. Say hello, Bad Boy One."

"Bad Boy One, here. What you say? Quiet Three, we gonna do some damage tonight or what?" This son of a bitch sounded as excited as if he had a new girlfriend. These guys got off on destroying things.

"You betcha, Bad Boy. Just bring along that big stick and we'll find you something to hit with it."

"Three, you want to be real careful after you cross the pass, the gooks got rail mounted one-zero-fives around there."

"Roger that, Bad Boy," I answered.

The North Vietnamese Army dug caves back into the mountain sides and put down railroad tracks to move their big guns in and out of the caves. No matter how much they were bombed, they simply took bulldozers, pushed the caves open, laid down a few new tracks and they were open for business again. When a one-zero-five tracer round was coming at you at night, it looked like a basketball that was burning bright orange. Not a pretty sight.

The North Vietnamese used proximity fuses on the rounds that exploded when they got within five feet of a target. When the shell exploded it spewed thousands of pieces of shrapnel in a large arc. We usually flew too low for surface-to-air missiles and we were mostly too quick for ground fire from Charlie's rifles. Whether they were shooting up or they were on the mountains shooting down, these track-mounted one-zero-fives were the biggest threat to the Mohawks.

"Quiet Three, this is High Flyer. We've got another flight of F4s just ten to the south and a third flight 40 klicks out. They're over Laos at this time. We're going to hold them all for your words. Headquarters wants this target real real bad."

"Roger that, High Flyer. It Goddamn sounds like they want it bad; hell, there's enough air cover to start World War Three"

"Three, this is Bad Boy. Say your ETA to the pass."

"We have the pass in sight, we're climbing to cross it now. Should be on the other side in two." The stop clock startled me as it began squawking; the 14 minutes were up.

"Roger that, Three. Bad Boy is going to make a look-see run down the other side now. We're coming out of the clouds"

The flight of F4s flew fast dead-ending right over my cockpit as it went down the back side of the pass.

"You know, Bad Boy, we really don't mind if Charlie don't want to come out and play tonight."

"Roger that, Three."

We heard a new guy check in. "Hey you guys, Thunder Flight here. Please don't start the party without us. We're peddling fast as we can to get there—four minutes max."

"High Flyer here. Is everybody blacked out down there?"

I transmitted, "Three is lights out and starting down the back side of the pass now. We should be over the river in zero-three minutes. We'll be making our run north to south and on the deck."

"Bad Boy, flight roger that we're blacked out and we're in the clouds at angles ten.

"Thunder Flight is blacked out and descending through 7,000 now. We're in the clouds, too."

As my aircraft descended on the back side of the pass, we were popping in and out of the clouds at 600 feet above the ground. I had to descend to 20 feet above the jungle since the target was 30 feet below the canopy. I was descending at a sharp angle and building all the airspeed I could. I reached over and pushed the throttles to full power; the engines screamed. The airspeed indicator was on 320 knots and climbing. The rate of decent showed

3,700 feet per minute as I continued to descend to the valley floor then turned south and followed the river looking for the loading docks that were our targets.

On the intercom I said to Jerry, "We'll be at 20 feet; we'll take our shots, pull up, and get the hell out of there ricky-tick quick.

Jerry came on the intercom and said, "Man, I hate this part, L-T."

I keyed my mike. "Just be cool, son. We'll be out of there in 30 seconds."

"God, I hope so L-T, I'm nervous as a whore in church."

There in the valley the bottoms of the clouds were ragged at about 1,100 feet. It had finally stopped raining.

"Okay, LT. We're on course, two klicks to the target. Cameras on. Klick-and-a-half now. One klick now, LT"

"Okay, High Flyer, we'll be dead on the motherfuck-er."

I transmitted, but before I could finish I saw the first tracer rounds crisscrossing in front of the aircraft. Two guns on either side of our flight path. They were way off target but coming closer. I was actually almost flying into them. It was so black, there was no way they could see us. They were just throwing the one-zero-fives down through the clouds; they'd heard the aircraft overhead. My instinct was to pull off, abort and try to get the hell out, but we were so close I persisted in the target run. Maybe I could get it.

Suddenly I saw a new row of tracers. I realized there were shells coming down on us from our right front. Then I heard Bad Boy leader screaming through the headset in my helmet.

"Break right—break right! Quiet Three, they're shooting them down at you from the side of the mountain. You better get out of there. We're rolling in hot to suppress. Oh shit, man, flares! Flares!"

None of us expected the flares. Charlie almost never

used them because they lit up the world and made them sitting ducks, too. In an instant, the burning orange basketballs were walking right up to my airplane. I realized that I would never get the target that night. I pulled off to the right just meters from the target.

I heard Thunder Leader and Bad Boy both screaming in my helmet. I heard Jerry say, "Let's break it off, LT." I heard High Flyer screaming, "Abort, abort!"

The world was glowing under the clouds and the radios were going crazy. Seeing Thunder Flight leader's bombs exploding a few thousand yards to our right front, I knew that was my escape route. The basketballs were close now and I was pulling back on the control stick climbing and turning hard right. I felt the G forces pulling me down into the ejection seat. Climbing, climbing to get into the clouds. We could beat these bastards. We were still very fast from the dive and at this airspeed we could make a maximum climb. God, just give me 20 seconds, I'll be in the clouds. Once we got into the clouds where we couldn't be seen, we'd be safe. But it was not to be.

"Get out of there, Three! Climb, climb, climb!" I think it was Thunder Flight leader screaming in my headset. There was chaos on the radios. Everybody was screaming at once.

Then Bad Boy leader said, "We gonna blow their little fucking heads off for you Three, over."

"What the—" Suddenly there was a blinding flash on the right front of the cockpit, then an unbelievably loud, booming explosion and the aircraft shook violently. The round exploded close, real close, like right at the aircraft and it tore hell out of us. The canopy was blown away and the air was rushing through the cockpit. It was like standing up in the slipstream at 300 knots. There was blood everywhere and Jerry had slumped over in his shoulder harness. I instinctively pulled the control stick full back and extended the maximum rate climb. I remember the aircraft was just 100 feet above the valley floor and I was climbing at almost 100 feet a second.

I felt a burning in my right shoulder. I died. Suddenly everything slowed.

It was all slow motion, I could see Jerry covered in blood and I thought he was dead, too. But Jerry couldn't be dead, he was still bleeding. Dead men don't bleed. I felt a weight in my lap. I looked down; Jerry's right arm and his hand were lying in my lap. His watch was still on his wrist. The shrapnel had completely severed Jerry's right arm at his shoulder.

In slow motion still, I was floating out of the cockpit. No, there I was. I was still in the cockpit, and I was still flying the airplane. Everything suddenly became totally silent. I didn't hear the radios any more. I didn't hear the engines or the wind. I watched from outside as I lifted Jerry's arm. It was heavy and bloody. I threw it at his feet on the floor of the cockpit. I could see that the airplane was climbing really fast; it was going almost straight up. Airspeed was 290 knots. As I watched myself and Jerry in the cockpit, I realized I was moving farther from the aircraft! I was scared. Where was the airplane? I had lost sight of the airplane.

I was cold — very cold — shivering. Everything was silent, and I was falling. It was freezing cold and dark and I was falling head over heels in a big tunnel. I had no control. I was falling farther and farther into this giant tunnel. Everything was slowing down again — almost stopping. I realized I was in a blizzard of raging wind.

I saw a pinpoint of light far away. I squinted to be sure it was real. I was moving toward the light. I wanted to be there, but it was all so slow and so cold and so far away. My shoulder was bleeding where the shrapnel hit me. I was getting closer to the light. The sleeve on my flight suit was soaked with blood from my shoulder.

Suddenly Jerry was talking to me. "It'll be all right, L-T."

I couldn't see Jerry. Where was he? I tried to answer him but no words came out. I wanted to say, "Jerry we're going to get out of this but I couldn't make the words come. I was scared. Was I dead?

As I got closer to the light I started to feel warmer air. It had been a long journey, but I was going into a lighted, warm, wonderful place. Rays of light were shining through the misty warm air. It was beautiful. I was safe there, I was standing and looking for Jerry. I couldn't see him anywhere.

This place was the end of my journey. It was a place of peace, of grace, of total well-being. I was resting. And I was very tired.

I stayed there for what seemed like forever. I lived there. It was my place. I was happy and I had total peace of mind and body. I missed Jerry. I wished I could find him. I wondered if he was all right.

My peace and the silence were suddenly broken by a woman's soft voice. I didn't want to hear what she was saying to me. The voice was kind and caring. Then I heard her say again, "Nelson, you must go back now. You must return to where Jerry is. He needs you very much."

She continued, "You must return. We are not ready for you here, yet. You have much to do before you come here. Please go back now."

"No." I resisted. "I'll stay here. I don't want to go back. I'm safe. I've come all this way and it took so long. I've been here a long time and this is my place now. This is my home."

I resisted for a very long time. I was afraid and shaking all over. I didn't want to go back into that tunnel and be that cold again. But no matter how much I didn't want to, I found myself returning to the tunnel. It was exactly like before. Slow motion, almost no movement. I was falling uncontrollably and it was freezing cold again. I was crying. "Oh, God, please help me." The wind was raging and the noise was unbearable. I was there forever and ever. Would it never end? I was so very afraid.

As suddenly as I had left, I found myself back. Back

in my ejection seat in the cockpit, still holding the control stick full back and climbing fast. I was instantly hyper-alert. I could see Jerry still slumped over, held in the seat by his seat belt and shoulder harness. He was still alive because he was still bleeding. His blood loss had been slowed by his shoulder harness pressing against the bloody stump of a shoulder. The more Jerry slumped forward in his seat the more restricted his bleeding was.

The radios were crazy again. I could hear the other pilots screaming in my headset, and I could see the flaming orange basketballs still coming from one gun above me. I could see the air caps bombs exploding on the jungle floor below. The Napalm was strafing the jungle and everything in it. Burn the bastards. The F4s were throwing everything they had at the big guns. I could see the cloud cover above and I was still climbing at full throttle. If I could just get into those clouds. My mind was racing; I was holding a hundred thoughts in my mind at the same time. It was like 20 movie reels on fast forward all playing at the same time.

I looked at my rate of climb indicator; it was still pegged at 6,000 feet a minute. My airspeed was still 290 knots. My God, how could this be? It seemed like I had been gone forever. I slowly mouthed the words, "What the fuck." Christ, my radio altimeter showed I'd climbed only 40 feet. It had to be a mistake.

Although it seemed like a lifetime, I couldn't have been out but a millisecond. This was all some supernatural shit. Was it actually happening?

Everything was racing at warp speed; we were finally into the clouds. Our altitude was almost a 1,000 feet. It had only been 11 seconds since I had been hit.

I made it to the clouds, but that looked like pretty much the end of it. Moments later the momentum started to run out. The airplane was getting sloppy and unre-sponsive. I had lost all power on the right engine. The big four-bladed propeller was wind-milling, adding resistance instead of thrust.

I could see where the shrapnel had taken chunks out of the blades. I felt the tip of the prop come off and the engine shuttered violently. The engine fire warning light was flashing. The prop tip hit the tail of the airplane and the controls jerked. I was losing airspeed rapidly. Instinctively I reached up and feathered the right prop, then shut off the fuel to the right engine. I pulled the fire extinguisher handle. Thank God the fire light went out.

The plane didn't want to fly on one engine. My airspeed was now down to 140 knots. The external wing tip fuel tanks were still full; each had 200 gallons of jet fuel in it, each gallon weighing 6 pounds, 2 ounces.

Again, training drove instinct as I reached over and pulled the release handle to jettison them and get rid of that weight. The tanks released immediately and they fell away from the wings. As they did I had more control. Hell, I was 2,500 pounds lighter. Even with that help I knew it was too late. Too low. Too slow. Too little power. The aircraft stalled and started to fall. It started spinning right into the dead engine. Altitude was falling fast.

"Quiet Three." I heard Bad Boy Leader screaming. "We've lost you. Did you climb into the clouds? Where are you, boy?"

Then High Flyer. "Quiet Three, this is High Flyer. If you hear me, come up on guard channel."

Shit, I was going to have to eject and at best become a prisoner of war; it was that or crash into the jungle and burn in the crash. There was still a 150 gallons of fuel in the main tank. What about an explosion? What about Jerry? I was in big trouble. This was my night to die.

I'd been taught in training, about instinctive reactions when faced with fight or flight. No matter how much training, though, I had no idea it would be like this. At this point, neither fight nor flight was an option.

When the aircraft came spinning out of the clouds the spin was almost flat. The chaos in my headphones was incredible; I couldn't tell who was transmitting. I had to force myself to keep my thinking rational. I had to regain perspective.

I had to get the aircraft back under control. I'd trained for hours in flight school to recover from spins. I had to build airspeed to pull it out. I pushed the stick forward and pointed the nose of the aircraft straight down. The airspeed built rapidly. The jungle was coming up fast. I thought about ejecting Jerry, but I knew that if I sent him out unconscious, the G forces would crush his spine. If he wasn't already dead, then death would be immediate.

Everybody was still transmitting on top of each other. I transmitted on emergency guard channel. "May Day! May Day! May Day! We're shot up bad. I'm out of control. I'm spinning in."

Bad Boy transmitted to High Flyer. His response came quick and clear. "Bad Boy has a visual on Quiet Three. He's out of the clouds and spinning through 800 feet."

Suddenly Thunder Flight leader was transmitting again. "Thunder Flight has a kill on one gun. Colonel Sanders would be proud of us. We cooked the motherfuckers extra crispy. Over."

With unbelievable calm I heard High Flyer say, "Everybody shut the fuck up down there. All aircraft in my control switch to guard channel and speak only when spoken to. Now. Quiet Three, will you assess your damage and situation for me, please."

I hadn't had time to comprehend what High Flyer said when I heard him say again quickly, "Talk to me Quiet Three. I can't help you if you don't talk to me."

I said, "Okay, High Flyer, let's chat. I don't have anything better to do right now, you moron."

High Flyer replied, "Okay, let's stay cool here. You're gonna get out of this, Quiet Three."

Sure, this son of a bitch could afford to be cool. He was flying in a big comfortable aircraft high above any guns. He was sitting in a leather chair looking at a scope. He and his crew even had a pilot to chauffeur them.

"High Flyer, this is Thunder Flight. We are strafing with the last of our Napalm, then we gotta get along home."

"High Flyer transmitted back. "Roger that, Thunder Leader. You guys saved the day, oops, I mean night. You're released back to your carrier."

I was gaining control of my aircraft again. I had the spin almost stopped and was slowing the dive. I wanted to talk to Thunder Flight. "This is Quiet Three, Thunder Leader, sure wanna thank you guys for holding the Indians back, we'd be toast without you."

I had broken the spin and recovered the aircraft only a few feet before I would have hit the jungle.

I continued on the radio. "High Flyer, I 'bout got this beast harnessed up. I think it may fly a little. I came so close to the jungle I scraped my ass."

"Roger that, Quiet Three. Just have some pretty thoughts and slow your head down. Think about those nurses in the field hospital back at home plate."

"Yeah that's a nice picture, High Flyer. I gotta get this son of a bitch back to home plate first."

"Three, they tell me them nursie girls love combat pilots, how is that round eye pussy anyway. Is it good stuff?"

This guy talking to me from High Flyer was a true professional. He had been trained in school to calm pilots who were in trouble. His pussy talk had worked. Just a tiny distraction helped ease me.

High Flyer was back on. "Quiet Three, talk to me, Son. What are your intentions?"

"Three here. I've got number two out and I've lost hydraulics, I've barely got the aircraft under control, repeat, barely under control. I'm going south down the valley staying on the deck. Around the mountains and out to the sea. I don't have enough power to climb. I'm just able to hold altitude at this time. Over."

"Status me on your tech, Three," High Flyer said.

"My tech is severely wounded and unconscious; he's lost a lot of blood. I'm not sure he's still alive."

"Roger that, Three. Just take baby steps and we'll get you home." High Flyer continued, "We have the cavalry coming. Nuck Flight is headed to you now and we have the Jolly Green rescue helicopters in position. They're holding five klicks off the beach and spread from south of Hanoi clear to Da Nang."

"Thanks, High Flyer," I said. "I'm hope I don't need them."

High Flyer came on with a warning. "This is High Flyer transmitting on guard. Advisory. Advisory. All aircraft over North Vietnam be advised, we have an emergency working — repeat emergency working, south end of Vector Mountain. All aircraft should avoid this area if possible."

I heard Nuck flight checking in. "Hello, hello, High Flyer. This is Nuck Flight leader, our location is classified." He paused and said, "No, I didn't mean that High Flyer, I'm just screwing with you. We're a flight of four hanging out here, nine southwest of Vector Mountain. We're descending through six grand at this time."

"Roger that, Nuck. High Flyer has you on radar. Hold at 2,000, please. You are 16 klicks west of your rendezvous point. Say hello to Quiet Three."

"Good morning, Quiet Three, Nuck Flight here. You can send the Air Force home now that the real fighters are here."

I transmitted. "Glad to have you here, Nuck Flight. I'm going to stay below the clouds close to the deck. This piece of shit I'm riding isn't in perfect condition at the moment."

Bad Boy Leader came on the radio. "We hate to give it to the Navy pukes, but we've done the heavy lifting, and we're outta go-juice. Good luck and God bless."

Things started to calm down and I realized there was at least some chance of getting the aircraft home. I just hoped that Jerry could hold on. His harness was acting as a tourniquet and it had pretty well stopped the bleeding. Either that or he was dead.

I heard High Flyer say, "Quiet Three, we have two extra Jolly Green rescue choppers at the beach waiting for you."

"If I get to the beach. I still can't eject my right seater. I plan to go for broke and take him home."

I was holding close to the tree tops because I knew that was the safest place I could be. I figured it was about 20 minutes to the sea and another 10 or so to the Demilitarized Zone. My airfield was only 7 kilometers south from there, and it was right on the beach.

"Quiet Three, this is High Flyer. Say your fuel stats, please."

"I've dropped my pod tanks and I've got one 30 in main at this time. I'll be on fumes but there's enough since I'm only drinking on one engine."

"Nuck Flight is rolling in south of Vector Mountain. We're going to let the gooks have a few tons of Napalm for their marshmallows. If we can keep the little buggers busy enough they'll stay out of your hair, Three."

"Quiet Three is approaching now. I see your barn fire. I'm just south."

"Nuck Flight has you in sight, Three. Your flight path is a good one. We'll spread a little cheer along from here to the beach and put a little light in your life. We have plenty Napalm, we'll make it daylight."

I was only a few miles from the beach now and I could see that the clouds had lifted over the water. Nice night for a full moon.

I heard High Flyer again now. "Quiet Three, we've notified North Flight Control of your situation and we told them we'll maintain contact with you until landing. The emergency vehicles are in place at Phu Bai airfield and you're cleared to land straight in."

Nuck Flight did exactly what Leader said they would do, they made it daylight along my flight path. I never saw bigger Napalm blasts than these guys were laying down. I could almost feel the heat as I flew just south of their line.

When I left the jungle and reached the beach I turned due south and transmitted again. "High Flyer, I'm pushing my nose right down on the sand, that'll let the ground effect help me keep flying."

I nudged the plane down to where the props were almost touching the sand. I felt the little bit of extra lift kick in and it lightened the controls. I had to start planning an approach and landing. I'd be at home plate in 12 minutes.

"Thank you for your help, Nuck Flight," I said. "You and your boys can come to my weenie roast any time. We're almost home now and all I have to do is dodge these damn fishing nets the gooks are drying on poles." The moon was so bright I had no trouble seeing them.

"We still have a few firecrackers left if you want some more light. Then you can see them nets better."

"No thanks, Nuck. I have a handle on it now. Thanks, anyway. Over."

"Okay, Three, Nuck flight is pulling out. We're going home. Good luck to you Three, you're a hell of a flyer, even if you are Army. Over and out of here."

I knew that the emergency backup system, a tank holding 500 pounds of high pressure air, would have to be used to blow my landing gear down at the very last minute. The drag on the airplane would be too great to continue flying if I lowered my landing gear too soon. As I approached the runway, I also knew I'd have to land at a much higher airspeed since I couldn't extend my hydrauli-cally-activated landing flaps. I'd been pumping most of my remaining fuel overboard trying to get as light as possible. More importantly, to minimize the danger of a fire if some-thing went wrong on landing. The aircraft was handling a bit better as it got lighter and with the ground effect work-ing for me, I felt pretty sure that I could land the thing. I didn't know what shape the landing would leave us in, but at least I could get it on the ground.

High Flyer came on and it was the first time I'd heard stress in his voice.

"Quiet Three, be advised we got a problem. Phu Bai tower has notified us that the airfield is shut down. They're under a rocket attack at this time. We show you crossing the Z now. You're nine miles from the runway. Your next alternate airfield is at Da Nang. State your intentions, repeat, state your intentions, please."

"High Flyer, we've dumped out fuel. We're running on fumes. We don't have any choices. My intentions are to put this son of a bitch on the Phu Bai runway, rockets or no rockets."

"Roger that, Quiet Three. Then continue your stroll to your house."

The clouds had rolled in again and I was flying through some light rain. I could see the sky lit up over the airfield. Anytime there was a rocket attack, it was standard operating procedure to put up lots of flares to light up the entire area. That made Charlie afraid he would be seen and most of the time it would stop him from slinging rockets.

"Quiet Three, High Flyer shows you two miles from touchdown, Check gear down. Over."

"I'm holding the gear, got enough drag for now."

I could see the runway straight in front of me and what looked like an armada of emergency vehicles. There were fire trucks, crash trucks, and emergency medical vehicles. They were scattered all the way down the runway. These guys were ignoring the rocket attack and had come out in force to scrape me up when I got there.

As I crossed the perimeter of the airfield I heard, "This is Phu Bai tower on guard. We have you in sight, Quiet Three and you're cleared to land. The crash trucks are standing by. Last check for gear down. Over."

I looked over at Jerry and said, "We're going to get you to the ship, boy. You just hang in." I knew he couldn't hear me. I was pretty sure he was dead. I was just yards from the end of the runway and not more than ten feet off the ground. I ran through the landing procedures that I would use. I was reaching for the emergency gear blow down handle when I sent my last transmission. "Quiet Three is blowing gear down."

I felt the landing gear come down and lock in place. I was over the end of the runway. I pulled the throttle back to cut off power to my good engine. I reached up to the overhead panel, cut the switches off and then pulled the fire extinguisher handle, just in case. My airspeed had fallen to 80 knots and the aircraft dropped like a simonized brick. It slammed onto the runway hard. This was an arrival much more than it was a landing, but at least I was down.

I quickly turned off all the electrical switches, then reached between my legs and turned my ejection seat switch off. I reached over my head and turned the second ejection seat override safety switch off. There were no brakes since they were hydraulic also. The airplane slowed and finally stopped almost to the far end of the runway. We were being surrounded by crash trucks and someone had a ladder up to the cockpit by my seat.

I knew these emergency crews were expert at pulling pilots out of cockpits and they proved it to me. As they helped me out I saw the medics working on Jerry.

"Is he still alive?" I asked.

I didn't get an answer and I remembered my earlier trip through the tunnel. The last thing I remembered was asking God to please let him live. As my feet touched the steel panel runway, I ran completely out of adrenalin and passed out cold. I learned later that when I landed the airplane only had three gallons of jet fuel left in the tank.

I came to in an operating room several hours later. I didn't know it until then, but I had shrapnel wound in my shoulder. The doc was putting a suture in it when he said, "You're one lucky dude, Dude. This is little more than a scratch, but this one suture will get you to the hospital in Hawaii and then home."

"I don't want to go to Hawaii. I want to go back to my unit. How's my tech? Where the hell am I?"

"You're on the Hope, and your tech is hanging in there, thanks to you. Right now he still owes you his life."

I kn,ew that the Hope was a giant hospital ship that cruised just off the coast of South Vietnam. It was staffed with military doctors and nurses and was capable of not only triage, but full medical treatment. The injured were flown by evacuation helicopters and treated as required. Then after being stabilized, they were picked up again and transported by helicopter to Saigon or Da Nang where they were put on an Air Force evacuation aircraft and flown to Tripler Air Force Base in Hawaii.

I got up from the operating table and reached over for the shirt of my flight suit; it was lying in a pile on the floor. As I picked it up I realized it was full of bloody stains and the sleeve had been cut away.

"Think you can find me a shirt?" I asked the medic who was in the room.

"I want to catch the next chopper back if that's okay, Doc?"

"What are you, fucking nuts? The regulations state clearly that any injury suffered in combat is grounds to evacuate out to Tippler," he said.

"I want to go home in the worst way, Doc, but not like this. My tour has got to be over soon and, if I make it, I'll go home with my head up and not from some sham injury."

"Fine, catch the next flight back, you dummy."

"Can I see my tech?"

Just then the medic came back with a blue Navy work shirt. He handed it to me and said, "Come on, I'll show you where his operating room is; it's just down the passageway."

"Right, I'll follow you. Thanks a bunch, Doc. I'll recommend you to all my friends."

"Just be safe, okay?"

The medic led me down the corridor for what seemed like a mile. Finally, he said, "Here, sir. You can look in the window, but I'm afraid you can't go in. Hell, he won't know the difference, sir. He's in bad shape, but the doctor says he thinks he's going to make it."

I could see several people working over Jerry. I said to myself, "God, make him better."

My thoughts went back to Rucker and flight school.

"Gentlemen," Colonel Tony Blevins said, "There are ten of you now; two of you will quit or be washed out of this training before the class ends. That leaves eight. Three of you eight will die in the airplane within a year. Learn to fly this airplane well, pay strict attention to your instructors. Every one of them has flown the aircraft in combat. Memorize every nut, bolt, and system on the Mohawk. Try to tame this flying machine with proficiency and knowledge. Good luck and God bless. I'm not at all sure that all of Vietnam is worth a tiny part of the price we are paying for it."

Now I knew exactly what Tony Blevins meant and I knew he was entirely correct.

I went out the flight deck door to a bright, sunshiny morning. I found a chopper on the helo pad. It was to be an hour before the next flight returned to the mainland. I went to the mess and had a cup of badly needed coffee. I really wanted a drink of whiskey, but I knew there wouldn't be any on the ship. No booze allowed onboard.

The flight back to Phu Bai seemed long, although it was only 45 minutes. The chopper set down and dropped me off in front of my company operations shack. The ops officer was surprised to see me come back; everyone thought I was headed home to the States.

When I entered my hooch, Jimmy Bill was pouring a glass of scotch. It was 10:00 in the morning and I knew it wasn't his first one of the day.

"Hey, pal, you're just in time for cocktails," he calmly said. "The rescue medics told us you were only scratched. I'm sure glad you came back. I bet 20 bucks you weren't gonna go home."

"Gee, I'm sure glad you're so happy to have me back, Jimmy Bill."

Jimmy Bill held out the scotch bottle. "Here, have a drink. Have a bunch of drinks; you'll feel better."

I did as instructed and soon I had enough in me to pass out, or go to sleep or whatever. That night I flew again.

When I went for my flight briefing at 10:00 that night, I saw some pictures of my airplane; there were 240 shrapnel holes in it, and the right prop had a foot-long piece missing from one of the blades. That piece was actually lodged in the tail. One of the briefing officers told me I probably shouldn't go out to see it. He said he thought it would be a real downer.

Several days later I received a promotion to captain. The citation read, "For heroism in the face of the enemy."

Along with the promotion were orders to go for a six-day rest and relaxation in Australia. When Jimmy Bill found out I was going, he borrowed one of the typewriters in the ops shack and, using my orders as a model, he wrote himself one just like it. All he had to do was change the name and a couple of numbers and he was all set. I had shown him how to do it earlier, just the way John Mills had taught me.

We caught a hop to Saigon, boarded an Air Force transport and were soon in Sydney. We headed out for our hotel. We washed up and put on civilian clothes. As we headed for the bar, Jimmy Bill said, "Pal, you have any idea how much I want some round-eye pussy. I'm so tired of fucking gooks, I'd almost rather jack off. Well, not really, but I need a refresher here for sure."

"Jimmy Bill, you know I just got married."

"Yeah, well, when you're 10,000 miles from home in a combat zone, you get a pass. Just read the small print on the bottom, that's all you gotta do."

"Yeah, and what does the small print say?"

"It says, 'Approved for unlimited pleasures of the flesh, but don't tell.'"

We had a big laugh.

Thus far I had made it without sex. I had sworn that I wouldn't screw around on Samantha. Oh, I had played with the gooks and like every GI who ever went to South East Asia, I got a few hand jobs after a massage at the local steam and creams. But in some irrational way, I decided that was all right.

There were a couple or six good-looking females in the bar of the hotel. The place was a meat house. Not only was it full of women, but each one was better looking than the other.

The Aussie women were all free-spirited, outgoing and happy. They loved American GIs. They'd tell you in a hurry that Australian men were "dickheads who had the staying power of a rabbit."

Late that night the combination of too much scotch, too many willing woman, too long away from Samantha and raging hormones allowed me to justify my decision. Jimmy Bill and I ended up back at our hotel room with three queens. Or, because my eyeballs were well lubricated by the scotch, they looked like queens. The party went on until almost dawn.

The next day Jimmy Bill and I were drinking lunch in the bar again when he said, "You know, there's something definitely different about the Aussie chicks."

"Yeah, what's that?"

"I can't put my finger on it, but they are for sure different than American girls."

I laughed and said, "Jimmy Bill, I think we should continue a scientific study of these women until we discover this difference you're talking about."

"That, pal, is the wisest thing you've said in some time."

We topped off our tanks with scotch all afternoon and without stopping for dinner, we diligently set out to locate that night's participants to further our study.

By the end of the week, Jimmy Bill and I had had or shared a good number of Aussie women. We talked about writing some new orders to extend our stay in Sydney another week. But when we examined that possibility thoroughly we both agreed it was very possible that continued indulgences in the study of Australian women could possibly be hazardous to our health. We could end up too weak to return to combat. Particularly with respect to the enormous quantities of scotch that had to be consumed during the facilitation of said study. Our experiment finally ended and we dispatched to the airport for our ride back to hell.

On the way back we were both so numb and fatigued that there was little talk. But Jimmy Bill did say, "Pal, I think I have reached a conclusion."

"Tell me," I said.

"Aussie women are just different, that's all there is to it."

"Brilliant. Fucking brilliant, Jimmy Bill."

Jimmy Bill and I arrived back at Phu Bai at 9:00 at night and went for a flight briefing at 10:00. The flights continued to drag on each night—taking off, going into a hot target area and waiting for Charlie to throw his shells at me. Just waiting to get blown out of the sky.

The night of my 329th mission I found a message in my info box. I would receive my alert orders in 48 hours and be going home in 7 days. What joy washed over me. Could it be I would get out of this hell alive? I started to turn and a clerk handed me a second message. Jerry was dead; he died at Tripler having never regained consciousness. I screamed and the tears ran down my face. Fuck! Fuck this whole fucking mess. Goddamn it all. I threw my helmet across the operations office and walked out. As I left the room I said to the ops officer, "I'm not going to fly tonight; just fuck it all. I screamed again. "Every son-of-a-bitch gook in this shithole country isn't worth Jerry. I went directly to my hooch and got piss ass drunk while I cried. I finally passed out.

The next night I was back in the cockpit. On the take-off roll in the dark rain I again thought, Could it be I'll get through this? Was I really going home alive? I did, but I was taking two incredibly damaging conditions with me.

The Post Traumatic Stress Disorder and the alcoholism would rot the rest of my life and all for nothing.

Chapter 2
The Start Of It All

I was sound asleep on my father's lap when he died. He flinched then farted and I smelled a terrible odor of poop. A big black car came and took him away; I never saw him again. Although I was only 7 at the time—he was 76—my memories are as strong as if it happened yesterday.

His name was James Bernard and for 57 years he worked 12 hours a day, 6 days a week. He never missed one day of work in his life and he only took off two holidays each year—Christmas and Thanksgiving. When he finally came out of the mine each night, his whole body was black with coal dust except for the whites of his eyes and his teeth. After work he walked the eight long blocks from the mine elevator to our house. My mother always had two buckets of hot water waiting for him on the back porch and she helped him scrub the coal from his body. Then he would put on his clean clothes and go into the house.

Every night the routine was the same. He went directly to his big chair in the front room, sat down, reached over, and turned on the console radio to listen to the Amos and Andy Show. My mother brought him his fruit jar full of white whiskey; he drank a pint every night of his life. Later my mother brought him his supper which he'd eat sitting in his chair. After supper he laid his head back and went to sleep. I never saw my father in bed. I believe he slept in that chair every night.

It was there that I experienced my first taste of alcohol. Many nights after my father ate, I climbed on his lap and listened while he told me stories of his adventures on the high seas. Sometimes he put his index finger into his whiskey and rubbed it on my lips. It tasted horrible.

"I don't like that, Daddy. That stuff tastes bad." I'd say, wrinkling my nose.

His reply was always the same. "Yes, it is bad, son, and it's bad for you, too. You promise me you will never drink whiskey."

"Yes, Daddy. I don't like it and I promise you I will never drink it."

When JB, as my father was known, was just ten years old, he and his older brother left their home in the Basque territory in the Pyrenees Mountains of Spain. He never returned. They made their way to the North Atlantic and signed on to work on a tramp freighter. They lived and worked on the same ship for 10 years. Since they had no papers, the captain treated them like captives. The captain knew they might run away, so they were watched closely when they were in port, loading and unloading the cargo.

Finally, when the ship docked in New York City my father, uncle and several other seamen were able to escape. It was 1888. JB's freedom lasted only a few hours until the New York police arrested them all for vagrancy. After several days in jail, a man from the Virginia Carolina Coal Company came and offered to pay bail for anyone who would come and work for him. Although my father couldn't speak English or even read or write, he somehow understood the offer and accepted. His brother refused and my father never saw him again. He never knew what happened to him.

At 20 years old, JB went to the Shenandoah Valley in Western Virginia to become a coal miner. It was there that he fathered me some 50 years later when he was 70, after being widowed four times. JB married a woman from the same community who was 40 years his junior. My mother, Alyffe Spencer, never went to school, and like my daddy, she couldn't read or write. When my father died, my mother was pregnant with another child. My sister was stillborn several months later.

The mining company paid for JB's funeral and that cost was added to the already large debt our family owed the company. My mother had no alternative but to go to work in the mine. I wanted to go to work to help her, but I was only seven.

Alyffe was not the first woman to work down the shaft, but there were very few. It was considered bad luck to be in a mine shaft with a woman and until she proved herself, work conditions for her were tough. Many times the men would leave her at the elevator and make her wait and ride by herself. They would harass her by asking her for sex and frequently she had to do the hardest jobs. My grandmother came to live with us and my mother started working the night shift so she could have more time with me. My grandmother was a non-person to me; she was cold and distant and she almost never spoke a word, especially not to me.

Many summer mornings I got up really early and raced to the mine elevator so I could be there when Mama came up. I carried her lunch bucket and held her hand while we walked home. I remember the feeling of pride I had, thinking I was taking care of her.

My life was as normal as it could be in that place during those times. My friends and I played, swam in the river, hiked the woods, and rode in the snow on homemade sleds. Everything we needed we bought at the company store. The store, which stood in the center of town, was a large, two-story building complete with a big covered porch on all four sides.

Our groceries, clothes, and every other item we needed to live came from that building. When I was nine I got my first job. It was at the company store. Every day after school I had to sweep off the porches; they were always dusty since there were no paved streets. My pay was three dollars a week. Every Saturday I received one dollar and the other two went to pay off our bill. I was filled with pride when I took that dollar and gave it to Mama. Each time she would give me 25 cents back to go to the store and buy anything I wanted. I always bought the same thing—an RC Cola and a Moon Pie. With the nickel that was left over I bought two pieces of hard candy and three pieces of bubble gum.

Our school was a ten-year system; classes were in a two-room building. One room was for children in grades one through six and the other was for the high school students. I didn't like school at all; I thought it was boring and a total waste of my time. The only thing worse than going to school was going to church.

Church, just like school, was not an option but a requirement. It was a Baptist church and the preacher was a big, fat man who blew spittle when he got worked up preaching his sermons. He looked like he was at least 100 years old. On Sunday he stood in the pulpit and I felt like he was burning a hole right into my very soul with his laser-like stare. He shook his fist, pointed his finger, and screamed that we were all sinners and we were all going to hell. I was raised to believe God was coming for us all and sooner than we thought. I was equally as sure that the preacher was going to hell for his sins, mine were nothing compared to his.

One day when I was finishing the sweeping at the store, my boss came out and gave me a package wrapped in brown paper. He instructed me to take it down to the church and give it to the preacher. When I entered the church. the preacher was sitting on the front pew talking to the man who was the director of the choir. He was another big, fat man. The preacher got up and told me to bring the package to his office.

So the preacher, the choir director and I went into his office; he took the package from me and closed the door. He then took me by the hand, pulled me to him, and started to hug me. I had strange feelings; it was the first time I had ever been hugged by a man. I wanted to pull away, but I was afraid to resist. I actually feared this man—after all, he was the preacher. I had been raised in his church. The choir director watched quietly while the preacher told me I had to stand naked before God to receive his blessing. He unbuttoned my pants and pulled them down. He then lifted me up, sat me on his desk, bent over and put his mouth on my penis. I was 12 years old and that day I received God's blessing both from the preacher and then from the choir director. They made me swear to never tell a soul about them blessing me and if I did I would go to hell for sure.

When I left the church I felt sick, ashamed, and dirty. I wanted to wash myself, so I went to the river and jumped into the water with my jeans on. I cried and stayed there until it was almost dark. When I got home my mother was still home. I wanted to tell her the truth, but I just said I had been swimming.

That was not the last time I received God's blessing in that church office. The blessing was periodically administered by one or both men for a couple of years. As time went on I seemed to become numb to what was happening; then sometimes I felt very guilty, particularly if I had an orgasm. Eventually they both lost interest in me. On Sunday I often overheard the preacher instructing the younger boys to stop by his office.

When I was fifteen I left my sweeping job and went to work at the Esso Gas Station next door to the store. One day a green sedan with U.S. Army written on the door pulled up. A tall, black sergeant got out of the car; his uniform decorated with badges and ribbons and yellow stripes. He was a recruiter and he spent an hour talking with me. He told me all about Army life and how much he liked it. This man was to change my entire life.

He explained that if I wanted to join the Army I had to work very hard in school, make the best grades I possibly could, and as soon as I graduated I should go to the recruiting station in Richmond. He wrote my name in his interview book and gave me his card. I stood for a long time and watched that green car as it drove out of sight. I was excited about what I had learned and could hardly wait to get home to tell my mother.

My mother was off work so we sat in the front room and I told her all about my opportunity to enlist in the Army after graduation. I think she was more excited than me. For years she had told me she would never allow me to work in the mine. She said we were blessed that God had provided me a way out of the coal mine. My grandmother thought it was a good idea, but she said she hoped I didn't get hurt. My mother always put a positive spin on everything. She told me she would be very proud to have her son become a soldier. She said I'd look handsome in a uniform. The challenge, though, was school. I gave my mother the soldier's card and asked her to keep it for me so I wouldn't lose it.

Although I had always made excellent grades, I had never really tried very hard to learn anything. Now it was different. I attacked my classes with a new energy. When my teacher asked about the obvious change, I announced that I was going to go into the Army as soon as I graduated. I became an honor student and at my graduation I was the top student in my class of 31. For my graduation present my mother gave me $40 to take with me to the Army. She also had wrapped the soldier's card she was keeping and gave it to me. She hugged me and said, "I love you, Nelson." Oh, those words were so very important to me.

Just two days after graduation—I was seventeen years old with a tenth grade education—I left for Richmond on the Greyhound bus. The trip took most of the morning since the bus stopped many times along the way. That was the farthest I had ever traveled from my home. Before dark that same day I was well on my way to becoming a soldier.

The Army recruiting station in Richmond was only a block from the bus station. The second floor of the building had large open sleeping areas with open bays and open showers. It took a good bit of courage for me to strip naked the next morning to start my physical exam. There must have been 50 of us going through our physicals at the same time. The physical, which included about a million shots, took all day.

That night we stood before the American Flag, put our right hands on our hearts, and swore to protect and defend the Constitution of the United States of America against all enemies both foreign and domestic. The third day we were administered several tests to determine our aptitudes, psychological profiles, and who knows what else. The last little nicety was burr haircuts that took each barber all of three minutes per head. There was much laughter and jousting as piles of hair fell to the floor.

Day four started at 3:00 a.m. when the 41 of us who passed our physicals were loaded onto an Army bus headed to Fort Polk, Louisiana and basic training.

After arrived at Fort Polk on a Saturday afternoon we were assigned to our barracks. We were off Sunday, and we all just sat around talking and learning about each other. There was a chapel service at noon and reluctant though I was, I agreed to attend with a fellow from New York.

When we entered the chapel I was greeted by a number of very happy people. There were several officers and sergeants as well as privates. I was stunned when the chaplain preached about God's love and grace. He said God wanted us to be happy and successful and to prosper. I had never in my life heard anything like that in church.

We were all excited when Monday rolled around because that was the day we all got our job assignments based on those tests we had taken. I thought I had done well and hoped for something more than being a rifleman in the infantry. We were marched to a personnel building and I waited in line for a couple hours to get my results.

When I entered the master sergeant's office he looked up from his desk and said, "Sit down, Nelson, I have some good news for you and I have some shitty news for you, too. First, the good news. You tested out with a genius IQ; your IQ score is 161. Anything over about a 140, maybe 145, is considered genius. Why hell, mine is a whopping 117. You'll be able do anything in the Army you want to.

Your future success is assured with a score like that."

Then he said, "The shitty news is you don't have an authorization release signed by your parents to enter the Army at 17. You can't join the service at 17 without a parent's signature. So, my good man, you are about to be a civilian again. You'll be discharged under honorable conditions. You get out now, but remember, you have not fulfilled your two-year obligation. So when you're 18 you can reenlist; if you don't, you'll probably be drafted."

I was so stunned that I found it hard to speak. "Sir, can I go home and get an authorization and come back?" I asked. "My father is dead, but my mother will sign."

"No, it doesn't work like that," he said.

"Do I have any other choices? I've planned to be a soldier for a long time now. I had hoped to be able to get some more education and make the Army a career."

"Sorry, bud. You're shipping out tomorrow and you'll be back in Richmond in a couple days and home by Friday."

I couldn't believe it, but that's exactly how it happened. I returned to Richmond and then went back home. When I showed up at the front door with my Army uniform on, it was almost dark and my mother was just getting ready to go to the mine. She was so upset that she didn't go to work that night.

We sat up in the front room. I sat in Daddy's chair and we talked until very late about what I was going to do. My grandmother seemed glad that I was home because she didn't want me to get hurt in the service. Granny said she was glad, but I wondered if she really was. She was so cold to me it was like I didn't exist. I had for years felt sure she didn't love me at all. That thought saddened me. I told my mother I thought I should go to the mine office the next morning and get a job. I never saw my mother so mad as when I said that.

"I'm only going to tell you this one more time," she said. "You're my son and you will do what I say; you will never go to work in a coal mine."

The only way I could calm her down was to promise over and over I wouldn't go to work there.

The Army had given me $250 mustering-out pay when I left Fort Polk and I still had it all, except for $4 that I'd spent to buy food on the way home. I also had the $40 that my mother had given me when I left home only one week earlier to go to the Army. Later that night we decided that I'd go to Richmond and try to get a job there.

The next morning, which was Saturday, I went to visit Janice, a girl I had dated in high school. Janice's father had a good job working on the railroad. Since railroad jobs were the best paying jobs in the county, they lived in big lovely home. I always thought her family was rich. Janice's mother was always nice to me, but her father didn't like me a bit. Once Janice told me that her father thought that I was mine trash and he didn't want her to see me. Her mother overruled him and told Janice to invite me over any time she wanted.

That Sunday morning, like every Sunday morning, everyone in town went to church. That day I reaffirmed that I liked the nice, loving God I met in the Army chapel much more than the angry God our fat preacher threatened us with. After church I told Janice and Mama about my experience at the Army chapel. Mama shrugged and didn't say much. I realized she had no way of understanding what I was talking about; the only preaching she had ever heard had been hellfire and damnation. I felt sad for that.

While we were at church that morning, one of the mine bosses saw me and asked why I was home so soon. I told him I was too young to go into the Army and I had to wait for a year to go back. That afternoon he came to our house to speak with us about me going to work in the mine. His visit was cut very short when Mama found out what he was there for. In just a quick minute, in no uncertain terms, Mama let him know that I would never go to work there. He said he understood and picked up his hat and left.

Monday morning bright and early I caught the bus to Richmond to search for a job. After hitchhiking and riding the bus back and forth to Richmond for almost two weeks, I landed a great job with the Virginia Electric and Power Company at the James River hydroelectric generating plant. My starting pay was $2.18 per hour. I would be doing shift work and on the interview I was told there was lots of overtime.

When I told Janice about my job and that the overtime pay was over $3 per hour, she was very excited. We had a big laugh when I said that soon I might be making more than her father. Janice giggled and said, "Well, you should, you're better than him."

My job started the next week. After I got my first pay check I was able to look for a place to stay in Richmond. I soon found a small but nice room in a boarding house and rented it. I worked all the overtime hours I could get. Many days I worked 12 or 18 hours, sometimes my paycheck would be over $150; that was a lot of money back then. I gave my mother some money to help with our bill at the company store and I bought little gifts for her and my grandmother. Mother loved the gifts, but she thought they were extravagant. My grandmother never said a word about them; she just frowned, and then took each one and put it in her dresser drawer.

My first job at the plant was to oil all the moving parts of the generating turbines and the water pumps that cooled them. It was no challenge at all—any monkey could have done it. The best thing about the job, other than the money, was meeting Samuel Goodman.

Samuel was a rough, tough supervisor who spent most of his time in the control room of the plant. He was my boss, but there really wasn't any bossing to do. After I finished oiling the pumps I'd go to his control room to visit with him. He became my first mentor; however some of the things Samuel taught me were questionable.

Samuel was 60 years old and he had been married six

times. One of his favorite sayings was, "I've made love to over 200 women; God knows how many children I've fathered. I think I have enough experience to say women are only good for sex, cooking, and cleaning."

He also liked to say, "You just remember this: It's a stupid son of a bitch that will turn down a piece of ass."

Samuel punctuated every sentence with a curse word. And he drank whiskey on the job. Several times I walked in and found Samuel in the locker changing room with one of the cleaning gals upside down on the benches. Once he even looked up at me and asked if I wanted to take a turn. I declined.

Samuel had been a DC-3 pilot in World War II and he told me endless stories about flying over the hump in Burma and India. His cargo contained everything from whiskey and supplies to paratroopers and whores. He told of harrowing experiences dodging a sky full of anti-aircraft flak and landing after having an engine shot out. I wouldn't have dreamed at that time that one day I would face the same kind of anti-aircraft fire.

One day Samuel told me something that neither of us knew would have such a profound effect on my life.

"Nelson, I want you to remember this. I know it's your dream to go in the military. If you do ever go in, you want to become a pilot," he said. "Pilots get the very best of everything compared to other soldiers. The living conditions and duty stations as well as rations and liberty are always the best." And in classic Samuel fashion he threw in, "If there's no pussy around, you could always fly to where it is."

Samuels's second lesson was just as important. "Remember this, too," he said numerous times. "The man who gets ahead faster and furthest is the man who is the first one to work, works the hardest, and leaves last."

When I had days off I usually caught the bus home to visit my mother and to see Janice. Our relationship had progressed to the point where we were engaging in some heavy petting and I really liked it. The truth is, she did, too.

Samuel had told me I should save my money and get myself a good used car. I figured that a car would sure make my life a lot easier. I had actually been saving most of my paycheck and after a short while I had a $1,000 saved up. I started visiting used car lots around town. I guess I was quite a hillbilly because every used car salesman I came into contact said he was offering me the best deal because I was a nice guy and he liked me.

After a few days of car shopping I met Hal who owned his own used-car lot—Hal's Like New Used Cars. He also provided financing on the spot. Hal ask me how much money I had and when I told him I had a grand, he said he just happened to have a great used Chevrolet that required exactly $1,000 as a down payment.

Hal led me to a really great looking Chevrolet. It was shiny black with chrome hubcaps and bright white wall tires. I fell in love with the car even before I sat in it. When I took it for a test drive, I knew that car was for me. When we returned Hal wrote up a contract. I would only have to pay the down payment and $65 a week for eight months. He explained he was doing me a special favor by letting me make my payments right at the lot every week. The contract seemed high, but I wanted that car. I did tell Hal the $3,000 price tag seemed a little high.

Hal just smiled, put his hand on my shoulder and said, "Look, young man; I have a son about your age and I just hope if he was buying a car from someone they would give him a deal this good." Deal done. I drove the car away.

The next day I left work at 7:00 a.m. and then I had the next three days off. I headed straight home. When I drove up to the house, Mama could hardly believe her son had an automobile. She made me take her for a ride right then. My grandmother didn't want to go. She said she was afraid of cars. I thought about it later and I suspected neither of them had ever been in a car before. Anyway, Mama just loved it and when I drove her past the company store she made me stop. She said she needed something, but I knew she just wanted to let everyone see our new car.

There was someone who liked that Chevrolet even more than my mother did and that someone was Janice. Even her father begrudgingly said that it looked like a good car, but that Chevrolets often had a lot of trouble. That weekend Janice and I rode around and used up over a tank full of gas.

Monday afternoon when I returned to work I proudly took Samuel out to the parking lot to look at my new car. He liked it and after examining it closely he congratulated me on selecting a good one.

Then he asked me, "Nelson, did you christen this baby yet?"

"I damn sure did, Samuel, right there in that back seat."

"Good man. How was it, pretty good?"

"No, to tell you the truth it wasn't good, it was fantastic," I responded, winking.

I was lying through my teeth, of course.

"How much did you have to pay for this baby?" he asked.

I took the contract out of the glove box, proudly handed it to him and said, "Samuel, the price is a little high, but I think it's a really good car."

Samuel frowned and said in a loud voice. "My jumping damn! You could've bought the whole damn car lot for this much money. This thing didn't cost three grand when it was new. How about you meet me here tomorrow morning and we'll go see this shyster."

"Okay, but what do you think we can do?"

"Nelson, I'm not sure, but you can bet your ass we'll do something."

I worked my shift and that night when I drove over to my room I was so nervous about the next morning I didn't sleep very much at all.

I pulled into the parking lot the next morning and Samuel was already there and he had a guy with him. The fellow was black and he looked like a cross between a tank and a bulldog. He must have been 6 feet 6 inches tall and weighed 300 pounds. His arms were bigger than my head.

"Hey, Nelson," Samuel said as I got out of the car. "This is a good friend of mine. His name is Louis Mines, but we call him Bigun."

"Hello, Louis."

"Just call me Bigun."

"Let's get going," Samuel said.

We all climbed into the Chevrolet and I headed to "Hal's Like New Used Cars." The closer we got to Hal's, the more anxious I became.

"What are you thinking about doing, Samuel?" I asked.

"Relax, relax, we're just gonna reason with this guy."

When we arrived Hal was standing in the doorway to his little office building, which was little more than a shed. Right above the door was a big sign I didn't remember seeing before "Buy Here. Pay Here, By The Week."

By the time we got into the office there wasn't much room left. Hal was shorter than any of us, he just came to Bigun's belly. He had to look up at Bigun to talk to him.

"All rightee," Hal said as he flashed a big smile. "You brought me some more business, huh, Nelson?"

Samuel moved to within an inch of Hal's nose and started screaming at him. I don't know if Hal or I was more shocked.

"You good for nothing son of a bitch. You're gonna make this contract right or we're going to make you wish you did," Samuel yelled.

Bigun moved a step closer to Hal who had to look almost straight up to see his face.

"I'm an honest business man and I sold this boy the best car on the lot."

"Yeah, well you should've sold him the best car on the

lot, you charged him five times what it's worth, you scum sucker," Samuel screamed.

Hal started to get nervous and was now looking around at each of us as he backed up a couple of inches. There was no place for him to go. Hal tried one more time to get the situation under control.

"What the hell do you think I should do, just give it to him?"

"Nope, we all think you're going to tear up this contract and he's not going to pay you another dime."

"Hold on here," Hal said to Samuel. "And what's going to happen if I don't?"

Samuel again got right up into Hal's face and said, "Well, I thought you would never get around to asking that question. What's gonna happen is Bigun is going to break one or maybe both of your arms. Then we're gonna do a little body work on the rest of those cars out there on your lot, including testing the windshields for strength with that baseball bat we got in Nelson's trunk. Then I'm gonna tear up this contract for you. Now have I answered your question?"

Hal raised his eyebrows and replied, "Hell, give me that damn contract."

Samuel handed it over and Hal quickly tore it into pieces.

"Okay, now you thugs get out of here before I call the cops."

As we walked back to the car, Samuel said, "Now this is an exceptional car and the fact that you bought it for a $1,000 is an exceptional deal. Congratulations, Nelson."

I came to love that car, not just for transportation, but because it became a temple of love for Janice and me.

One Saturday night, shortly after the incident at Hal's, the inevitable happened when Janice and I went to the drive-in movie. We had been to the drive- in a number of times, but we always walked there and sat on the bleachers down front near the screen.

This time was different. We found a spot way in the back where there were no other cars. The movie was a love story of some kind, but I was so worked up that I didn't pay much attention to it. I finally got my hand under Janice's bra and for the first time in my life I felt a real live breast. It felt wonderful. Janice's nipples got very erect and very hard; they weren't the only erection in the car at that time. Finally, we got in the back seat, and I didn't have much trouble getting Janice's panties down and then off. I was smoking hot and my penis was so hard a cat couldn't have scratched it.

After some convincing, Janice was ready for us to have our first sexual encounter. I moved on top of her and between her legs, with my mouth nursing her breast like a newborn. I was supporting myself with both arms around her. After a couple of misses, Janice reached down and took hold of me to guide me in. When she took hold of me it was all over. Bam! I lost it all over her and the car seat. It seemed like it was a cup full. God, I was so horrified. I don't even remember what I said, I was so embarrassed. I do remember, though, that Janice was very nice. She said that it wasn't meant to be that night. And even though I tried again in the next hour or so, she just wanted to watch the movie. She didn't even want my hand back in her bra. She did say that we would try again sometime soon.

The next couple times I had time off to go home, Janice was having her period. After what seemed like a year of waiting she finally agreed it was time. I was like a rabid dog. I was so anxious to have her I was going nuts. When it did happen it was absolutely fantastic for both of us. Janice and I both were totally uninhibited and passionate; she made so much noise screaming I was worried we were going to get a visit from the owners of the drive-in. I decided there and then I wanted to have sex forever.

Every time I had at least a day off, I quickly headed home to see my mother and Janice. By then we were enjoying sex every time we saw each other. Several months after

I bought the car, Janice said she had something important to tell me.

"I'm pregnant; we're gonna have a baby."

Of course, I was shocked and surprised. Unfortunately the first thing I said was, "Oh, shit, your daddy is going to kill me, Janice."

That was for sure about the stupidest thing I could have said because Janice started to cry.

"You don't love me. I know you don't," she said.

"I do love you. I do. I promise."

"I'm so sick every morning; I don't know what to do," she said, sobbing.

By that time I was petrified. I didn't know if it was more that I'd made her pregnant or that her daddy was going to kill me. Whichever, I didn't have to wait for morning for my sickness, I had it right then. We sat in the car for a long time and finally started talking about it.

"What are we going to do, Nelson?"

"If your daddy doesn't kill me, then we're going to get married, I guess."

Janice looked at me and started screaming and crying even harder.

"You guess? You guess? You don't love me. I know it. You don't want to marry me."

"Of course I want to marry you. Whether you're pregnant or not, I want to marry you. Okay?"

Again stupid ass me spoke before I thought. "I just wasn't thinking we'd have to do it so soon. Did you tell anyone else?"

"No," she snapped.

"Well we're going to have to tell someone sooner or later."

The next day at the plant I worked fast. As soon as I was finished I went to the control room to talk to Samuel.

"I need to talk to you in private," I said.

I couldn't believe it when he replied. "What's the matter, you get her pregnant?"

"Yes, Samuel, Janice told me this weekend she was pregnant," I said as we walked outside. "Man, I don't know what to do; her daddy is gonna kill me."

"Nah, he ain't gonna kill you. He's just gonna be super pissed."

"What do you think I ought to do, Samuel?"

"You ought to do two things. Tell him quick she's pregnant and tell him even quicker you love her and you're gonna marry her."

We talked a while longer and when I started to leave to go back to work, Samuel said, "Hey, it ain't so bad, son. I been married six times, you know."

That didn't make me feel any better, but at least I had decided to tell Janice's folks.

By the time I had my next day off and went home, Janice had already told her mother and her mother had told her daddy. When I drove up to her house, she came out and said that they knew and her daddy wanted to talk to me, but he was at work and wouldn't be home until about 7:00. So I went home and from 2:00 until 7:00 I was just sick with fear.

At exactly 7:00 that night I knocked on Janice's front door. She opened it and led me into the dining room where the inquest was going to be held. We all sat around the dining room table. Janice's father looked at me and opened the conversation by saying, "Are you gonna marry Janice?"

"Yes, sir. I love her."

"I don't care whether you love her or not," he said. "I just want you to get married as soon as possible."

Janice and I were married by a Justice of the Peace the next week and our son Nat was born seven months later. We moved into a little apartment near Richmond and I continued to work at the plant. After the baby was born we were having a hard time paying the bills. When I talked to Samuel about it he said that he knew of an opening in the meter reading department and it paid a lot more money.

Soon I was interviewed and hired for that job. I found that I had landed a much better position than I'd even thought. I went to work at 8:00 each morning and as soon as I finished the day's route I was off until the next morning. I learned to jump fences and run from one meter to the next and as a result I finished my route right around noon on many days.

I had a lot of interesting experiences during the time I was reading meters. Once I was working in a very low income area in Richmond, in a neighborhood of two-story houses. Most of them had two apartments upstairs and two down. The electric meters were inside each apartment.

On that particular day I bounded upstairs to one of the apartments. Like always I was rushing to finish. As I reached out to knock on the door, suddenly it flew open. As it did I heard a woman say, "You better get me to the hospital quick or I'm gonna drop this kid in the middle of this flo."

There, right in front of me, stood a totally naked woman, who looked like she was 20 months pregnant. She didn't even move as I reached for the door knob to pull the door closed. I was so embarrassed.

"Oh, please excuse me. I am so sorry," I said. As I pulled on the door knob, it came off in my hand.

"I thought you was my husband, what you doing here?"

I put my hand on the edge of the door to close it, but she held it open and just stood there.

"I'm here to read your electric meter."

"Well you bedda get yo white ass outta here 'cause my husband gonna be here any minute to take me to the hospital."

"Yes, ma'am. I am so sorry."

Suddenly I heard a male voice coming from the stairs behind me.

"What you doin' here, honky? Don't you be staring at my wife bein naked like she is," the man said. "I'll kick yo

honky ass if you don't get outta here. 'Sides, I gotta get her
to the hospital fo' she has this kid right here."

I did exactly as instructed and I got the hell out of
there real quick. I don't think I hit three steps as I ran down
and out the front door. I wrote an estimated meter reading
for that house as well as the next four or five houses down
the street.

During my rounds I saw many drunken men and
woman, too, not to mention lots of partially clothed wom-
en as well as nude sunbathers. More people than I could
count—men and women—opened their doors in their
underwear and invited me in to read their meters.

Several times ladies came on to me and once so did
a man. Another day I had to get into a lady's basement to
read her meter. She led me down to the basement and as
we started back up the steps she said. "I been out of work
for almost a year and I ain't got enough money to pay a big
electric bill."

"I am sorry, Ma'am, but I can only record what the
reading is, I don't have anything to do with the billing."

"If you'll make me a low reading on that bill, I'll give
you the best lovin' you ever had."

"I'm sorry, Ma'am, but I've got a lot of meters yet to
read today and I'm kind of in a hurry."

"Look here, do you understand I'm offering you a
good screwin' if you fix that bill?"

By this time she was between me and the front door. I
just wanted to get the hell out of there. "I'm sorry I have to
finish my route and if I have time I'll come back later this
afternoon," I lied.

"Well, you just remember my offer. I mean it. You ain't
never had the kind of screwin' I can give you."

"Okay, I'll remember." I went out of the front door
as fast as I could and, thank God, I never had to read that
route again.

During this time I was trying to save money so that
I could go back into the Army. I knew the Army pay

wouldn't support my family, so having some set aside would help out. However, even though I was making what seemed like pretty good money as a meter reader, something always came along to take it. There was never even enough to last from one payday to the next.

Not only that, but my son was having a lot of ear infections. It seemed that as soon as he got over one, he had another. The doctor bills were expensive and sometimes we didn't even have the money to pay for them. We'd have to set aside some money to give the doctor each payday. There just didn't seem to be any way to get ahead.

Then one day I came home from work and Janice said she needed to talk with me and that it was real important. Some little voice in my head immediately told me I had heard this before. And sure enough, Janice announced she was pregnant. A short time later I told Janice I was going to look for a part-time job. She wasn't very happy about that, but I told her I was going to do it anyway.

Chapter 3
Part-time Jobs and Frogs

After coming to the realization that I was getting further and further behind on the bills and the doctors started dunning us for money, I decided that I was going to look for a part-time job. Something I could work evenings and nights.

I started searching the Richmond newspaper help wanted ads every day. I soon found one I thought I had a shot at getting—it was driving a delivery truck—and when I told Janice that I was going to apply for it, she started yelling.

Janice was screaming as loud as she could. The veins in her neck were dark blue and bulging from the strain.

"You'd better stay here and take care of me. I'm knocked up with your baby, you know."

"Janice, the last time I checked it takes two to get knocked up, okay? I'll stay here and take care of you, but who'll pay our goddamn bills for us?" I screamed right back.

"Well, why don't you just leave and forget about Nate and me? You don't want to be with us. Why don't you just forget about us?"

"You just shut up. I'm gonna go apply for this job. That's it. Now shut the fuck up."

When I went to fill out the application, I found that the company delivered bakery goods from 11:00 p.m. to 7:00 a.m. I excused myself after explaining I had a full-time day job and I couldn't work those hours.

When I got home and told Janice about what I had found she was happy. I thought to myself no way did she have enough sense to realize there was no other way.

It wasn't as easy as I thought it would be to find a part-time job where I could punch out around eleven or midnight, which would still allow me to get some sleep. That was just fine with Janice; she didn't want me to get the part-time job anyway. She was getting bigger every day and it seemed like each day she was also getting more irritable.

We rarely argued before, but now it seemed we spent more and more time at war. She told me she didn't like living near Richmond because it was too far from her folks. Me, I kind of liked not having to see her father very often. The only nice thing that man ever did for me was to take me out to the river and show me how to catch and clean frogs.

I remember one Saturday afternoon after Janice and I had just had a battle about I don't remember what, I went with a friend to catch a mess of frogs. I loved fried frog legs and Janice could really cook them up good. Well, we were having great luck but it started raining and we decided to quit froggin early. We each had a canvas bag with a couple dozen frogs in them. My friend had a pickup and he dropped me off in front of our apartment. I was sopping wet when I got home.

I usually cleaned my catch before I went home, but since it was raining, it seemed the thing to do was to take them home and clean them in the kitchen sink. When I walked in the door soaking wet and with a sack full of bloody frogs in my hand, Janice went nuts.

"You're messing up the whole floor," she hollered. "I have to do all the cleaning around here, you know."

I got mad and started yelling back. "The hell you do all the cleaning. The place is spotless because of my efforts, too."

We got into a real battle.

Janice yelled again, "Get out of here with those damn frogs, you shithead."

I screamed back as I took the frogs to the kitchen sink. "You can kiss my ass. I'm gonna clean the sons of bitches right here; it's raining outside."

I dumped the bag of frogs into the sink and to my surprise it was immediately apparent that a lot of my catch was still alive and still jumping.

"Oh, shit," I muttered.

About that time Janice picked up a plate and hurled it at me. I ducked and it broke on the wall into a million pieces. The world suddenly erupted. Janice was enraged. I was grabbing for bloody, jumping frogs trying to stay out of the way of her barrage of projectiles—she was throwing anything she could get her hands on.

Nate was jumping up and down. He was loving all the excitement. He thought it was a hell of a fun game. He grabbed a nice big frog and held it up to his chest saying, "Frog, Daddy. Frog."

The walls in that kitchen that had been white before, were splotched with blood and slime, as was just about everything else in the room. By the time I got my catch recaptured and back in the sack, Janice had gone into the bedroom and thrown things into a small suitcase. She cleaned up Nate, put a nice shirt on him, and stood in the hallway screaming. "I want you to take us to my mother's. Right now, damn it."

I left the whole mess where it was and said, "Get your ass to the car; I'm damn sure ready to get rid of you."

I drove Janice and Nate to her mother's. Neither of us said another word. When I returned home it took me hours to clean up the mess. It pissed me off, but I cleaned the frogs and gave them to a neighbor. When he came to the door he took the bowl full of frog legs and said, "Gosh, thanks man. It sounded earlier like Janice didn't want frogs for dinner tonight."

Janice stayed at her mother's for a couple of weeks, then one day when I came in from work she and Nate were back. She was as cold as ice to me for another two weeks or more. She hardly spoke to me and, of course, she wouldn't have anything to do with sex. One night I went home with a bouquet of flowers and a box of candy. I waited until

Nate was asleep and I presented them to her. I hugged her and whispered into her ear. "I love you and I'm so sorry honey, maybe we can screw off our mad at each other. Whaddya think?"

She put the flowers and candy down on the table, smiled at me and said, "Come with me." She took my hand and led me into the bedroom. I was thinking, man, I'm gonna like this. I was big time ready.

When we got close to the bed she turned around, put both arms around me and whispered into my ear. "You see that bed right there?"

"Sure, honey," I said as I started unbuttoning my shirt.

"Well, you get a good look at it so you can remember what it looks like because you aren't ever going to get into my bed again, even if you live to be 200 years old."

It didn't matter how nice I was to her, she wasn't giving it up. Lots of nights she wouldn't even let me come into the bedroom so I had to sleep on the sofa.

During all this I was still trying to find a part-time job. One day I found an ad for a job that I knew was the one for me: "Part-time work, six to nine daily, make full-time pay. No experience required; we train you. Good conversational skills required. Earn $50 per evening."

Sounded perfect since it was evenings and $50 was more than I was making at my full-time job. I decided to go put in an application for it. I still vividly remember the instructions in the ad: "Apply in person at 6:00 p.m., 3330 Broad Street, Richmond."

When I got off work, still sweaty and in my white T-shirt and jeans, I drove to the address in the ad. The office was in a very cute house that had been converted to business use. The landscaping was perfect. Bright green grass, flowers lined a winding walkway and there were beautiful potted flowers on the porch. A small sign in the front yard read Seagate China Company.

After parking I entered through the clear glass door. I realized I was half an hour early. Inside the large waiting room, a very pretty receptionist greeted me. She handed me a clipboard and a pencil and asked me to complete an application. I completed it and returned it to her. She said, "Mr. Johnston will see you in a few minutes. You're early, you know."

Soon four other men came in. They were all were wearing suits and ties. Each one completed his application and waited too. Soon Mr. Johnston opened his office door and invited the guy who came first after I did. It wasn't long until the office door opened again and another applicant was invited in. Two hours had passed and everyone had been seen. Although I had been the first man there, I was still sitting and waiting.

The phone rang. When the receptionist answered it, she said. "Yes, sir, I'll tell him."

She got up, came over to me and said, "Mr. Johnston will not be able to see you this evening. We'll call you to come back the next time there's an opening."

"Ma'am, I came half an hour early and I've been waiting over two hours. He saw four people who came in after I did," I said.

At that moment Mr. Johnston opened his office door and as he came out he was putting on a navy blue blazer. He was wearing a red and blue striped tie, a starched white shirt, and khaki trousers. Johnston looked to be about 35 and was the picture of preppy.

He walked directly to me. I stood up. He looked at me and said in a very not-so-nice tone, "If you don't think enough of yourself to dress for an interview before coming here, then I don't think enough of you to interview you at all."

Then he shoved a large envelope into my hand and continued, "If you can memorize every word of this sales presentation, and you can get yourself some presentable clothes, then you come back here and I'll interview you. Now good evening.

To say I was devastated, crushed, insulted, belittled,

and very hurt was an understatement. As I watched Mr. Johnston walk out the front door I had to fight back the tears that welled up in my eyes. The receptionist could see my pain. I think she was as embarrassed as I was. She kindly said, "I'm very sorry."

I went back to my car, hurled the envelope into the back seat, pulled away from the curb and headed home. After a few blocks I couldn't fight the tears any longer. I started balling. I pulled the car over to the curb and cried for a long time. I had never been so hurt in my life.

At that moment I would never have thought that Douglas Johnston would be the next mentor in my life. During the next five years he taught me more about life and how people interacted with each other than any other person I ever met. He was always brutally honest with me regardless of how much it hurt my feelings and just as quick to praise and compliment exemplary performance.

He taught me to believe in myself and in my ability to achieve any goal I set. Most of all he taught me how to make money. He had a masters in marketing and a PhD in psychology. He ran two-hour sales training classes twice a week and required his sales people to attend at least one of them.

He was one of nine children born to a sharecropper father and a blind mother. Despite his humble beginnings, Doug was able to pull himself out of that poverty. He worked summers as a traveling Bible salesman knocking on doors and put himself through college at The University of Virginia. He then went on to build a profitable sales company. Doug was a true inspiration to me; he was the best motivator, teacher, and sales trainer I ever met before or since.

I would never have made the many millions of dollars that I did if I had not learned from this master. Many times in my life, when faced with a difficult situation, I thought about Doug and asked myself what would he have done.

While driving home from that awful experience, I decided I would never tell Janice about what had happened. For several weeks that envelope stayed right where I threw it. After driving in a rain storm with my back window open it got soggy wet. Several weeks later while cleaning out my car I found it. I opened the envelope for the first time. The document was as thick as a book and every page was typewritten.

I started to read:

"Hi my name is _____. I'm with the Seagate China Company and it's my job to speak to single working girls and young married couples. I'd like to show you our hope chest items. We have beautiful china, crystal, silverware, and cookware. Just for looking at them, and giving us your opinion, you receive a beautiful free gift. I wonder if you'd have a few minutes to just look at our nice things and give us your opinion."

Johnston had said, "Learn it word for word."

Memorizing it wasn't much of a chore, I didn't know at the time, but memorizing was easy for me maybe because of what the Army called a stratospheric IQ. After reading through it twice I was able to recite every word of the presentation. I recited it every day on the drive to work and back. Wasn't long until I was smooth and comfortable with the presentation.

I still found it difficult to return to Johnston's office, but finally I got the courage. After buying a nice pair of pants, white shirt, tie, and sport jacket I returned on a day off. When I entered the door the receptionist didn't recognize me until I explained who I was. She went into Johnston's office, and in just a few minutes I was sitting in front of him. The receptionist had given him the application I filled out the last time and as he looked it over he said, "We sell china, crystal, and cookware to single working girls and young married couples. It's done by appointment and you can make $50 for every sale you make. What do you think of that?"

"I'm very interested and I really need a job to make

some additional money for my family."

"You don't look old enough to have a family."

"Yes, sir, I have a wife and a baby and my wife is pregnant with our second."

"Have you learned the presentation I gave you?"

Without another word I launched directly into the presentation; Johnston was obviously surprised and impressed. After a couple of minutes he put his hand up and interrupted me. "You've memorized the entire thing?"

"Yes, I have and I can continue if you want me to."

"No, no, that's okay. You know, I don't think I've ever interviewed any applicant before who had actually memorized it. Meet me here tomorrow afternoon at 5:30 and you can go with me on an appointment; you can see how this all works."

The next evening Mr. Johnston was ready for me when I arrived.

"We're going to go downtown to the phone exchange building where all the phone operators work," he said. "Richmond is a unique city in Virginia. Young girls from country towns all over the state come here after high school or college to live and work. There are areas where large, old two and three-story boarding houses are occupied almost entirely by them. And they work for companies like the phone company, hospitals, the electric company and many others."

As I stood there listening, he continued. "These boarding houses sometimes have up to 20 girls living in them. Most of the girls ride to and from work on the buses. The nurses and phone operators number in the hundreds, and since they work three shifts, there's always a multitude of them coming and going to and from work. These are the girls we want to sell our hope chest items to."

Mr. Johnston and I got into his big Cadillac and headed off on an adventure that would be a learning experience and a financial windfall for me. We drove downtown and went to the telephone exchange building.

"By the way, I want you to call me Doug," Johnston said as we stood in front of the building. "Now remember don't you say a word. Just watch and listen while I make us a couple of appointments for tonight."

"Yes, sir. Believe me, I'll listen and watch. I want to be good at this."

The shifts were changing so there was a steady stream of girls coming out of the building. The very first two girls who came out onto the sidewalk headed right toward us. As they started to walk by us, Doug stepped directly into their path and said, "Excuse me, I wonder if you could help us."

The girls stopped, but before they could say a word, Doug continued, "My name is Doug Johnston and this is Nelson. We're with the Seagate China Company. It's our job to speak to single working girls and young married couples. We'd like to show you our hope chest items. We have beautiful china, crystal, silverware, and cookware."

With great enthusiasm he said, "Just for looking and giving us an opinion you get a beautiful free gift. I wonder if you girls would have a few minutes to just look at our nice things and give us your opinion."

My first thought was, wow, is this gutsy or what?

"Sure," one of the girls quickly replied.

"When can we look at them?" the other girl asked. "What's the free gift?"

"There are several you can choose from. You can select a polished stainless steel pizza pan, different kinds of perfume, or several other nice items. We'll bring them over tonight and let you pick any one you like," Doug continued. "Is that okay? Say around 7:00? It will only take a few minutes to look."

The girls agreed and gave us their names and their address.

"By the way, if there are any other girls at your boarding house who would like to join you we'll give each of them a free gift, too."

I was amazed, but it was that easy. We soon had two appointments arranged for that night. "That was easy, wasn't it?" Doug asked.

"Yes, it was, and I can't wait to do it myself."

As we got back in the car Doug said, "Let's grab a bite of dinner and I'll introduce you to the other guys who work for me."

We drove to a small diner where he and his sales crew were regulars. There I met four of his salesmen and had dinner. Doug introduced me. "Do you guys believe Nelson memorized our presentation completely, as in every word of it? If you don't believe it, I'll have him recite it to you right now."

As we ate and chatted about their appointments for the night, my thoughts were racing about this opportunity, the money I could make, what I'd do with it, and on and on. The meeting broke up and everyone went his own way. The plan was to meet back at the office after our appointments.

When we arrived at the first appointment, there were two additional girls who wanted to see the hope chest items. Doug carefully sat the girls around the dining room table and placed me next to him where I could see everything. He placed his large sample case on the floor next to his chair. He then got up and turned off the ceiling light, leaving only a lamp burning on a small table. The low light made the atmosphere in the room very soft. Next, he took a beautiful deep blue, velvet cloth about a yard square and spread it on the table. This made the mood almost romantic. He proceeded to open his sample bag and took out a full place setting of fine china one piece at a time. After carefully polishing each piece as he told the story of the patterns, he set each piece in its proper place on the cloth.

It was spellbinding; he was a professional showman, saying his lines like a seasoned Broadway actor. I loved his performance. I could see myself doing the same thing. Of course, the girls were mesmerized. Finally each of the four

girls picked her favorite china pattern and Doug handed
each of them a salad plate in her favorite pattern to hold
during the rest of the presentation.

Next came the silverware, and then the cookware—
everything was polished and gleaming. Lastly, he added
three stems of crystal. He carefully took his second finger
and rimmed one of the crystal goblets, making it ring.
"Crystal sings love songs, you know," he said, smiling and
nodding his head.

Each girl followed his lead and nodded yes.

"I have one more thing to show you girls," he said.
"I'd like each of you to hold your plate in your lap and
then close your eyes. Close them tight now; no peeking."

As if they were in a trance, each did exactly as instructed. Quickly he placed two small crystal candle hold-
ers on the table and lit the candles. Next he silently moved
to turn off the lamp. This left the most beautiful table setting imaginable. He spoke very low, now.

"When I say open, I want you all to open your eyes
and just imagine how your boyfriend or husband will
feel when he sees this in front of him at a beautiful dinner
you've prepared. Okay, open your eyes now. I want you
to think about the man you fall in love with and the first
night you prepare him a lovely meal." Johnston continued.
"Just think how you and he are going to feel when you sit
him down in front of what you're seeing right now. It's
going to be a very romantic evening. Concentrate now on
how proud you'll be, and how impressed he'll be."

In just a few minutes Doug had written four orders;
each for four place setting of china, crystal, and silverware,
and each order included a beginner set of cookware. Each
girl signed her $299 contract and gave Doug a $50 down
payment. The balance was to be paid in small monthly
payments. Lastly, each girl choose her free gift. As a bonus,
each was given a small bottle of evening in Paris perfume.
They were all very excited as we left.

I was carrying the sample case as we walked back to

the Caddy, Doug was busy talking to me. "Now, Nelson, you have the opportunity of a lifetime here. You can do exactly what you have seen me do tonight. In fact, after a little practice, you may be better at it than I am."

"Doug, I know for sure I can do this and I know for darn sure I will, too. I want to be your best salesman," I said, excitedly.

Doug opened the trunk and I put the samples in. Next he reached into his pocket and took out five $10 bills, handed them to me, and said. "Here's your proof that you can make $50 dollars a night. We just made $200 so far."

I was blown away. All I could think about was $200 in one night. That was more than I ever made in a week.

"Mr. Johnston, if you'll give me this job, I know I'll be your top salesman."

As we got into the car he said, "Remember, please call me Doug, and there's one more thing that's great about this job. As soon as your customers pay off their contracts you just go back and sell them more place settings. The starter set of four place settings isn't enough; they have to buy more from you. Just remember, every sale is not as easy as tonight's was, but you can always see another prospect and make another sale."

Sure enough, our second appointment that night was a bust, but it was still a hell of a night's work.

When we returned to the office I got my sample kit issued. Doug told me since the upcoming weekend was Labor Day and we had three days off, he expected me to practice enough to be perfect in my demonstration the following Tuesday evening. Doug also loaned me a small cassette tape recorder to record myself, listen to the recording, and correct any mistakes that I heard. Since I had already memorized the presentation, all I had to do was keep rehearsing it and synchronize the entire thing while presenting the samples.

During my time working with Doug Johnston I learned many things. Perhaps the single most important thing was that when you're trying to persuade someone to do something, you have to give a very convincing performance. Rehearsing your performance over and over until you get it just right is extremely important as well.

Unfortunately, my relationship with Janice continued to deteriorate rapidly. A week before I made my first $50, Janice had left and taken Nate back to live with her mother. She was five months pregnant with our second child. Just as she had told me, I never got back in her bed. The longer she stayed away, the less I seemed to miss her. I rationalized that it was easier not to have anyone to answer to. Besides, with her gone I could turn my total attention to making money and I did just that.

Since the apartment was empty and I didn't have to work over that three-day Labor Day weekend, I had nothing to interrupt me from practicing my presentation as Doug had instructed. I sat in front of a big mirror and worked endlessly to perfect my sales pitch. By Monday night I had it as perfect as I could get it. I couldn't wait to go back to Seagate and show off.

On Tuesday afternoon I finished my meter reading route about 1:00 and went to the company shower room to clean up and change. I walked into Doug's office at 3:00. Doug and three of the other salesmen watched as I went through my presentation.

"Perfect, perfect, perfect," Doug said. "You're gonna kill 'em."

Doug had already made us two appointments for that evening. He said he wanted to see me with a real live prospect, and then I could go out on my own. That night I made the first three sales of my life and picked up a $150. After congratulating me on how well I'd done, he said, "Okay, sport, you're on your own. Go get rich."

Just after our second son Earl was born, I was presented with legal papers saying that Janice's family planned to adopt both boys. A day later the divorce papers arrived. By that time I was the top salesman in the office. The second month I set a sales record for our office. I continued to be the top salesman for the next two years. The money rolled in and the more I made, the more I forgot about Janice and my sons.

I started wearing expensive clothes. The divorce went through first and then the adoption went through. I didn't oppose either one. Without dependents I knew I could be drafted again, but that didn't bother me since what I had wanted all along was to go into the Army. Sometimes I realized I was angry and hurt and bitter about Janice, but I was busy, much too busy to dwell on my feelings. I pushed the thoughts out of my mind and went to the next appointment.

My sales performance was also making me renowned within the company. Soon I quit my full-time meter reading job. I was able to make much more selling china. I was invited to speak at sales meetings at other Seagate offices including those in other states.

The life of a superstar salesman was flattering and the attention was an ego trip. The accolades and the attention propelled me to do even more.

I decided it was time I shared my success with my mother. I hadn't seen her in six months. When I showed up on her door I was driving a big new Cadillac and I was wearing a suit that cost more than she made in a couple of months. She opened the door, stepped out on the porch and said, "I don't have but a minute I'm going to work early. I need the overtime money."

"What's wrong, Mama? I have money, can I give you some?" I asked.

Then with a cold harsh stare she said, "Nelson, I'm ashamed of you for abandoning your children and your wife. I think you've lost your mind. The devil has entered your body and money has become your god. It's made you crazy. All that money you're making has made you more. I don't want any of your money, ever."

I felt like a bucket of cold water had just been poured

down my back. I reached out to hug her and said, "Oh my God, Mama, I didn't leave Janice, she left me. Besides, her mother and father caused all this. You know her father has always hated me."

Mama stepped back out of my reach and said, "Nelson, I've prayed over this and I've talked to the preacher about it. He said the devil has entered your body, that you're sinning and you've turned away from God. He said I should tell you not to ever come round here again."

I stood motionless and watched my mother turn and walk back into the house. I would only see my mother one more time in her life. I wanted to crash in the door and tell her about the goddamn preacher and his oral blessings. I wanted to cry and tell my mother I was sorry. I wanted to go straight to Janice's house and beg her to come back to give me another chance. I wanted to never sell another piece of china. So many thoughts raced through my mind as I got into the car and drove back to my new apartment.

My apartment was on the top floor of a five-story building in Richmond. It was right on the James River and the all-glass sliding door opened onto the patio. This gave me a perfect view of the river to the south and east. The windows also afforded me a full view of the city's main airport. Byrd Airport seemed to have airplanes taking off and landing all day and night. I loved to sit and watch them in the morning while I had my wake-up cup of coffee. Sitting there thinking about where I was in life. I still had dreams of an Army career and being a pilot. I often thought about the things Samuel had told me. The problem was I was making so much money that I couldn't afford to quit my job at Seagate.

While thinking of the money I was making, I looked around. The place was drab. It needed to be decorated and I could afford it. So why not? New furniture and a few rugs, maybe even a picture or two. Not long before, I'd been to dinner at Doug's home and had seen how elegantly it was decorated. During one of those dinners I asked if they had a professional decorator. Doug's wife, Betty, told me about her friend, Penny Moss. Penny was an interior decorator and Betty had known her for a long time.

I arranged an appointment for Penny to come over and take a look at my place. The morning she came over I knew the minute I opened the door what Doug meant when he'd said, "Be careful, my man."

Penny, a woman of at least 50, bounced in the door saying, "Hi, call me Moss. Please, don't ever call me Penny. My goddamn husband calls me Penny. I hate him and I hate that name. I wonder why my mother didn't name me 'ten dollars'? Oh, what the shit, just call me Moss. Okay?"

She swooshed by me and started strolling around the apartment, talking all the time. I followed her listening to, "Oh, oh, ohhhhh, this is going to be spectacular. This corner is special. Oh shit, what an opportunity this bathroom is. Betty tells me you're single and rich!"

"Yes, that's right. About the single — I'm divorced actually. I've got a ways to go on the rich part, though."

About that time I realized I was absorbing the fact that Moss was wearing spiked heels, and a skirt that was cut about an inch below her crotch. Her blouse was stretched so tight over her full breasts that her buttons were straining to hold them in check.

After she finished the tour she walked up to me, put her hand on my arm and looked directly in my eyes. She spread a broad smile, winked, and very dramatically said, "Well, honey, don't you worry. When we finish with this place, the ladies will be climbing all over it — and you, too."

Moss placed her other hand over the middle of her breast, batted her eyes and said, "That's if I don't keep you all for myself, lover."

It was very obvious that Moss had more to offer than decorating. I hadn't had much sex since Janice left me. There were a few casual one-nighters. The only regular sex I had was a couple times a month with Doug's receptionist, but nothing hot and heavy — nothing like the kind of sex I always had with Janice. I made a quick decision and remembered something Samuel had said, "It's a stupid son of a bitch that turns down a piece of ass."

"Moss, does sex come with your decorating?" I asked with a big smile on my face.

"Only if it's sport fucking. I don't want any damn falling-in-love shit," she replied, as she began unbuttoning my pants with one hand and her blouse with the other.

The job went pretty fast. When Moss was finished decorating, my apartment looked great. We added new furniture, drapes, wallpaper and a couple of large etched glass mirrors, as well as pictures. I was in an all new environment, and it made me feel good.

Moss and I had sex more times than I could count during the next six months — at least a couple times a week. I was home most mornings if I wasn't traveling for Seagate and that provided a perfect cover for her.

One day I asked, "Moss what does your husband think you're doing on these mornings you go out?'

She giggled and said, "That bastard thinks I'm going to work out at the gym and then to work. He doesn't have a clue I'm going out to have some pleasure with indoor sports. So come here, lover, and give me some exercise and some pleasure."

I got the distinct feeling that her activities were not only for her physical pleasure, but for some kind of psychological payback because of her anger toward her husband.

My fame and my fortune continued to soar. There was a time when I made over 20 sales in a row. I became the top salesman nationally for the entire company. Life moved faster and faster. I soon began training new salespeople. Seagate sent me to several sales training courses at different schools. I learned from Doug's classes about time management, goal setting, and the psychology of selling. Several of those classes were expensive and they were also often taught by psychologists. Seagate, of course, picked up the tab for all of it as well as the national travel I was doing. During all this, Doug Johnston was a fantastic supporter. He pushed me and prodded me to higher and higher accomplishments.

Training required a lot of travel around the country. Sometimes I'd be away for a couple weeks at a time speaking and training. Traveling provided me with a lot of first-time experiences. I was the keynote speaker at my third national convention in New York. There were 700 people in the audience; the place was electric there was so much excitement. The president of the company came to the podium to introduce me. When he did he said. "I want to introduce you to Nelson, the new national sales director of Seagate China Company."

First I thought he misspoke, then I was almost too surprised to stand up. This was a fairytale. Everyone in the audience was screaming and clapping their hands and standing up. The scene was dramatic, the stage lights went out, and a spotlight came on me. The most exciting thing that ever happened to me. Rock star status was what ran through my mind. I wished Mama could have enjoyed it. I wished Janice could have been there with me. Oh well, what the hell. Screw it; just enjoy it. I knew it would be a charge to tell Samuel. Hell, he'd love it.

One of my best experiences to come out of all this was my first flight on an airplane. I was flying from Washington, DC to a regional sales meeting in Chicago. When the airplane accelerated down the runway pushing me back in my seat and the nose rotated skyward, it was so exhilarating. I just sat there, closed my eyes and let the pleasurable feeling sweep over me. It was far beyond anything I had imagined.

How could I know that someday I would be at the controls for thousands of takeoffs, some even from an aircraft carrier.

My new position with Seagate kept me flying quite regularly. I loved the travel and, of course, I got to visit lots of cities and states I would never have seen. An additional benefit of my travel and being recognized as a kind of celebrity was the endless opportunity for sex. I abided by Samuel's advice and had every girl I could. Many times when I got back home and had a couple of days off I'd visit Samuel. I didn't know which one of us got more pleasure from the telling of my exploits.

There were countless opportunities to extend my activities to my customers, but there was a hard and fast company rule against that. Dating company receptionists and secretaries was okay, but there was a total ban against dating customers. I had seen one pretty good salesman fired for it.

My salary as national sales director was over $50,000 and I made my normal commission on every order I sold. During one of my visits with Samuel he shocked me when he said, "Nelson, you ought to be whipped for not sending some of your big earnings to Janice and your mother."

"Samuel, my mother told me she never wants me to come around her again and Janice had her folks adopt my boys so she would never have to deal with me again," I said. "Hell, man, I don't know about sending money to them. I have the money, that isn't the problem. I just have a lot of anxiety about doing it."

He frowned and shook his head. "My advice is just send it."

The next day I went to the bank and bought two $1,000 cashier's checks — one for my mother and one for Janice. I also bought two $500 checks for Nate and Earl. I mailed them immediately and on the way back home I felt good for doing it. Samuel was right, as always.

There were black clouds on the horizon, though.

About now Moss and I lost our heat for each other. One morning she laughed and said, "You know I'm tired of you, lover. Let's both go find somebody new and exciting."

"Moss, it's been a hell of a lot of fun, but I feel the same way," I replied, laughing.

"Good, lover, you got plenty without me, you're so famous they must be all over you."

Although we had never talked about it, Moss knew full well I had been banging everything I could get to lay down.

It was a year before I saw Moss again. I was attending a birthday party for Betty Johnston. Moss and her husband were there, too. Moss introduced her husband. A little bitty skinny and ugly guy; I could see why she was screwing around. I thought making love to this guy must be like screwing a broom stick. In a couple of minutes Moss was standing just a foot behind him, when she gave me a big wink, rolled her tongue around her top lip, wrinkled her nose and smiled. I wasn't the only one who saw all that. I looked away and looked straight into Betty's face; she too, gave me a wink, then walked over to me and smiled. She put her palm up and waved her arm. "Oh, Nelson, I forgot that you knew Moss. She decorated your apartment didn't she?" She chuckled and walked toward another guest.

There was no question; Betty knew that Moss and I had been lovers. Later that evening people started to thin out and those who were still there were quite well lubricated. Moss came out on the patio where I was standing enjoying the view of the pool. No one else was around. "Shithead hubby's had too much to drink," she said. "He's asleep in the guest room. You wanna do something wild and crazy?"

"Oh, I don't know. What do you have in mind?"

"How about a little natural swim?"

"You know, Moss, the moment we hit the water there'd be a dozen people out here looking at us."

"Look here, lover, I been watching you all night and I'm horny as a kangaroo in heat. I wanna jump on something. Now get your ass over by the pool house and let's solve a little problem for both of us."

"Moss, I must say you have a way of explaining things so people can understand them. Let's do it."

We made pretty quick work of the act and were back in our clothes and inside the house before any one missed us. Anyone except Betty, that is. Before I knew it, Betty was standing beside me, "You two rabbits enjoying the party?" She smiled and walked away before I could answer.

The party ended and as the last of us were saying our goodbyes, Moss came over, gave me a peck on the cheek, and stuck something in my jacket pocket. She and her husband were going to stay the night since he had had so much to drink.

On the drive home I started thinking about my situation; I took my inventory. In my 20s, over $30,000 in the bank, great apartment, plenty of women, fantastic job, respected in my company and all after the beginning I had had. But I was drawn back to the other side of reality. There was a giant crater there, when I looked into it. I could see Janice, the boys and my mother. No matter how hard I tried, I couldn't reach them. Well, at least I was able to sooth the situation a little by sending the money.

Unfortunately though, sending the money would turn out to be a disaster.

In a few days I had an appointment to meet Samuel for lunch. I was headed to work after our lunch and had on the same Jacket I'd worn to Betty's party. When the waitress brought the bill, I took it and reached into my jacket for my wallet. I felt something I didn't recognize. When I pulled it out it was Moss's panties. I remembered she stuck something into my pocket at the party. Damn, I was embarrassed. I looked at the panties and started to speak. Samuel said with a huge smile. "I bet you look nice in those."

The waitress followed with. "I'm sorry. That's my color, but they're a bit small for me."

That following day my mother returned my letter unopened and marked "Return to Sender." Janice also returned hers. She put my letter into a larger envelope that required a signature to provide proof that I had received it.

When I opened it, there were the three checks torn in half
and a note that simply said, "Don't ever do this again."

We all had a big laugh. Before we left Samuel said,
"Hey, sport, all you can do is all you can do. Remember
I've told you several times all women are crazy. Don't
worry about the money thing. Now I suggest you get over
it and go do something that's fun. Get laid, fly an airplane,
go visit a foreign country, just do something."

"Damn, Samuel, I love you. The answer is right there
in front of me. Fly an airplane," I said. "I love it so much
and I can afford to take lessons, I manage my own work
schedule so I can take time off to take lessons. I'm gonna
do it."

"Nelson, that's great. You know, if you go out there
and get all your flying licenses, then you're a shoe-in to be
a pilot in the military. I've said all along that's the best life
you can find. I know it's hard to believe but being a flight
officer in the military is better by far than the fancy life
you're living now."

After a visit to several flight schools in the area I found
one I liked a lot and signed up for lessons. I loved flying.
Having the controls of an airplane in my hands was much
more fascinating than just being a passenger.

I soon discovered that no matter how good things got,
nothing lasts forever. One Sunday morning as I was getting ready to go to the airport for a flight lesson, my phone
rang. To my surprise it was the preacher from back home.
He said. "Nelson, I want you to know we miss you back
here at church, and if you ever want to repent and stop the
sinful life you're living, you can come back here. God will
take you back, you know. But I really called you to tell you
your grandmother has died. Her funeral is going to be on
Tuesday afternoon at 4:00."

My God; this couldn't be happening. Even though I
never really felt close to her, I realized I had never known
until that moment that I did love her. I was sickened by
the guilt I felt for not going to see her when I learned she

was sick, but I didn't think she was going to die. No matter what my mother said, I should have gone immediately. I wondered what kind of person I was. Maybe I was a sinner; maybe the preacher was right. I cried alone for hours. I looked down the river and at the airplanes coming and going and thought about whether or not I'd attend her funeral. That town only held bad memories for me.

I vacillated back and forth about whether I would attend right up until I drove into the mining town on Tuesday. I was feeling so many emotions I almost couldn't deal with them all. The streets were muddy from rain and the trees were bare. The whole scene was almost morbid. The temperature was balmy, but I was freezing cold. There were only a few old cars, a couple of muddy pickups and one very old logging truck at the church.

Driving a new Cadillac added greatly to my guilt. When I went inside there were only a handful of people. I recognized my mother from the back. Her hair was up in a bun the way she always wore it and it was much grayer than I remembered. She was sitting in the front row.

Directly behind Mother were Janice and my two sons. They were six and four years old. Janice's mother and father sat beside them. The rest were other people from the mine. Some I only recognized and some I knew well. Everyone looked over their shoulders to see who had come in. I walked halfway down the aisle and took a seat several rows behind them.

In a moment the organ started playing. The preacher got up from his seat, went to the pulpit, and took hold of it with his massive hands. Myself and these two fat men were the only ones in the church wearing suits. Those two men and I also had something else in common—we shared the same horrific secret. A secret that I had never told another human.

The preacher opened with the same shit I had heard all my life. "You are all sinners. And know, too, that this dead woman who lies here in front of us, was a sinner too.

He pointed down at the coffin. You must all pray and ask God to forgive her sins and allow her into heaven. For as surely as you don't, she will go to hell."

Looking straight at me he continued, "This was a woman who has had much heartache in her life, the loss of her granddaughter who God favored, and saw fit to take before she came to this sinful earth, and a grandson who sits here choosing to live in sin."

He raised his hand and his voice, pointed directly at me and shouted, "You know you are living a sinful life and you know you must repent your ways. You have abandoned your mother and you have abandoned your fine wife and these two fine little boys. They sit here fatherless today. Let us all pray that you repent and you do it right now, this minute."

He started waving his arms and shaking his fist and screamed even louder.

"Right now, for if you don't repent now, it will be too late; you will never have another chance. God will never take you back if you don't do it now. No matter how hard you try, this is God's last chance for you. Get up from your seat and crawl to this altar begging God's forgiveness"

Every head had turned toward me and every eye was burning into me. I slowly got up from my seat, turned, and walked quietly out of the church. I felt like I was an ant escaping from an elephant. It was horrible. God, how I hated that preacher. I wished I could have killed him. I wished I had told my mother about the son of a bitch the first time he abused me. I wished I could have gotten up in front of all those people and told them what a horrible bastard he was. As I got to my car I spoke aloud, "Oh, God, can I be this bad a person?"

I was really upset on the way back to my apartment. I fought back the tears. I felt like someone had ripped my heart out and stomped on it. My emotions were all over the place. I was overcome with guilt—guilt for leaving the funeral, guilt that I didn't go to the cemetery, guilt that I never went to see my grandmother when she was sick. There were two little sons I now felt I had abandoned, a mother for whom I felt both love and contempt. I knew that neither God nor any living human being on earth could love me. I would never love myself; I hated myself.

I had no way of knowing that being alone like that was a feeling I would come to know many times over in the course of my life. When I got home I laid down across the bed and started to sob. I went to sleep crying and didn't wake up until the next morning.

The next day I was beat up with a moral hangover with guilt oozing from my every pore. But I still went for an early morning flight lesson. Then it was shower, shave, dress, and go to my "acting" job to sell more china and make more money. During the next few days I forced myself not to think about my sadness and over time I made myself feel better.

My flying lessons were advancing rapidly. I soon passed my private pilot's exam, and then advanced right into working toward my commercial license.

In civilian flying, everyone started out as a student pilot; next you earned your private pilot's license, followed by commercial, multi-engine, and then instrument pilot's licenses. Instrument pilot training taught you how to fly in bad weather using only flight instruments. After earning all those licenses you could go back and get your instructor's pilot licenses. My goal was to get my instructor's licenses, just for the status it would bring, if nothing else. Very few pilots are skilled enough to successfully pass the instructor pilot's exam.

I wasn't sure I could get it all done since I was racing the draft; I just knew that if it was possible, I would do it. Each license was, of course, successively more difficult than the one before it. Having successfully conquered my private pilot phase, I found working on the commercial much more difficult; I was also doing some training toward my instructor's testing; both at the same time and while working, It was almost more than I could do. I loved the challenge and was getting lots of satisfaction from my accomplishments.

Although I was spending lots of time working on my flying, my income didn't slow down at all. Selling something to someone was a rush, but it didn't compare to the rush I felt every time I flew an airplane.

I was doing so well I was even starting to sell repeat orders to girls who had finished paying their contract. Kirsten Burnett was one of my first repeat customers. I made an appointment to sell her an add-on order. I didn't remember all my customers, but I did remember Kirsten. She was 18 when I sold her the original order and I remember thinking when that girl filled out a little and got those braces off, she was going to be a knock-out beauty.

When I arrived for my appointment I found out just how right I was. I could hardly believe how beautiful Kirsten had become. She was 20 and had filled out perfectly. Her hair was blond and fell below her shoulders. Her breasts were perfect and with her long legs, she was an absolute beauty. She knew it, too.

I was waiting in the community room of the house when Kirsten came down the steps. I stole a quick look at the place where her long legs disappeared into her short skirt. Wow, this babe was gorgeous, a real world-class kitten. Kirsten bought the add-on order that night. It was all I could do to follow the company's no-dating-customers rule and not ask her out.

I finished writing up the order, put the samples away and got up to leave. Kirsten said, "Nelson, why don't you stay and talk. I'll fix us some popcorn, if you'd like, and a Coke."

"Sure, I don't have another appointment tonight." That was a lie. Although I had never stood up an appointment, I was going to that night. The longer we talked, the more I liked her. That was the kind of gal that would make a trophy wife. She talked with some brains, too; she was no dummy. I liked the fact that her wit was almost as well developed as her body.

Kirsten wasn't shy about telling me she'd enjoyed some pretty good times with more than one guy during her three years working and living in Richmond. She also let me know she loved to drink beer. The boarding house had a curfew — no men visitors after 11:00. We had talked for three hours nonstop and I hated to have to leave. Driving home that night I couldn't get Kirsten off my mind. I thought about Samuel's rule, "Never pass up a piece of ass."

This girl hung around in my head on and off for a couple weeks until I decided I liked Samuel's rule more that Seagate's no-dating-customers rule. I figured I could date Kirsten just once and not get caught. When I called her, she was easy. We set a date for Saturday afternoon to catch a movie and then go for a burger.

That Saturday was a perfect weather day. When I picked Kirsten up she was wearing the shortest and tightest shorts I'd ever seen; those and her halter top made her look like a Playboy pin up. She was waiting on the porch when I pulled up and she bounced out to the car. When she climbed into the seat I got a cleavage shot that rolled my eyes back. This was going to be worth breaking any damn rule.

"What movie would you like to see, Kirsten? Or is there something else you'd rather do?"

She surprised me when she giggled and said, "I want to get a few beers and go to the park."

Well, that statement set my thoughts off like a volcano erupting. I saw myself sitting on my father's lap shaking my head, making a bad face and saying, "I don't like it, Daddy; I promise I will never drink it."

I sure didn't want to tell Kirsten that. Hell, she'd think I was much less of a man if I didn't drink beer.

"Okay, it's your day, we can do anything you want to," I said, hoping one of those wants included wanting to get into my pants.

I stopped at a small grocery and we went in together, I thought to buy a six-pack. We walked up to the beer box and Kirsten reached in and picked up two six-packs. "You get a couple, four should hold for awhile," she said.

As I paid for that beer I knew I was in trouble. The moment we returned to the car, Kirsten opened a can of beer and handed it to me. She then opened one for herself and said, "Didn't you tell me you had a beautiful apartment?"

"Yes, I'm very proud of it. It was professionally decorated and I think it's super."

I thought of all the times I had screwed Moss there. This was great; I was getting ready to replace Moss with a younger woman.

"Let's go there, I want to see it," she said, "Besides we gotta put this beer in a refrigerator or it'll get hot before we finish—it." Then she looked at me and grinned.

Once in the apartment it was full steam ahead. We drank beer, turned on the TV, and watched the University of Virginia football team get the shit kicked out of it by a team I don't remember. Soon we were both naked and screwing on the living room floor. It took Kirsten a lot more beer than it took me, but she was persistent and we both got shit-faced drunk. We drank and screwed until we were too drunk to do it anymore. I couldn't take her home that night; I was too drunk to walk, much less drive. It really didn't matter; she was too drunk to know where she was.

When I woke up Sunday morning my bladder hurt more than my head. I was so sick I felt green, and my mouth felt like a tribe of homeless people with camels had camped out in it for a month. I forgot for a minute that Kirsten was there until I rushed into the bathroom. She was standing in the shower drinking a can of beer.

"Want some?" she asked.

"Oh, God, no. I'm too sick to drink anymore."

"Not beer, dummy. I mean do you wanna screw some more."

I drank about a gallon of coffee while Kirsten got high again. After a while she asked, "Who won the ball game last night?"

Later that afternoon I composed myself enough to take Kirsten home. We did have goodbye sex first, though. On the way home she did something that was great for my ego; it was the first I had ever had a woman describe in detail how good I was in the sack. Maybe all my practice hadn't been for naught.

I suffered with a moral hangover for several days, remembering that I had promised my father that I would never drink. I did it. I couldn't undo it, but I did promise myself never to do it again. I decided that I wasn't going to date Kirsten again for three reasons: First I knew there was no way to date that girl without having to drink beer. Secondly, I broke the company's rule once and didn't get caught; I figured I'd better not try it again. Thirdly, Kirsten was the kind of girl that a guy like me would end up marrying and I didn't have time for that shit.

It was a couple of weeks when I got a call from Doug Johnson's secretary. She sounded a little strange when she asked me if I could come in early that afternoon and meet with Doug. When I walked into his office he stood up and without even saying hi, he fired me.

Doug very harshly said, "Nelson, you are fired. I sold a friend of Kirsten Burnett's some china last night and she told me all about your date with Kirsten. Seems Kirsten has told every girl in that house about your sexual skills and ability. You've always known the rule, no dating customers. So, you're fired."

I couldn't believe it. "Come on, Doug, I swear I only dated one girl, one time. I'll never do it again."

"Sorry, you know the rule, you broke the rule and you're fired."

"C'mon, man. I'm the company's national top producer, the national sales director."

"Doesn't matter," he said. "We're a big company and we'll survive without you. That's it."

"Man, I can't believe this shit."

"Well, believe it and speaking of shit, leave your display kit and get your shit out of your desk—now. Goodbye."

There was no way I was going to talk Doug out of firing me. It was horrible the way he did it too, so cold and so quickly. Goddamn it, those bastards were crazy firing their best salesman. But that's exactly what they did.

When I walked out of Doug's office, his secretary whispered to me, "I'm so sorry about this. He wouldn't let me tell you when I called you."

I put my macho on and replied, "Jean, don't you worry your pretty self about this, it's Seagate's loss."

"Can we still get together again when my husband is out of town?" she asked.

"Wouldn't miss it for the world, you just call me."

Jean and I had been to bed several times and I saw no reason not to continue that, besides she was a pretty good lay. I went into my office, packed my shit and left. I figured what the hell, I had money in the bank and I was going into the service soon. I didn't need that damn job.

When the reality set in, it made me feel like shit. Getting fired, especially the brutal way Doug did it, was a real downer. But I realized I couldn't waste any more mental energy on it. I had a lot of work to do with my flying career. I had to do it quick too—the draft was pushing. I also knew I had to do some preliminary work to investigate which branch of the service I wanted to enter and exactly when I wanted to enlist. I soon decided to make a trip down to the recruiting station to see what my options were.

Chapter 4
How Many Roses to Get Laid?

To my surprise, when I walked into the recruiting station the first person I saw was the tall, black sergeant who had talked me into joining the army when I was in high school.

"Hey, sergeant, I can't believe it's you! Do you remember me?"

"Yes, sir, it's little ol' me, here in living color. And I sure remember you. How are things in the coal mine?"

"That's a long story; I'll save it for another day."

After a brief exchange, I learned he'd served two tours in Vietnam since I last saw him and he hoped this was his last duty station.

"I'm going to be retiring in two more years and then I'm gonna go out and get a real job." He had a laugh and continued, "What in the world brings you in here? You're ready to go in the Army, right?

"I'm almost ready to come back in now."

He had no way of knowing about my experience at seventeen. He asked. "What do you mean back in?"

I then told him all about what had happened and what I had learned from my testing back then.

"Well that's all the damnedest thing I ever heard," he said. "I went away to Slope Land and missed all of that, I guess. A 161, huh? You're some hot piece of merchandise."

"Yep, that's what they told me." I also told him about taking flying lessons, how far along I was, when I planned to be finished, and when I'd be ready to enlist.

"Man you're to good to be true, let's get into see my captain," he said. "He's an aviator, and he's been to Nam, too."

"Actually, I thought I'd come down here and talk to all the services to see who had the best deal. I think I might like to be an Air Force pilot," I responded.

"You just go ahead on and talk to them if you want to." He leaned his head over as if to indicate where I should go and he continued, "Come on, I'll show you where they are, we hide them and the jarheads around the corner. They embarrass us when people see them picking their noses."

As we walked down the hall, he said, "There you go my man." He pointed to the office door. "You come back by my office after these guys make their bids; because we're gonna beat any offers they make."

"You got my word on that," I said. "I'll come back over before I leave."

It didn't take long for the Air Force recruiter to learn that I only had a high school diploma. He was a nice enough guy and very polite, but there was no chance of getting into the Air Force to fly without a college degree. Back to the Army sergeant I went. The Air Force guy said he'd save me some time and explained that the Marines and the Navy both required a college degree. The only service I could get into without a degree and be a pilot was the Army.

When I returned and stuck my head through the sergeant's doorway he looked up and winked. "I knew they didn't have enough brains to take you."

"I don't know about that, but they only accept college graduates in their flying programs," I said.

He came around his desk and said, "Let's go talk to my commanding officer, Captain Riley. I told him about you already."

Riley was a tall, good-looking fellow, about 35, who had a square jaw, a light complexion and short-cropped red hair. He also had three rows of awards and decorations on his chest with aviator wings pinned above the top row. Riley quickly stood and welcomed us in. I kind of got the feeling the two of them were actors in a play that they had performed many times before.

The captain reached over the desk as he put out his left hand to shake mine. His right hand looked deformed and I could see that there was a black leather glove on it. The thumb was missing. I tried not to be obvious, but my surprise must have shown on my face.

"Don't mind the glove, we're expecting snow, and I don't want my hand to get cold," he said, smiling as the sergeant laughed.

"Captain Riley uses that line every time he meets somebody," the sergeant said as he smiled, showing his mouthful of pearly white teeth.

"Seriously, my hand was severely burned when Charlie shot my chopper down in Nam. We caught on fire, and I almost lost my whole damn arm." Riley sat down and motioned for us to do the same. "Not that it makes any difference, it's not doing me any good. After I finished rehab, the Army started trying to put me out. They would have, too, if I hadn't gotten a good Army lawyer. Now I think we're going to beat them and I'll be able to stay in until I retire. I've got nine years in and only eleven to go."

"I'm very sorry about your hand, I respect you for your service, sir," I said.

"Yeah, well, thanks, but the real shame of it all is I'll never be able to fly again," Riley said as he began to slowly shake his head. "Besides that, it's all for nothing. We're in a fucking shithole war where we're not allowed to fight to win."

I don't think I fully understood what Riley meant at that moment, but I later learned firsthand that what he had said about Vietnam was an incredible understatement.

Finally, the sergeant brought the conversation back to recruiting, saying, "Sir, this is the man I was telling you about a few minutes ago, the guy with the genius IQ. How about that warrant officer helicopter course? Think we could get him in that?"

"With your high IQ score and the fact that you'll already have all your civilian pilot licenses, you can be assured of getting into a fixed-wing program right away," Riley said. "Almost everyone goes to helicopters, but fixed-wing is a lot better."

"I'm not quite finished all my licenses yet, but it won't be very long," I said

Riley then told me about the advantages of flying a regular fixed-wing aircraft versus helicopters. "The main reason fixed-wing is better is life expectancy. In Vietnam the life expectancy of a fixed-wing aviator is about ten times the life expectancy of a chopper pilot."

We all had a good laugh about that, but I knew he was serious. He continued, "Fixed-wing aviators are an elite group — sort of the best of the best, if you know what I mean."

There was more. "Only the top 5% of students out of each class of 225 are selected for fixed-wing training. The rest go to chopper school."

As we stood at the end of the meeting, Riley said, "Nelson, you're a cinch to get a slot in a fixed-wing class. I'd like you to let me know about one month before you're ready to enlist."

"Yes, sir, it won't be very long. Thank you very much for your time."

On the drive back to my apartment I thought about the day's experiences, and what I needed to do. I figured the first thing to do was go in to talk with Sydney Holmen who owned the flying school I was attending. I had enough money saved to finish and I really wanted to hammer down. I knew Sidney pretty well, and I knew he'd do anything he could to help me finish as quickly as possible.

Next morning I drove to the airport and went up the steps to Sydney's office. Julie Barnes, Sydney's long-time secretary said, "He's on the phone with his wife, I think. She must call here 20 times a day."

"No problem." As I sat down I thought about how Julie would be in bed — good, I bet. I could smell the aroma of her perfume. She had a world class body and was in her early 30s. It seemed like forever since I'd had sex. After I'd gotten fired, it seemed a lot of my energy for chasing girls subsided. I thought about calling Moss to see if she had any interest—just one for old time's sake. Not a good idea.

The word was that Julie and Sidney had been lovers for a long time. Seems everyone knew about them and the stories were white hot. I had no personal knowledge of their affair and didn't care, but I did smile inside anytime I saw either of them. Several people had said they saw Sidney screwing Julie in one or another airplane seat in the hanger. Of course they thought their relationship was the best-kept secret of all time, and they were sure no one knew about it.

I had waited only a couple of minutes when Julie got up from her desk and went into Sidney's office. As she walked by me I got another whiff of her perfume and it excited me a bit. I wondered if she would like to see my apartment. Lucky Sidney.

Julie returned and said, "Okay, Nelson, he's all yours."

Sidney was a short, thin little man with a huge ego. And his nose was almost as large as his ego. He was in his 50s and had been a World War II flying ace. He also flew Saber Jets in Korea. His office was large—about half as big as a basketball court. It consumed one-quarter of the second floor over the main airplane hangar.

Sidney's passion, other than Julie, was big game hunting. His office attested to his experiences. There were dozens of trophies that he had bagged from all over the world. Many were fully stuffed animals. There were lots of animal heads lining the walls and hundreds of pictures of Sidney standing over dead animals. They were hanging in every available space. It all reminded me of a dead animal museum. It smelled a little like it, too.

Word was Sidney was a lot more proud of those trophies than he was of his family and Julie combined. From my observation, I figured that was true. Numerous times during a conversation Sidney would stop talking and look up at one of those trophies, it was as if the animal was talking to him. Then after a moment or two, he'd continue with his conversation. After every meeting with Sidney, he'd walk me to his office door. On the way, he'd stop by one of his trophies and give a detailed description about where, when, and how he shot that particular animal.

As I entered, Sidney was already on his feet and crossing the office toward me. "Hey, Nelson, how you doing this morning?"

"I'm fine, Sidney." We each reached out to shake hands. "Do you have any exciting hunting trips planned?"

"No, not right now. The old lady has put the brakes on my damn hunting for awhile. The crazy bitch thinks all I do is go out whoring around when I'm on a hunting trip."

I smiled and said, "Well, I don't have that problem anymore."

"Yeah, I heard you used to be married. One of the flight instructors told me you were divorced. Well, Nelson, what can I do for you?"

"Sidney, I came to talk about finishing my flying lessons as quickly as possible. I'm going into the Army as a fixed-wing pilot."

"Hey, that's wonderful! Following in my footsteps, eh? I was an ace, you know." He smiled and looked around at his trophies, like he was about to take a bow. "My chief instructor told me last week that you'd made a lot of progress on your licenses."

"Yeah, I only have instrument and instructor left to finish. I passed my multi-engine exam last week," I said. "If all goes well I should be able to finish everything up in the next two months."

"Well, what can I do to help you?"

"I need to get about 30 hours of commercial pilot flying in to meet the minimum hours requirement. I was hoping I might get you to use me on some charters."

"Absolutely," he said. "I can always use an extra pilot around here. In fact, I have a contract coming up that should allow you to get more than 30 hours."

"That's great; tell me about it, please."

"The contract is to ferry 15 airplanes from the Cessna Aircraft factory in Wichita, Kansas to Panama. They're going to Howard Air Force Base to be used by the Air Force to teach Central American military pilots how to fly. If you want, I'll give you credit toward your flight training instead of paying you."

"That's perfect; it sounds too good to be true. How many days you figure we'll be gone, and when will you know about the contract?"

"Even if we have a weather day, it shouldn't take but five days max. The Air Force will take care of all the clearances to over-fly the countries we'll be crossing. That way we don't have to fool with the immigration and Visa requirements of the different countries."

"Man, I'll take your offer, if you get the contract. You just tell me when you know."

"The truth is I have it already. I just have to wait for the paperwork to come in. Should be all completed by next week. Your timing is good. I want to take four pilots and myself. We'll make three trips back to back; taking a total of fifteen airplanes. These planes won't have radios or navigation equipment," he said. "That's going to be added in Panama. We'll fly in a loose formation, and we'll be led by an Air Force C-130. When we get there, the Air Force C-130 will fly us back each time."

"Man, I'm up for this deal; I can't wait!" I replied.

A big smile crossed Sydney's face. "You know, those Central American babes down there are all so hot that their underpants are on fire."

"As I told you, I'm so up for this deal; I can't wait!" I said, laughing.

Damn, that was a big time truth. For many years I availed myself of those burning underpants.

I was on a roll. It was only mid-morning, so I went over and took an airplane out for a couple hours of practice. When I returned, I saw Teddy Benson standing over by his airplane. I'd gotten to know Teddy at the airport. He owned his own twin-engine plane and took it out a couple of times a week. Ted also owned a real estate firm in town and told me if I ever needed help with real estate to come see him. I headed over to talk to him.

"Hi, Teddy; how's it going?"

"It's going great, Nelson, how about you? You getting any strange ass?"

"Oh, I'm doing all right, but I have a little real estate challenge coming up. I need to sublet my apartment soon. I have about half a year lease left and I'm gonna join the Army as a pilot as soon as I finish my flight training."

"That's a piece of cake."

"Yeah, I'd like to sell my new furniture with the lease, if I can."

"That, too, is a piece of cake. Why don't you come by the office tomorrow and we'll get the particulars and write up an agreement. How about 4:00 tomorrow afternoon?"

When I walked into Teddy's office the next day, I had to do a double take. I couldn't believe how beautiful his secretary was. Teddy had spoken about how perfect she was, but I'd forgotten about it. Her name was Samantha and she was a double wow—easily the most beautiful woman I had ever seen.

I inhaled deeply, fully inflating my ego and boldly said, "Woo, you are about the best looking thing I have ever seen, lady."

She smirked sarcastically and proceeded to put me down, as in slam me down. "Listen, I'm not interested in what you think. I'm not on the make, and I don't like men who are. So we understand each other, right?"

I was too embarrassed to speak. I caught my breath and apologized for my comments. "I'm so sorry I offended you." Then I lied. "I wasn't trying to make you; I only meant to compliment you."

She responded without even looking up from her work. "As I said, we understand each other."

A few minutes later when I got in to see Teddy I told him about the shark attack. He said, "Man, I been trying for two years to get Samantha in bed, ever since her divorce. No luck; not even close. She's got a little girl and she doesn't want another man around, now or ever she says."

I nodded my head, saying, "Damn, I don't know if she's a shark or a barracuda, but what a fun challenge."

"Hell, Nelson, I doubt if she'll ever give it to another man. She caught her old man in bed with another woman and she ran his ass off right there on the spot."

"Well, Ted, a couple things. I'm a lot better at chasing tail than you are. I've probably had a lot more experience than you, and I've got much better moves than you do. Additionally, I'm hornier than a nine-ball tomcat. You wouldn't be jealous if I gave her a try, would you?"

"Get after it. Hell, you may just chase her right into my bed."

We had a good laugh and then I said, "Ted, I bet you a hundred I get her."

"You're on, Romeo. How many years you think this little job is gonna take you?"

"Not years, my man, just two or three months. I'll get her before I go into the Army. May just double up my efforts since I don't have much time to invest."

"Whoa, you misspoke there," he said, laughing. "Invest is when you get a return, spend is a more appropriate word. You'll be spending time, not investing it, understand that there'll be no return."

"Two months, Teddy, three max."

"It's a bet."

Teddy agreed to help me find a renter for my apartment, and he thought he could find someone who might also want the furniture. By the time I finished shooting the shit with Teddy, Samantha had already left for the day. To my sorrow, I didn't get to see her on my way out. I headed home and was back at the airport the next morning.

I flew almost every day for at least two hours, some

days I did a double period. The rest of the time I spent studying for my exams and running back and forth to Ted's office to keep the moves on Samantha. I used every occasion I could to see her again. She was cool to chilly with me no matter how smooth I tried to come across. I did learn her daughter was almost two and her name was Emma. Each time I left the office I went back over our conversation, I was improving on my approach for the next time I saw her. I was seriously taken with this woman and I was thriving on the challenge she presented. It was fun.

It must have been about ten days after I first met Samantha that I phoned her and asked her to lunch. She was polite, but firm, and declined. Later the same day, I saw Teddy at the airport coffee shop and told him about my call to Samantha.

"Listen, man, I told you she was off men," Teddy said, laughing. "There's less chance of getting in her pants than the Navy putting screen doors on their submarines."

"Well, there's no indication yet that she's falling in love with me, or if she is, she's hiding it well."

As I left Teddy we were still laughing at the stories we shared about our exploits with women. Although he was very married, Teddy played with the girls. His feeling was that everybody needed a hobby. He swore, too, that he'd seen Sidney and Julie making out in an airplane in the back of the hanger and not just one time. As I left Teddy, I thought about Samantha again.

Actually I had a twinge of guilt thinking about what I was doing. It was fun rushing Samantha and it was fun joking with Teddy about it, but it was also kind of crappy. By the next day I had blown off the possibility that she could be more than just a potential roll in the hay. I needed to put on a full-court press. There was money and sex on the line, so I made a plan to initiate emergency action.

I went to a little local flower shop and ordered a dozen red roses to be sent, without a card, to Samantha. I told the florist I wanted the order repeated every day until I called and stopped it, and I wanted every order delivered before noon. I didn't return to Teddy's office for a week; I wanted the flowers to have time to do their work.

Then when I did bee-bop in to see Samantha, the first words out of my mouth were, "Hey, who died?" There were roses everywhere. Her office looked like a funeral parlor.

"No one yet, but when I find out who's sending these darn roses there's going to be a funeral because I'm going to kill whoever it is."

"Now that isn't very nice, I expected to get a thank you," I said, shaking my head. "If you really want them to stop coming I—"

She cut me off short and said, "Look this is ridiculous. It was funny for a day or two, but now it's starting to be embarrassing."

"Okay, okay," I said, smiling. "If you'll go to lunch with me, I'll stop sending them. An innocent little lunch, come on, what can it hurt?"

"Where do you want to go?" she said finally.

Since I was making such great progress, I asked, "Would you like to go flying with me on Saturday? I have to get a couple hours of flight time in this weekend, and we could stop at an airport I know that has a nice little coffee shop."

With bait like that how could she resist? I knew she had never been in an airplane. I decided to put the finishing move on her. "You can bring your daughter if you like. She'll love flying."

I was right; she took the bait. She agreed to meet me at the airport late Saturday morning, and I promised to have her back early. She didn't want to bring her daughter, though. I figured that was a good sign and maybe we were going to do the deed that weekend. Perhaps I could even get her initiated into the mile-high club.

The day was fantastic and we had a wonderful time. By the time we returned to the airport and landed, I realized I could get serious about this girl. During the next few weeks, we saw each other several times and each time was more magical than the last. I had to make a tough decision about where I was going with Samantha. Was I going for just sex so I could collect my hundred bucks or was I going for a relationship? Or could I have both? Inadvertently, Sidney helped me with the answer.

Although it had been delayed, the airplane ferry contract came together without much notice. Sidney called a meeting of three other pilots and myself and told us he had made arrangements for us to be flown to the Cessna factory in two days. An Air Force major was at the meeting and he gave a long briefing on our flight plans, which included maps and charts covering the trip, refueling and overnight stopovers—it was all laid out for us. I was totally impressed with his professionalism and preparedness He had a flight bag for each of us with everything we needed to navigate the trip. I was going to like going into the Army and being a professional. After the briefing, I phoned Samantha and told her the schedule.

Samantha knew it was coming, but she seemed surprised that I was leaving so quickly. She made me feel terrific when she said she couldn't wait until I got back and could tell her all about my adventure. Little did I know exactly what an adventure it was going to be!

Early in the morning on the day of departure, an Air Force C-130 cargo plane landed to pick us up. Sidney was there and he was panicking because one of the pilots hadn't shown up. A decision had to be made—were we going to leave without him or delay the departure? The Air Force major who briefed us two days earlier wrecked Sidney's world when he announced the flight plans and departure clearance times and said we'd have to leave very soon. Sidney went into full vibration mode. He started stuttering and shaking his head. He couldn't believe it, it couldn't be happening! I watched the whole charade selfishly thinking that if we didn't leave that morning perhaps

I could see Samantha that night.

Sidney finally made a decision. "We go without the bastard."

The Major thought that was a great idea. "Let's move it," he said.

Just as we started walking to the C-130 our missing pilot showed up and we were off as per plan and on time. We loaded in and sat on strap seats in the cargo bay for the flight. Next stop — Wichita, Kansas.

We arrived in Wichita, and it didn't take long to identify the planes we were to fly. After a thorough preflight inspection of all the aircraft, we took off right on schedule. The plan was to follow the Air Force C-130 in a daisy chain, each pilot following the plane in front of him. I was feeling excited and loving every moment of it. The expedition was making good progress and we spent our first night at Davis-Monthan Air Force Base in Tucson, Arizona.

The next morning we were in the air shortly after sunrise. We soon crossed the border into Mexico and spent another uneventful day trailing each other south. The flight plan called for us to spend the second night in Guatemala and all went as planned. The airport in Guatemala City was for joint use — civilian planes on one side and military on the other.

When we landed, the control tower directed us to the military side of the airport where we were provided a large parking ramp. A Guatemalan military bus provided transportation to our hotel in the downtown area. The heavily armed soldiers in full battle dress were intimidating, but the major assured us they were friendly. When we got to the hotel, everyone was tired so we all went to our rooms to wash up and rest before dinner.

That night the entire group, two Air Force pilots and three crew members, plus the Army major liaison officer, had a rather loud and fun time in the hotel dining room. Beer and wine were consumed, but I declined as I thought about my one drunk and my father. The party wound down about 10:00 that evening. The Air Force guys, who had been in Guatemala before, cautioned that we shouldn't stray too far from the hotel. They told us most of the country was in political turmoil and sometimes the unrest spilled over onto the streets. Muggings and street robberies were not uncommon, particularly against foreigners. After receiving this information, no one had very much interest in leaving the hotel.

Not so with Sidney. He had also been to Guatemala before on some kind of leopard hunt. He knew where the nightlife was and he wanted to head there. After a good deal of coercion, most of the group agreed to go with him provided we took taxis so we didn't have to walk on the streets. I thought we were going to a nightclub of some kind, but the destination turned out to be something far different. We arrived in a Boys Town area, an area populated with only bars and bordellos.

It was a short ride from our hotel. Here in Guatemala City, Boys Town was a walled off area about four city blocks square. This time I was happy to see the armed soldiers standing on every street corner. The girls were young, cute, and very bold about what they had to offer. I swear some of them looked like children. Some couldn't have been more than twelve years old.

Many of them were more than willing to display their wares right on the sidewalk. There were a few other gringos, and a lot of other foreign tourists. It seemed the gringos got special attention in that part of town. I must admit the offer to partake of some of the indoor sports the ladies were offering was enticing. Soon most of our group had a girl selected and went directly to a bordello. Some made a stop or two at the bars first. No doubt, though, they all ended up participating in the same event. Sidney was one of the first to, as he said, have a closer look at the opportunities presented and we didn't see him again until breakfast.

Meanwhile I was taking some heat from several members of the group since I was resisting the temptation. I

had promised myself I wasn't going to drink and I wasn't
going to buy sex either. I made it through the entire night
without having anything to drink, but I didn't keep my
other promise.

Samuel's rule prevailed and I carefully picked a girl
who said she was 20 years old. The price was cheap — $20.
I chuckled when I thought of her as 20/20. In fact, I called
her that since she couldn't speak a word of English and
didn't have a clue what I was saying. Some of the group
had longer fuses than the others and took longer to do the
deed. Some departed quickly taking taxis back to the hotel.

Interestingly, my very first prostitute only cost me $20,
but in my future I would pay thousands of dollars for one.

The next morning at breakfast, the conversations were
lively and the tales were interesting, to say the least. Sidney wouldn't tell us anything of his evening's entertain-
ment except to confirm that the girls did have hot pants.
Those who had any at all, he joked. Sidney spent more
than an adequate amount of time insuring that he had everyone's vow of silence about the activities of the previous
night. Obviously he was extremely concerned about tales
getting back to either Julie Barnes or his wife. After a jovial
breakfast we loaded on the bus back to the airport.

I was about to learn a lesson in how the world works
south of the border. It was one that would serve me well in
my future.

As we approached the aircraft parking area, our bus
was stopped at the entrance gate and then diverted to a
military headquarters building. There were a few tense
minutes; the soldiers were pointing their rifles motioning
for us to unload the bus and enter the building. None of
those guys spoke English, but that didn't stop them from
carrying on a running conversation with us just as if we
understood every word.

A Guatemalan officer, who appeared to be in charge,
came into the room where we were being guarded. The
major had a short conversation with him in Spanish, then

informed us that we were not under arrest, rather just being temporarily restrained. He was going with the Guatemalan to get the situation all straightened out. He assured us it would only take a short moment.

The short moment turned into three hours. When he returned, he gave us the good news that we would be allowed to go to our airplanes and leave within the hour. By noon we were airborne again and headed south to Honduras. The problem was solved with the passing of ten $100 bills to the Guatemalan officer. The major said graft was a way of life in Central America and the Air Force never let them go anywhere without a wad of cash. That was my first experience with how business was conducted in Latin countries south of the United States.

We spent the third night at Tusche Air Force Base, a small base located right in the middle of what looked like a million miles of Honduran jungle. It was not a secret base, but rather it was considered silent. I guess that meant that you just didn't talk about it.

The next day it was on to our destination in Panama. The planes were delivered per the plan and a day early. We had a new crew on the C-130 flight back home, but the major liaison officer remained with us. On the return flight he told us the second of the three flights would start in two days. Since we were landing late at night, I would only have one night to try and see Samantha before I was off again.

Samantha seemed excited to hear from me, and we set a date for dinner. She wanted to know everything about the entire experience. I told her about how much fun it was flying in a daisy chain and about the magnificent scenery. I described the entire trip except, of course, the educational experience of Boys Town. She asked a ton of questions as we sat and talked in the restaurant. It took us two hours to have dinner. I was getting to like this girl a lot and it was increasingly obvious the feelings were reciprocated. Our conversations ventured into my future plans to enter the Army.

We both knew that as a pilot I would likely go to Vietnam. Unless, of course, the conflict ended, which seemed unlikely. I asked Samantha if she would ever consider moving from Richmond and she was quick to let me know she'd have no reservations about leaving. She said she had dreamed of living some other place. The scene at dinner with Samantha repeated itself immediately after the next two flights, except there was a warm and wonderful goodnight kiss when I took her home after the third flight. That was a "wow" experience! I was making progress.

The rest of the flights were also carbon copies of the first one, including further educational ventures into Boys Town. I had decided by then how I was going to handle the wager with Teddy.

I made it a point to find out when Teddy was going to be flying again. I met him at his airplane when he showed up.

"Hey, Nelson, how did the international flights go? I bet it was interesting, huh."

"That's an understatement, Teddy. It was the most fun thing I've ever done with my clothes on." We had a big laugh and I continued, "I'd do it again in a heartbeat including being taken hostage by the Guatemalan Army".

"Well, tell me about that. What in the world happened?"

I spent the next half hour describing the experiences and telling Teddy what an adventure it was. He wanted to know if Sidney behaved himself on the flights; he had always heard the stories about Sidney's escapades anytime he was away from home.

"Teddy, as far as I know he was a good boy the entire time," I said.

"Well, if you ever want to blackmail him, you can threaten to make up some story and tell it to Julie. I bet you could get anything you wanted from him."

"Man, I don't even want to think about that happening," I said. "By the way, Teddy, I want to give you the hundred I owe you; I've decided to call off the bet on Samantha."

I took out my wallet to pay him.

He laughed out loud and said, "You calling the bet early, what's the problem? You finding out what I told you is true, huh? I tried to tell you she was never going to let you have it."

"Actually, Ted, I've decided to stop trying. A very strange thing has happened—I think I'm falling in love with her."

Teddy shook his head and smiled a huge smile. "I knew it, I knew it. I've got to tell you, I could feel it happening. I've never seen her as happy as she's been the last few weeks. In fact it's the first time since I've known her that she seems truly happy."

"Yeah, well, she isn't the only one who's happy about it. Here's your hundred, let's just say I lost." I removed the money from my wallet.

Teddy reached out for my hand to stop me and said, "Hell, I could no more take that money than I could piss over this airplane hangar. Nah, I want you two to buy your first wedding present with it."

"Hey, I said I really liked her, I didn't say we were getting married!"

Teddy gave a little laugh as he opened the door on his airplane. "How about doing me a favor—years from now, let me know how she is in bed. Will you do that?"

I didn't answer. Teddy winked and climbed into the cockpit and I walked away smiling. I had to get ready for a flight test. I heard him starting the engine on his plane.

Life became good for me during the next month. I was finishing up the last of my requirements for my instructor's license. It was the last one and when I successfully finished it, I was done. Samantha told me that she and Emma planned to give me a little party when I finished.

But the best laid plans can go wrong quickly. It shouldn't have been a surprised when I picked up the mail and, bigger than life, there was my draft notice. The bastards were giving me only 25 days to report to be drafted or enlist. I didn't know what to tell Samantha.

I had been getting along well with two-year-old Emma. She was a great kid and very smart, too. She had the brightest yellow curls, and she was a little daredevil who'd try anything. We always had fun.

I had visited Samantha's family once while we were dating. They lived in the country about 25 miles west of Richmond. They had a small farm and her stepfather had an interesting career. He made and sold corn whiskey. He always offered me a drink when we went there, but I told him I was having trouble with my stomach and I'd better not drink it. While I was enjoying Emma, Samantha, and her family, I was also rapidly running out of time. The Army was getting closer and closer. I had to do something with the situation and fast.

I hadn't sublet my apartment and that had the potential to be a real problem. It would be hard to get rid of the furniture and even harder to keep paying rent on the apartment after I left. I was days from finishing up my flying, and it was time to talk to the recruiter again. Most important of all, I wanted to get some understanding about my relationship with Samantha. I decided I would talk the situation over with Samuel Goodman.

On a visit to the power plant, Samuel and I went to the coffee room to talk. On the way, we passed two of the cleaning girls in the hall. When the girls saw us they started to giggle. As we passed, Samuel turned and gave one a big pat on the butt.

"You gals aren't messing with any of these other guys are you?" he asked.

The one he patted jumped and the two of them went off down the hall laughing and joking and looking back at us.

"You never did partake of my harem here, did you?" Samuel asked.

When we got set down with our coffee, I told Samuel about my dilemma. "Man, I have a lot on my plate right now."

"Tell me what's going on, boy." He said.

"Samuel, I'm due to enlist in just a few days. I haven't rented my apartment or sold my furniture yet, and I don't know what to do about Samantha and me."

"Woo, this is big shit! Let's take them one at a time. You told me last time I saw you about this gal, Samantha, and the bet you had to screw her. Did you get in there yet? How was it, anyway?"

"I'm sure it's gonna be great, but I haven't had her yet. Hell, Samuel, I think I'm in love with this one."

That didn't faze Samuel a bit. "Okay, that's big stuff. First things first. The most important thing here is you gotta screw Samantha. If you're serious about the relationship, and you sound like you are, once you screw her good, she'll be a lot more likely to hold still while you get settled into the Army. Remember, a good one is usually loyal after they think you love them. So making love to Samantha is your number one priority."

"I like that answer. I'm sure she's going to let me have it before I enlist. I mean, hell, I know she's is in love with me from the way she acts."

"Another reason you gotta nail her before you go is, if she ain't any good in bed, then you don't wanna waste your time hanging on to her."

"Shit, I never thought of that."

"Now, I got an idea. Where does Samantha live?" he asked.

"She lives in a little basement apartment with her two-year-old little girl. Her uncle owns the house."

"Okay, perfect. Why not let Samantha move into your apartment, pay whatever rent she can, and hang there until you can have her come to where you are in the Army later. That's all provided you want to continue on after you check her out in bed," he said. "Man, I fucked up one time and married a bitch that couldn't screw worth a shit and I liked to never got rid of her."

"Well, why'd you marry her?"

"She was the best cook of any of the wives I ever had and, like a dumb ass, I thought I could teach her to screw, but I couldn't."

"Samuel, you're a genius, I know Samantha will go for this 'cause the place she's living in is the pits."

"Now about the Army; you go to the recruiter and tell him you need another month to get your affairs in order before you enlist."

"Will they let me do that?"

"I'm 90% sure they will, all you gotta do is ask them."

"Tomorrow morning I'll go over there and try."

Samuel and I talked a while more and then I left. I had a date with Samantha. She was coming over after work and we were going to barbecue some chicken on the grill. God only knows why I stopped on the way home and bought a large bottle of champagne. Sometimes when we were out to dinner Samantha would have a glass of champagne, but the second one always made her giddy. I never drank with her; I just had a Coke or tea. I guess I figured I might need to get her giddy that night.

We were sitting on the patio with the champagne iced down and each of us holding a full glass. Samantha was surprised to see me with the champagne. I said this was a special evening and I had a big surprise for her. I had told her about Samuel before and my relationship with him.

"What did Samuel say about what's going on with you. Did he have any recommendations?"

"Yeah, he sure did." I spent the next 20 minutes telling Samantha all about my visit and the conversation with Samuel, except, that is, the part about checking her out in bed, and the little part about the cleaning girls in the hallway at the plant.

She really liked the idea of moving into the apartment. However she had a surprise announcement for me too.

"Nelson, I know all about the bet with Teddy, you better hurry up and make love to me or you're gonna lose a hundred dollars. Teddy's never been one for keeping a secret, he must've told every real estate agent in the office. One of them told me the day after the bet was made."

"You mean you've been holding out just so I'd lose that bet? I can't believe it!" I didn't know whether to laugh or not.

Samantha smiled and said, "Nelson, after the first week when you took me flying I knew I was going to give it to you. I just didn't know when."

"You're not pissed?" I asked.

"I was totally pissed when I first heard about it, and those damn flowers didn't help my attitude any. As time went on, though, and I got to know you, I sensed that you were having feelings for me and I knew I was for you. I wasn't pissed anymore.

"Damn, I'm sure glad to hear that! I stopped trying to win the bet, you know."

"Yeah. I can tell you, though; if you would have pushed me just a tad more I would have gone down. But, hell, you just stopped; it was like you suddenly decided to be a priest. Right when I was all worked up and ready."

We had a big, big laugh.

By now the champagne was starting to let me know I should stop and I'm proud to say that I did. I thought about my promise not to drink, and then I rationalized it by only drinking a little. That was my second experience with alcohol and I didn't need a repeat of the fiasco when I got drunk on beer with Kirsten. And in this same apartment, too.

I poured Samantha another glass of champagne and put water in my glass. We continued to talk and I finished cooking the chicken.

"Somewhere along the way I decided this relationship was more important to me than just the sex. I decided to wait until it was right for both of us. I had no idea you knew about that sick bet."

"Nelson, I made a bet of my own; I bet myself that I could get you out of your clothes before 7:00 tonight and if you don't hurry your ass up and get naked, I'm gonna lose my bet."

"Samantha, you never cease to amaze me. Bet I can get naked before you can."

We both jumped up and ran for the bedroom stripping off our clothes as we went. It was like a comedy movie. Suddenly consciousness came to us both and we stood as still as statues, I reached out and Samantha moved toward me. What a beautiful moment. I took Samantha's hand and gently pulled her to me. Our bodies touched and we embraced, never breaking eye contact.

"You are a magnificently beautiful woman, Samantha."

She closed her eyes slowly and we kissed deeply. That evening we made love again and again. I knew, at that moment, that I had never truly loved a person before. Certainly not like I loved this creature. We slept in each other's arms that night. When I awoke, Samantha was sitting on the side of the bed with the sheet pulled over her generous breasts. She was looking directly into my eyes. We embraced and made love again.

It was early afternoon when we realized we hadn't eaten since Friday lunch, so we ate the barbecued chicken and Samantha drank mostly flat champagne on ice. We didn't leave the apartment all weekend. By early Monday morning, we had our future planned. Samantha went to work and I went to the recruiting station to try for a short extension before enlisting.

Chapter 5
Choose An Aircraft to Die In

As I approached the recruiting station I saw police cars, fire engines, emergency ambulances, military police, and about a million people in uniform. Traffic was being diverted two blocks from the building. I parked four blocks away and by the time I walked back, the entire scene was disbanding. I still had to stand outside the building for a few minutes until the vehicles and people were all cleared out. I heard a policeman tell someone that a crazy Marine had gone berserk and had been shooting off his pistol inside the building. When I was finally allowed to enter the building, there was no one in the Army reception area.

I proceeded down the hall to Captain Riley's office. "Captain Riley," I said as I stuck my head through the door of his office. "Sorry to barge in, but there's no one in the outer office."

"Hey, Nelson, come on in. We've had a little excitement here this morning. A Marine corporal came to work this morning and found he had orders back to Vietnam for a second tour. The crazy son of a bitch went out to his car, came back with a pistol, and announced he wasn't going back. Then he started shooting off his weapon."

"Damn," I said. "How'd they subdue him?"

"When he'd emptied his weapon, he threw it at his commander and gave himself up. He kept screaming, 'Go ahead, you mother fuckers, put me in the brig, but I ain't going back to Nam.'"

"We gonna make you a fly boy, now?" Riley asked, rubbing the black leather glove on his right hand. "I've got you an enlistment contract. I think you'll like it."

"I've been ready since I was seventeen, sir. I'm sure ready, now. I got my draft notice, but I need another month and then I can report. Can you help me get that approved?"

"Oh, that's right!" He put out his left hand to shake mine. "I'd forgotten about the fiasco you went through the first time you joined the Army. I think we'll do a little better this time. The month is no problem at all. I'll handle it for you."

I shook his hand and said. "Yes, sir. Last time it started and ended all in one week, right here in these offices."

"Let's go into the conference room across the hall and I'll explain it all to you," he said.

Riley went to his file cabinet, quickly removed a folder, and led me to a small conference room. He went on to tell me that I would be enlisting as a Private E-1, and would go to basic training for eight weeks. After basic training, I wouldn't have to attend flight school, because I already had all my flight licenses. I actually had more flight experience than the Army provides an individual in flight school. So, without going to flight school, I was going to be immediately appointed after basic training to Warrant Officer One, commonly referred to as W-1.

Warrant officers were officers with special skills in a particular field, and they worked only in that field. Unlike warrants, regular officers still had the responsibility of commanding troops and performing staff jobs.

After basic training, my first flying assignment would be to a fixed-wing detachment at Fort Rucker, Alabama. There I would either teach flying or become a VIP pilot flying high-ranking officers around the country. Next, I would most likely go to Vietnam.

After carefully explaining it all, Riley said, "Well, you think you're willing to sign up for two years for all this?"

"Yes, sir."

A month later I kissed Samantha goodbye when she dropped me off in front of the recruiting office. I repeated exactly the same procedures as I had when I was 17.

I signed the forms and was sworn in and was soon in Fort Polk, Louisiana. Basic training wasn't very interesting for me. The classroom training was extremely easy and it seemed most of the instructors, who were sergeants, were morons. There were exceptions, but few. They were as bored with their jobs as the trainees were with the subject matter.

There were a lot of guys who had a very hard time with classroom subjects, and I spent as much time as I could helping them. The physical training was another story. At 26, it was a challenge for me to keep up with the 18-year-olds who made up most of my class. Those guys could out run, out jump, and out climb me. I passed all the physical training tests and while I was never last, I was never first, either.

Somehow I made it through and graduated close to the top of my class. Everyone in my class, except me, was shipped off to points all over the world; many went directly to Vietnam with rifles in their hands. After graduation, I was told I didn't have orders to my next duty yet. While I was waiting for my orders, I was assigned to a casual duty slot, which meant I was sent out daily on all kinds of work details. I swept driveways, pulled weeds, painted, washed vehicles, and did any number of other "challenging" jobs.

Finally, after two weeks, my orders came. I was being sent to flight school at Fort Walters, Texas. I explained to my senior sergeant that I was supposed to go to Fort Rucker. All he said was, "Just shut up and get on the fucking bus. Tell them at your next duty station."

"Sergeant, this is not where I am supposed to—"

He cut me off. "Look, private!" he screamed. "They'll get it all straightened out when you get to Fort Walters. Now just get on the fucking bus, okay?"

I did as instructed and felt certain that as soon as I arrived at Walters, I would get this mess corrected. I was anxious to get my promotion and start flying.

But it made no difference what I wanted or what I had been promised, or what my contract said for that matter. I quickly found myself at primary flight training and assigned to a helicopter training company along with 250 other men. It took me two days to find an opportunity to speak to my platoon sergeant and explain the foul up.

When the time came, I politely explained to him. "Sergeant, I'm not supposed to be in a helicopter class and, in fact, I'm not supposed to go to flight school at all. I already have all my civilian pilots licenses. Additionally, I signed an enlistment contract that said I would have a direct appointment to Warrant Officer One when I finished basic training and I wouldn't have to go through flight school. I have a copy of my enlistment contract right here."

"Let me have that, I'll check on it," he said. "Until I get you an answer, you'll have to start helicopter school with everyone else."

"Yes, sir, but do you have any idea how long it will take to check on it?"

"I'll get you over to personnel as soon as I can," he told me. "Just be patient."

It took three days to process us in. Then we were informed that our class would start on the following Monday morning. I wasn't feeling good about that. In fact, I was angry as hell. My trust level in the Army was very low at this point. Thoughts kept running through my mind about the first time I joined. This had all the indications of a major SNAFU which in the Army meant "situation normal, all fucked up."

This bad dream continued for a week; that's how long it took me to get to see a senior personnel sergeant. I explained the entire story to him. He sat back in his chair, pushed the brim of his hat back, scratched his head and said, "Your contract says exactly what you've told me. Your orders say different. Only thing I can do is query the Department of the Army at the Pentagon."

"Sir, how long you think that'll take?" I asked.

He offered a frustrated smile, shook his head and said, "I haven't a clue. Could take a few weeks, could take a few months, or it could take a few years. This is the Army, you know"

"Is there anything at all that I can do?"

"Unfortunately there isn't," he said. "All your licenses are verified right here in your file. I do have the authority to put you into a fixed-wing course if you want that. I think that will be a lot better for you."

"I really don't want to fly helicopters."

"Hold in place a minute, let me confirm with the commander."

He got up and went into another office down the hall. It seemed like a long time before he came out and waved to me to come in. When I walked into the office, I was really impressed. There were more plaques, awards, certificates, pictures, and diplomas than I had ever seen in my lifetime. Almost every inch of wall space was covered. I gave a salute to the major who was standing behind his desk. I was trying to keep my eyes on him and off the walls, but he noticed that I was impressed.

He motioned me to sit down and said, "I'm Major John Mills. I see you like my ego walls."

"Sir, how long have you been in the Army? I'm genuinely impressed."

"I've been in a long time, son. When I came in, Christ was a corporal in my platoon." He laughed and continued, "I went through helicopter flight school during Korea and then fixed-wing school just before Nam started. I had a tour in Nam flying a spook plane, an OV1."

He went on. "The sergeant here told me about your problem. I want to help you out, but chances are you'll be finished flight school and graduate before this mess straightens out."

I felt myself wilting. "Crap, they've done it to me again," I muttered. I closed my eyes and shook my head. I told Major Mills the entire story from the first time I entered the Army until that very moment.

He opened my personnel file that was lying in front of him. He read and thumbed through it for a long time. Then he said, "You know, I don't think it matters, but I see everything you have told me. It's all documented in your file, but I don't find any discharge order from when you were seventeen. Like I said, it don't matter a damn."

It would be years later, but eventually the fact that there was no record of my discharge would turn out to matter. In fact, it would matter a whole hell of a lot.

He pushed back in his chair, put his feet on the desk, shook his head and said, "Shit." After a long pause he continued, "There's an opportunity here for you — and me, too. I don't have the authority to appoint you to be a Warrant Officer One, but we will move you to a fixed-wing class. I have a slot that's unfilled in a 15-man class."

As angry as I was, I was also a bit excited. My emotions were jumping up and down faster than a roller coaster. Major Mills and I talked for most of the afternoon. Although he had both helicopter and fixed-wing flight ratings, he'd never had any instrument training. I found that peculiar since, without that training, a pilot was restricted from flying in the clouds or any kind of bad weather.

After I understood what he was telling me, I said, "Sir, that seems almost unbelievable. I wouldn't think the Army would want to restrict its pilots like that by not having instrument training."

"It is restricting," Mills told me. "It's damned insane, but only a very few pilots get instrument training. No telling how many hundreds of pilots and crews have crashed after getting caught in bad weather because the pilot had no instrument training"

"That's scary," I said.

Mills smiled and said, "I have a feeling I'm going to have that training real soon, though."

"I hope so, sir"

He about half closed one eye while a smile spread across his face, then said, "You remember I said there's an opportunity here for both of us?"

"Sir, I don't understand. How does me going into a fixed-wing class benefit you?"

"Why hell, son. You got an instructor's license and you're gonna teach me how to fly instruments. Now that's what I call a good deal for both of us. FTA. In case you don't yet know what that means, it means fuck the Army," he said, laughing heartily.

The major laid out his agenda and I was absolutely dumbstruck.

His best friend was the commander of the airfield there at Fort Walters and that meant that all the airplanes were under his direct control. Consequently, Mills had access to any airplane he wanted to fly and at any time he wanted to fly it. Just as Mills said, I started primary fixed-wing flight school the next week.

The curriculum was no challenge. The ground school and the flight portion were all stuff I had already mastered. After a couple weeks I was giving Mills regular lessons and by then he had instructed me to call him John. While on one of those flights, I told him how crappy it was that I had to learn to fly for the second time.

He responded to that. "Okay, do you think you can live with attending half the time?" he asked. "I'll square it with the class commander."

"Sure! He's a friend of yours, too, right?"

From then on I started attending school only when something was coming up that I wanted to review. My primary responsibility for the next six months was to teach instrument training to Major Mills and several of his friends. Some days I'd teach as many as four of Mills' officer friends. Most of those guys had the same agenda — to retire from the service and get a civilian flying job. Life was good. I could go to class when I wanted to. I made my own appointments to instruct and on weekends I was free to go anywhere I pleased. Many weekends I'd catch a military hop to Andrews Air Force Base in Washington, DC. Samantha would drive up from Richmond and we'd get a motel room and spend all weekend together.

Major John Mills and I became best friends and since

he was also single, we caught a hop on a military transport or he arranged for us to fly one of the trainers. Several times a month, we went somewhere almost every Friday. We returned on Monday or Tuesday or whenever Mills wanted to come back. John always wrote his own orders to travel. The inference was, we were on military business no matter where we were. He showed me how to counterfeit official orders. It was quite simple, actually. I wrote hundreds of my own orders for the rest of my military career. I never, ever had one challenged.

Once he decided we should go to the world hot air balloon festival in Pueblo, Colorado. We took an Army twin engine trainer and flew from Texas to Fort Carson, just outside Denver. There Mills signed out a staff car and we drove to Denver and then on to the balloon festival. Each night we went back and slept at the fort. That trip lasted four days. Those six months were a sweet time for me and I hated to leave, but I was anxious to get on with my career, too.

Graduation time came around and even with my terrible attendance record I graduated first in my class. At graduation I was promoted to W-1 and John was there to pin my aviator wings on during the ceremony. I never knew what happened to the direct appointment from my original contract; it never came through, of course. As the honor graduate, I was given my choice of aircraft to transition into. Samantha came for my graduation and while she was there, I proposed to her. She accepted. We planned to have a quick, no-frills ceremony as soon as possible.

We told John our plan at the graduation ceremony and he immediately insisted we go to the officers' club for a celebration. John and I had traveled together enough for him to know I didn't drink, but he insisted we go anyway.

Once there, John raised his glass and proposed a toast. "I want the two of you to always be as happy as hogs in mud."

"Why, thank you John, that's the nicest thing anyone has ever said to me," Samantha replied, smiling.

"When are you gonna do it?" John asked.

By that time Samantha had a couple of cocktails in her and she said, "ASAP, John; that's Army talk for quick. Hell, I've been chasing him for over a year. I don't want to take any chances of him getting away."

We were having a big laugh when suddenly John said, "I have a hell of an idea."

I raised my Coke and said, "Another toast, John?"

"No, no, not that."

"What pray tell could it be, sir?" I asked, smirking. I could only call him by his first name when we were in private. Otherwise it was sir or major.

John went on. "It's Tuesday. Samantha, how long are you staying?"

"I don't have to go back until Sunday, my flight is Sunday morning. I have to be back at work in Richmond next Monday."

"That's great," he said. "Nelson, you have two weeks leave between schools and I'm going to take off a few days myself; I deserve it."

"Oh, you sure do, sir," I said, smiling.

I want you both to be at the flight line tomorrow morning at eight o'clock," he said. "We're gonna take a little trip you guys will never forget."

"Where are we going?" Samantha asked, excitedly.

"Just trust me. Pack a bag for two or three days and be ready to board at 9:00."

That night Samantha and I talked about all the risk taking and rule breaking that went on in the Army, something I learned more about later in my career.

"Do you think you'll be like that when you get back from Vietnam?" she asked, referring to taking risks and breaking rules.

"I sure hope I get back so I get the chance to find out," I said.

She didn't much like that line. "I don't find that so funny," she said.

We sat on the bedroom floor of my apartment in the bachelor officers' quarters and talked about the events of the day. We agreed that the next day was going to be interesting, and we committed to make it fun, no matter where John was taking us.

"Samantha, I bet we're going to the Texas coast or to New Orleans."

"I'm not going to even guess. I just want to be surprised and excited. I'm not a world traveler like you."

We fell asleep early in each other's arms, anticipating the next day.

When we walked into the transit depot at the airfield the next morning, John was standing there with a big shit-eating grin on his face. "Come on, cats," he said. "Our chariot awaits."

We walked out the door onto the tarmac and saw a ten-passenger VIP airplane sitting on the ramp with both engines running.

"John, how in the world did you do this?" Samantha asked. "And where are we going?"

"I've got friends, my dear, friends," John replied as he ushered Samantha onboard.

I knew exactly what John had done. He had gone to his buddy the airfield commander and told him what he wanted to do and his buddy made it happen. I was learning that almost anything could be had in the Army if you knew somebody who controlled it, and in many cases, even if you knew someone who knew someone.

Onboard the airplane were two pilots and a crew chief. We just settled into the big plush seats and let ourselves be chauffeured. After takeoff, John told Samantha that he thought it would be nice to run on up to Las Vegas for a couple of days and we could get married while we were there.

"There's no waiting period in Vegas; you two can be married immediately," he said. "We're going to land at Ellis Air Force Base. It's only a 15-minute cab ride downtown and there's a wedding chapel on every corner."

Samantha looked at me and asked, "Did you know about this?"

"Honey, I absolutely did not know, but it sounds like a good program to me. John can be our best man."

"Why not? I'll have something to tell my grandchildren," Samantha said.

The next few days were a fairytale for sure. Samantha and I were married that afternoon in a small wedding chapel right on the strip. Then John picked up the tab for a nice room at the Sands.

We all had a great time. Just seeing the place was an experience in itself. Everything was open around the clock and there were gamblers constantly laboring over the tables and machines. We spent our last night at the air base since we had an early departure back to Fort Walters.

I had just over a week left of my leave. I had to pick an airplane to transition into by the time I reported back for duty. While we were away in Vegas, John picked a time when Samantha was taking a nap to talk to me about what plane he thought I should choose. We talked about the different VIP airplanes. He also told me about the Army Security Agency's fleet of Listeners. These were twin turboprop Beechcraft Planes that had been converted and loaded with electronic eavesdropping equipment.

"They're in the air 24/7 over Nam, high above the guns and SAMS," he said. "The plane is great to fly, but the fucking mission is 12 or more hours and it's boring as hell. It's always flown with a copilot and navigator. That makes the pilot's duties much easier, but it's no challenge or fun."

John told me the pilot put the autopilot on and napped while the plane went around and around like it was on a big racetrack. Then when the mission ended you turned off the autopilot and flew home.

"John, I'm going to rely on you to advise me. You know the planes and the missions. You also know that my flight schooling before the Army was in planes that were almost all trainers."

John continued to educate me. "There are two things that a military pilot considers when he picks his aircraft. That is, if he's lucky enough to have an option as to what he wants to fly. First, there's the challenge of flying the aircraft itself. You have to consider whether it's large or small, whether it's a single or a multi-engine plane, and of course, whether there'll be a copilot on board. The second thing you have to consider is what mission the airplane is performing in the field. There are cargo planes, training aircraft, troop transports and planes that fly VIP-only missions."

John told me the most demanding of all the missions was the surveillance and intelligence-gathering missions known as spook missions.

"I know I want to fly an airplane that will challenge me. I know that much for sure."

"Quick question," He said. "Is the type of aircraft more important than the mission though?"

"Absolutely. I want to fly the most complicated and sophisticated airplane I can qualify for."

John's reply was just what I expected. "Nelson, I think for you there's only one airplane to fly. It's the same bird I flew last time in Vietnam. Let me tell you all about the OV1 Mohawk. With this option you get the best the Army has to offer."

"Didn't you tell me the missions were almost all at night?"

"I can't tell you very much until you get your security clearance," he said. "Both the airplane and the missions are Cryptic Top Secret."

"Well, just tell me what you can."

"The Mohawk's a large combat, hard, twin turboprop that's designed for short take-offs and landings. It's actually the only aircraft the Army flies that was specifically designed for combat."

"I like this John. I bet a STOL would be a hoot to fly, and its single pilot, too — right?"

"Yep, a single pilot who sits beside an enlisted tech who operates the electronic surveillance systems. The tech is the pilot's right hand. The plane's so powerful that it'll fly straight up. I can't say too much about it because it's a Black Program from start to finish. The entire Mohawk program is very small and elite and any pilot who's not chickenshit would want to fly that plane. Not many can qualify, though, since it's extremely demanding."

"Please, is there anything else you can tell me?"

"Just a little more. There were only 200 of the aircraft built. Probably 20% or more of those have been lost. Of course, you know full well it comes with a very dangerous mission."

"Where's the school?"

"Flight training is at Fort Rucker, Alabama. The system school is at Fort Huachuca, Arizona. You'd also have to qualify for carrier landings and that's at Pensacola Navy Air Station. You learn about the ejection seat while in the flight training portion."

"John, do you think I can get a slot in the Mohawk program?"

"If you want it, you got it. Hell, man, I'm a fellow with friends, remember."

"I want it."

"Okay," John said with a big smile as he put his hand out to shake mine. "You'll have to go to Black Training School first. I'll get you a slot there as soon as we get home. After that you'll go directly to Rucker. You'll have to be very careful what you tell Samantha."

It took John less than a month to get me a slot in the Black Training School, which was then followed by Mohawk School. Samantha went back to Virginia and rejoined me when I got to Rucker. Before she left she was very curious about what I was going to be flying there. Since the entire program was secret, I asked John how to handle her questions. He arranged a meeting to talk with her about what I was getting into. I don't know to this day what John told Samantha, but so help me, from that day on Samantha never once asked me about my work.

Black Training School, commonly referred to as BS, was required before a person could get an Encrypt Top Secret Clearance. ETSC was only one level below a White House Clearance. I had heard many rumors about this type of clearance. It turned out that the rumors paled in comparison to what it was really about.

The BS course was eight weeks long and was taught for four weeks at the Army intelligence center at Fort Huachuca, Arizona and for another four weeks at CIA Headquarters in Langley, Virginia. There were twenty-five people in each class and two new classes started every week. The students were from every military service, many departments of government as well as the CIA, FBI and the White House. Several of the women in the class were gorgeous and more than once I thought how distracting they were to the class.

For the most part, the students were all very bright, well-educated, and highly motivated professionals. I was two out of three and planned to get well-educated part as soon as possible.

When I first realized how many students there were in BS, I wondered how we could possibly keep secrets if we all had access to them. I soon learned that regardless of the level of security clearance, all military intelligence, which is an oxymoron in itself, was on a need-to-know basis.

We were told it was going to be a tough, fast-paced class. It turned out that was an understatement. The classes went from 5:00 each morning until 11:00 at night, seven days a week. The material was interesting and challenging. It was the first course I had ever taken that was demanding for me. Each subject was taught in one day-long block and almost every night there was an exam.

There were a lot of recycles and washouts in the class. Students got two chances to complete the program. If they failed the first time, they were sent back to start all over in the next scheduled class. If they failed the second time they were sent back where they came from. I was amazed that the entire course ran with the precision of a Swiss watch; it restored a little of my faith in military and government schools.

The course material covered everything from how to answer someone who asked what your job was to how to encrypt messages. There were a couple of days dedicated to how to recognize a person trying to glean secret information from you. There was a day about body language and how to read people's eye movements and facial expressions. I called this paranoia training.

There were several days spent on federal laws having to do with secret information and the restrictions on disclosing secret data. Of course, there was also a class on the punishment for disclosing secret data. The punishment was simple — it was treason.

There was no ranking when you completed the course. But by the time the class was over, the number of students had been whittled down to seventeen. And I received one of the four commendation letters passed out at graduation. When the school ended, I had two weeks leave before I had to report to Mohawk transition at Fort Rucker.

Since the second half of my BS training was at Langley, Samantha drove up after the school ended. It was a Friday and we decided to stay in DC that night. After checking into a motel, Samantha went into the bathroom before we headed out to dinner. I lay down on the bed, and went out cold; I didn't wake up until the next morning.

I awoke when I heard someone knocking on the door to the room. I was so groggy, I thought Samantha was still in the shower. "I'll get it," I called out to her. I got up, went to the door and opened it.

"Well, good morning, sleepy head. You sure fizzled out last night," Samantha said as she walked in the room with coffee and donuts.

"What time is it, anyway?" I asked. "I thought it was still last night."

Samantha put the box of donuts down and said, "Nope, it's almost 11:00. You haven't moved for 16 hours. Don't you have to go to the bathroom?"

"Oh yeah, thanks for reminding me."

"That must have been a fun school you were in," she said.

"No, actually it was bullshit," I replied.

We spent a week visiting Samantha's friends and family, where we spent one night. We had arrived about noon on a Saturday. I found it very interesting to see how her father's bootleg whiskey business was conducted. They lived in Orange County, Virginia and there was no legal alcohol sold in the county. There was a steady flow of customers all afternoon. Her father had an old shed out back, and when a customer drove up to it, he'd leave the house and go make the sale. He seemed to know them all and he gave curb service. His customers didn't have to leave their car.

While we were there, I made a special trip to see Samuel Goodman and just as always, the first thing Samuel asked was, "Hey boy, you getting any strange pussy?"

"Hell no, Samuel. Can you believe Samantha and I are married?"

"Congratulations, I figured you were going to marry her, but what does that have to do with getting strange pussy? Anyway, tell me all about it and the flight training."

We spent a couple of hours visiting. I told Samuel all that I could, skirting the parts I couldn't talk about. Finally, we said our goodbyes.

While Samantha and I were in town we stayed at my old apartment where she and Emma were still living. After she went to bed one night, I thought a lot about Samuel and how much I had benefited from our relationship. Samuel was always there for me no matter what the problem. In December 1965, Samuel Goodman died of a massive heart attack in his control room at the plant. He was supervising an emergency shut-down drill on a hydro generator. I didn't attend the funeral. I was 10,000 miles away at the time.

By now Samantha had quit her job working for Teddy and was mostly packed and ready to move to Fort Rucker. I think Emma was the most excited of any of us about the move. We had lunch at the airport once and I went up to Sidney's office to tell him goodbye. Julie looked and smelled as good as ever. When she got up to tell Sidney I was there, I smiled a big smile because I couldn't help but think about how good she probably was in bed.

Sidney gave me a chance to practice my avoidance training from BS as he asked a hundred questions about flight school. He wanted to know where I was being assigned and what kind of aircraft I was flying. I was quite proud of myself just giving him partial answers.

Before I left, Julie gave me a big hug goodbye. I told her how good she looked and said to myself, I'll bet you're a screamer.

As I was walking down the steps out of Sidney's office, I saw Teddy coming across the hanger.

"Hey, good buddy," Teddy said as he walked up and gave me a big hug.

"Teddy, I just got a big hug like that from Julie. Can you believe it?"

"Lucky you," Teddy said. "Could you tell if her boobs are real?"

"Oh yeah, they're real all right."

We both laughed and I said, "You're looking good, Teddy. How's everything?"

"Things could be better. You know, some dude came to town and took my secretary away."

I smiled and said, "Isn't love wonderful? You think you'll ever find it in your heart to forgive me? I never really meant to fall in love with her, you know."

"So, tell me all about the airplanes you're flying. Bet it's really exciting stuff, huh?"

Again I did the BS tap dance, avoiding giving Teddy

any specific information. I was getting pretty good at that spook stuff.

"To tell you the truth, Teddy, I don't know exactly which plane I'm going to be flying next." He forced me lie to him. "My assignment's to Fort Rucker, Alabama. We're pulling out tomorrow morning."

Teddy just couldn't stand it any longer and asked, "Hey, you gonna tell me how she is in bed?"

I gave Teddy a slap on the shoulder and smiled. "Oh, one day I probably will, but right now I don't have time, I've gotta go pack."

The next morning Emma and Samantha were up before the sun. Emma chattered away asking questions about where we were going to live. As we drove out of Richmond. I thought about what an adventure this was for all three of us.

As we passed through the main gate at Fort Rucker it was obvious that it was the home of all Army aviation. I'd never seen so many airplanes in one place. Not only were there airplanes I'd never seen, there were some I had never even heard of. Since I was on temporary assignment and had my family with me, there were no quarters available on the fort. It wasn't a problem and it didn't take long to find a little furnished apartment in Ozark, the town right outside the gate. Samantha had us settled in and comfortable in two days.

Our second morning, I went back on the post and reported in for duty. I learned the Mohawks were parked far back from the boundary fence. I could hardly wait for my school to start.

On the first day of school, I was in class at 5:00 a.m. The Army started everything it did at an unreasonably early hour. To me that was just further confirmation that one of the Army's main missions was the practice of misery.

I met the other nine guys in my class. There was supposed to have been fifteen total in the class but we were told that a SNAFU caused six not to get orders on time.

I immediately recognized that my classmates were some sharp folks. Most of them had been in the Army for several years. There were also three guys who were transitioning from helicopters and four others had been to Vietnam.

Although I had less military time, I fit in nicely. I was about their age and I had developed excellent people skills during my sales days. Additionally, my prior civilian flight time and licenses commanded a high level of respect, not just from my classmates, but from the instructors, too.

Our initial orientation was given by Colonel Tony Blevins. Blevins was also known as Little Tony Blevins. Little Tony was five feet six, but he could roar like a lion. Little Tony was commander of all the Mohawk training at Fort Rucker. He had flown two 12-month tours in the Mohawk in Vietnam. After complimenting us on earning the right to fly that airplane, he went into great detail to explain just how much of a privilege it was. He also told us that 90% of the Mohawk's mission in Nam was flying low level at night over the North.

We were all ears as Little Tony continued to explain about the airplane's high casualty rate and what caused it. He had us all spellbound as he continued on about the demands of flying over hostile mountainous terrain, low level, at night, in a sophisticated, single-pilot, high-performance, high-risk airplane. Throw in the requirement of supervising the enlisted observer sitting in the cockpit next to you and you've hatched a situation where even the tiniest mistake was lethal.

"While you're getting all that shit handled, don't forget the anti-aircraft fire. There's always a bunch of gooks down there trying to knock you out of the sky." He smirked and continued, "You will have your hands full, that's for fucking sure."

At the end of Little Tony's briefing he said, "Men, I've described as honestly as I can what you have to look forward to. So listen very closely to this and remember it every time you go near that airplane. There are nine of you now; two of you will quit or be washed out of this training before the class ends. That leaves seven; three of you seven will die in the airplane within a year."

After a long silence he continued, "Learn to fly this airplane well and pay strict attention to your instructors. Every one of them has flown the aircraft in combat. Memorize every nut, bolt and system on the Mohawk. Try to tame this flying machine with proficiency and knowledge. Good luck and God bless."

Blevins then added something I didn't understand at the time. "I'm not at all sure that all of Vietnam is worth a tiny part of the price we're paying for it."

He then turned and left the room. Before my Vietnam tour ended, I knew exactly what Tony Blevins meant. He was so right—it wasn't worth the hideous price we were paying.

That afternoon, we had our first hands-on introduction to the OV 1 Mohawk. It was everything I had envisioned and more. As I walked around the aircraft, I felt a sense of intense pride. I thought about my upbringing and, just for a moment, about my father. I wondered if he would have been proud of me. Day two we got down to the business of learning how to tame that flying machine.

We spent each morning in the classroom and each afternoon in the air. Our first training day was spent on the ejection seat, which of course was critically important. Positioning in the seat had to be exact or the 13 Gs experienced on ejection would crush a man's spine. The simulator itself was essentially an ejection seat mounted on a 25-foot tall rail that was tilted back about 15 degrees. The apparatus had large impact bumpers at the top to stop the upward trajectory. Each of us had to ride the seat three times. The instructors had a morbid standing joke about the seat. They told us that they had no way of knowing for sure, but they thought the seat had about a 50% failure rate. There was no way to be sure of that because when a seat failed, the pilot was never around to complain.

I went home after school the third day with my head spinning. I must have felt like the astronauts felt before their first lift off into space. The next afternoon I was going to fly the Mohawk.

My assigned flight instructor was a Warrant Officer Three named Lee Toms. His nickname was Gun. Gun was six seven and weighed 170 pounds. He was born in North Dakota on a sugar beet farm. He told me his daddy felt the same way about him working on that farm that my mother felt about me working in the coal mine. Anyway, Gun had married a Vietnamese woman while he was stationed there and they had a kid. When I asked him if it was difficult being married to a girl from Vietnam, he said the mechanics were easy, but getting people to accept her was quite difficult.

We were walking across the tarmac to the airplane the first day I met him when he said, "I see you've got the preflight manual with you. You won't be using it; you'll have to memorize every step because in the Mohawk there's no co-pilot to read it out to you. That's also true of the pre-takeoff, pre-landing, and emergency procedures checklist. They all must be memorized."

None of that bothered me since memorizing was easy for me. It did, however, present a problem for most of my classmates since the total number of items on the combined list was almost 300. Gun walked me through the preflight inspection, and then we climbed into the cockpit and buckled ourselves into the ejection seats.

The training aircraft were configured with duel flight controls. The instructor took the observer's ejection seat. His space was rigged with flight controls instead of the electronic infrared system. I expected my first flight to be a demonstration ride, but that didn't happen. Instead Gun talked me through the startup and taxi. My heart was pounding pretty fast as we were cleared onto the runway for takeoff. I held the brakes and pushed the throttles to full power. The aircraft had big 13-foot-long propellers with four blades. As they bit into the air, the airplane started shuttering as the engines fully spooled up. The first takeoff and every one after that was a great thrill.

I released the brakes at full power, and the machine lunged forward and screamed down the runway. I was pressed back in my seat so hard I couldn't hold my helmet off the back of the ejection seat. We were at takeoff speed almost immediately and had covered only 600 feet of runway. I had been used to flying airplanes that needed several thousand feet to take off. Of course, their engines were one-tenth the size of these, too. I eased the control stick back and the airplane seemed to leap into the air. We quickly climbed at 4,000 feet per minute to 16,000 before leveling off.

I could hear myself breathing through my oxygen mask. The rest of the flight was almost too much for words. Before returning to the airfield, Gun took the controls to demonstrate the aerobatic capabilities of the aircraft. He did inverted flight, rolls, loops and spins. Although the Mohawk was not designed to dog fight, aerobatics had to be learned before a pilot could be certified in the plane. That first time, and every time I ever took off in the Mohawk, it was the most exhilarating thing I had ever experienced.

The entire Mohawk school was incredibly demanding. Classes were 12 hours a day, 7 days a week. Toward the end of the school, I spent three days with the aircraft and Gun at Pensacola Navel Air Station in Florida. There we did carrier landings on an aircraft carrier stationed off the coast in the Gulf. Quite an experience is the best way I can explain that part of the training. When approaching a carrier to land, it looked like a postage stamp in the ocean. I had some tough competition in the class, but I was able to pull off another honor graduate, first-in-class again.

About half way through the transition my alert orders to Vietnam showed up. We knew they were coming, but it was a jolt back to the reality of what was coming next.

Although my reporting date was not set, I knew it would be soon after graduation. The orders confirmed that after graduation I would have to stop off at Fort Huachuca, Arizona, for eight weeks training on the infrared surveillance system used in the Mohawk.

The night of my graduation at Fort Rucker there was a party at the officers' club. Someone brought a wall map of the United States and everyone, instructors included; put an X on the map where they were from. Toward the end of the party, Samantha, who was well-lubricated from red wine, took a dare that was to determine her future.

Samantha agreed to be blindfolded and then randomly place a pin on the map — where that pin landed was where she and Emma would live while I was in Vietnam. It wasn't a place I would have picked, but three days later we took off for Wilmington, North Carolina. Wilmington would be their new home while I went to win the hearts and minds of the Vietnamese people and save their country. What a goddamn joke.

Chapter 6
Returning From Nam

A man came out of the crowd yelling at the top of his voice, "Welcome home, murderers! Killers of babies!" He was just a few feet from me. He then turned and ran away.

"Go to hell, asshole," I hollered, as I started for him.

I felt a strong hand grab my shoulder.

"Just let it go man, just let it go," a sergeant standing behind me said softly.

"Yeah, yeah, okay. Let's get the hell out of here."

"Come on. The terminal door is this way," he said.

We had just deplaned after our 19-hour flight to Seattle from Saigon. My flight back to the states was on a Boeing 707 under contract to the government and flown by Continental. Although my flight to Vietnam seemed to take a few hours, my return flight seemed to take an eternity.

Something else was different on this flight, as well. I knew several of the other guys on the flight, some were even from a unit next door to mine in Phu Bai. For the first time in the history of the United States, the senior psychiatrist in the military decided to conduct an experiment and not send units to Vietnam. They decided to only send individual soldiers. That was done in an effort to prevent unit bonding and cohesiveness. The theory was that when units lost soldiers in combat, it would be less disruptive if they weren't all old buddies from back home.

I couldn't believe I was back in the States. It was like a dream that was happening to someone else.

The Army considered me a returning hero. I had another opinion. I was returning as a captain. I had flown 336 low-level night combat missions over North Vietnam. I was one of the most highly decorated Army pilots to come out of the Vietnam War. I had been awarded a Distinguished Flying Cross, two Bronze Stars for Valor, 34 Combat Air Medals, and a Vietnamese Cross of Gallantry. I also had a chest full of other shit.

However, I had become a habitual heavy drinker. My horrible, near-death experience resulted in chronic Post Traumatic Stress Disorder. The indulgent, or overindulgent, use of alcohol and the psychological scars destroyed the rest of my life. At that moment, all I wanted to do was pick up my wife Samantha, our four-year-old daughter Emma, and go hide for the rest of my life.

That first night, the sergeant from the flight and I—I don't even remember his name—shared a hotel room near the airport. We enjoyed a hard night of drinking in our room. We didn't want to go out for fear of running into more anti-war crazies. Seattle was a major returning point for Vietnam vets and because of that, the entire area was full of protesters just waiting for a confrontation. The next morning, wearing civilian clothes, we went back to the airport to catch our respective flights home.

At 7:00 a.m. American Air Lines notified the waiting passengers that the flight to Washington, DC was going to be delayed for three hours. I went to the bar and did battle with myself—I would only get high, not drunk. I just wanted to drink enough to try to feel better. Flight time finally came and, after boarding, I found myself seated next to a mature and sophisticated looking gentleman and his wife.

They wanted to talk; I just wanted to be left alone. The man asked me where I was headed and I told him my wife was meeting me in DC. I knew right away I shouldn't have said that for fear he would find out I had just returned from Nam.

"Where have you been, young man?" his wife asked.

"Well, I'm just coming from Seattle," I replied, hoping she would leave it at that. But no such luck. They were too friendly and I figured they probably didn't want to talk to each other.

"I'm Sarah Banning and this is my husband, Andrew," she said. "We're from Seattle and we're going to Washington for a church convention, Andrew is a Lutheran minister."

I thought back to the preacher I knew as a child and wondered if Andrew also gave God's blessing to little boys.

"That's very nice," I said, hoping that was the end of it. Well, it wasn't, she just kept after it.

"And what were you doing in Seattle?"

I didn't know what to say.

"You're returning from Vietnam, aren't you?" Andrew asked.

I couldn't process all the crap that was running through my mind. Goddamn it, couldn't they just leave me alone? I didn't want to lie to them, but I didn't want another encounter like the one in the airport, either.

Finally I said, "Yes."

Dear Sarah just had to ask, "Did you have to kill anyone over there?"

"Son, don't be ashamed of your service there," Andrew said. Not everyone in the United States thinks harshly of you boys."

I didn't reply for a long moment.

Then I said, "Yes, sir."

"I know you've seen a lot of news about the anti-war marches and demonstrations and I know what the press is saying about the atrocities you fellas committed over there."

Now he was really twisting my mind. Was he putting me down? Was he going to berate me, too? I decided to level with him and hope he would just leave it alone.

"Sir, I was told to go and I went. I just did my job. I would like to not talk about it if you don't mind."

He completely ignored me and went right on. "It must be very difficult for you boys returning to this mess we have in our country. I was in World War II and when we came home we were heroes. The marches and demonstrations were to honor us, not to dishonor us."

"Yes, sir," I said.

Sarah came alive again. "We all think you're heroes, even if you're not."

To this day I don't know if she said it as a compliment or a slap.

"Yes, ma'am."

Then Andrew said, "Let's just not talk about it anymore."

"God, let these people stop," I thought.

"Yes, sir," I responded.

I just wanted to melt into the seat. I could feel eyes on me from all around as I closed mine and quickly pretended to sleep. When Andrew and his wife finally left me alone, I made a commitment to myself that I was not going to drink anymore, ever again.

Samantha and Emma met me at the DC airport. Samantha had put our furniture together in my apartment and now the Army movers had taken everything to storage. The apartment lease had expired and they'd move and deliver our stuff wherever we wanted it.

We had a warm and wonderful reunion. Samantha drove and we stopped in Woodbridge, Virginia, and checked into a little roadside motel. I showered and cleaned up and then we went out to eat.

Before we left the room Emma came over and gave me a big hug and said, "I'm so happy you're home, Dad. I'm so glad you didn't get killed in the war. Please don't ever go to a war again. Promise me, please?"

I was paralyzed, as I sat on the edge of the bed holding this precious, innocent, beautiful little girl in my arms. My body was seriously sick from the unusually large amount of scotch I had consumed the night before in Seattle. I thought about the promise I had made my father not to ever drink. I had to quit.

A million other memories ran through my head — the

shell exploding when it hit my airplane; Jerry Thompson's arm in my lap; and the protester screaming, "baby killer."

I came back to reality and realized I was crying. I reached for Samantha and held the two of them there for a long, long time.

"God, I'm so glad to be home," I said, sobbing. "Emma, I promise you, I will never go to another war."

After a bit I got up and went into the bathroom, threw cold water on my face and composed myself. We went out for a nice seafood dinner. It was the best meal I had eaten in 15 months. Emma drank soda, Samantha had wine, and I drank iced tea.

Emma and I stayed up and watched television all night. I hadn't seen a TV in over a year. Late the next morning we drove down to visit Samantha's parents.

Although in the past I had always resisted when Samantha's stepfather offered me some of his fine product, this time I gave in. I felt shitty; it had only been hours since the last time I promised to quit drinking. I got pretty drunk a couple of nights during our visit. I started to realize that I didn't only want the whiskey, I had to have it.

After a few days it was time for us to leave. So we packed the car and were off to my next duty station at Fort Huachuca, Arizona. Our trip from Virginia to Arizona took four days and we had a delightful time visiting and bonding on the way.

Fort Huachuca was a beautiful, old installation set in the high desert of the Parker Mountains in southern Arizona. The fort was just a few miles north of the Mexican border. There were three streets of old, restored Civil War era homes. These were assigned only to officers and we were lucky enough to get a nice one. The home was fully furnished, including linens and silverware. Samantha and Emma were super excited about our new home. There were huge old cottonwood trees along the street and in the yard. There was even a little park across the street.

Huachuca was the home of the Army Intelligence

School. However, my experiences were rapidly leading me to believe "Army Intelligence" was an oxymoron. It was also the home of the intelligence gathering airplane, the OV 1.

One of the best parts of the whole new scene for me was the fact that the sun shone brightly every day, unlike Nam, where it rained almost every day. The fort was 5,000 feet above sea level, which made it comfortably cool as well.

I was assigned to flight duty as an instructor in the Mohawk. The difference from flying in Nam was that here I flew half nights and half days. And, of course, there were no anti-aircraft guns firing at me. I taught new pilots how to fly the aircraft at low level and how to navigate low level to distant targets at night. Our targets were as far north as Idaho and as far east as Tennessee.

Samantha went to work for a local real estate firm. She was very good at sales. Emma started first grade at the elementary school on the post, which was only two blocks away from our house.

On the trip out to Huachuca I had also spent a good deal of time thinking about the promise I had made to my father that I would never drink. Finally, without saying anything to Samantha, I resolved to once again quit drinking. It was kind of a Catch-22, though. When I didn't drink, the nightmares and flashbacks increased in frequency and intensity. Sometimes the devastation from the aftermath of those wretched nightmares was almost debilitating—much worse than any hangover from alcohol.

The nightmares were always exactly the same. I was sitting in the cockpit of the aircraft flying straight down into the jungle. Jerry's arm was lying in my lap, and we were moments from crashing and dying. I would awake with a sheen of heavy, cold sweat soaking me and the sheets. Often I would be kicking my legs and swinging my arms, trying to get out of the cockpit.

My efforts to stop drinking soon ended. Again and

again I drank until I passed out and then I slept. The shrink's term for drinking like that was "self medicating." I still called it drinking too much. I knew I was drinking too much and, although I frequently resolved to stop, I couldn't go without the alcohol.

I worked a variety of shifts, and on nights when we flew I was off all day until late in the afternoon. That gave me time to do other things. Just a few months after arriving at Huachuca, I decided to go to the education center on the post and check into taking some college courses. I was very apprehensive because I knew that my previous education in no way gave me any foundation to study at a college level.

During my interview, the counselor reviewed my personnel records. When he saw my IQ score and other test scores, he said he felt I might qualify for a Test Out program. The Test Out program allowed me to study the textbook and course material of a number of courses and then take a final exam. If I got the equivalent of an A on the exam I would get the credits for the course without having to actually attend it. I could proceed as rapidly as I wanted to and take any level of courses, in any order I wanted.

I completed an application for that program and the counselor said it would be reviewed by a board of professors at the University of Arizona. He would notify me of the results within two weeks.

That was my first experience with an Army Education Center and I found it very impressive. They offered both military and civilian courses. They offered in-house classes from three universities as well as a seemingly unlimited number of correspondence courses from many different universities. A soldier could take casual courses of interest or work toward any degree from a GED to PhD.

I was called back to see the counselor in just a week. He told me that I had been accepted in the Test Out program for courses up to and including the master's program. After that, if I wanted to go on I could apply for the same program to earn a PhD. I was very excited about that and immediately took the study material for my first three courses. I also enrolled in two weekend courses that I was required to attend since they were not part of the Test Out program curriculum.

The pace was a killer, but I found most of the courses to be little challenge. I liked the management and marketing courses best.

One of my professors was a very sophisticated gentleman named Benjamin Cain. Benjamin was a retired attorney and judge. He moonlighted at the University of Arizona and commuted 70 miles from Tucson to teach those classes at Huachuca. Benjamin had previously done a stint in the Army and it was obvious that he loved being around the troops and on the post itself. Near the end of my second course with him, he called me in for a meeting. We sat down across from each other in the classroom after everyone had left.

"Well, Captain, what do you intend to do with all this education you're getting?" he asked.

"I don't know, sir. I know I'm going to get out of the Army soon. I've thought about getting a job in business with a company somewhere. I guess I've also thought about going to law school."

He smirked. "Oh, god, that's just what the world needs — another lawyer. I advise you to do anything but that."

"It seems there's a good living to be made as a lawyer and it's certainly a stable life, isn't it?"

"You have no idea the ends to which my colleagues will go to make money. There are a very, very few who have even an iota of either ethics or morals. From the street lawyers all the way to the big corporate boys, including the many who are serving in the Congress and Senate, the level of ruthlessness, deceit and self-serving is unparalleled."

I couldn't believe what I was hearing.

He continued, "Besides, you're probably too smart to be a lawyer. Most of them aren't too bright."

"Well, I've never had an experience with a lawyer, so I'll be sure to remember what you're saying."

"You will be well-served to never forget what I have just said. I have experienced this firsthand for many years."

"Sir, I am fascinated by what you're saying. So what would you advise I consider when I get out of the Army?"

He pushed back his chair, stood, then said, "Nelson, you have a brain and that is something few people possess. Additionally, you have exquisite people skills. Your drive and motivation are proven, considering where you started. My first advice to you is stay in the Army and get that general's star. You know it will come and come early the way you're going. Finish your master's and PhD and you may get several stars. If you do decide to get out, then you must go into business for yourself. The quickest way to make big money is to own your own business. I don't mean a hot dog stand. Start something that has big growth potential. For years I've been a lawyer and represented many business owners who make up to 25 times as much money as I do."

Our meeting ended and I assured Benjamin how very much I appreciated his time and his advice.

One thing was for sure, during that meeting I made up my mind I'd start immediately working toward my master's degree.

That night Samantha and I talked for a long time about my session with Professor Cain. I told her I was planning to get out of the Army at some point. She wasn't too keen on the idea, but she said it was my decision. We agreed that I would sit tight until I had finished my master's degree. If all went well, that would be less than a year away.

Soon life seemed to settle down and it actually became routine. I was pretty happy with my flying job and I had also started working on a double master's in management and marketing, with a minor in language. I was working on three degrees at one time as well as working full time every day. I was extremely busy, but it seemed I still found time to drink too much.

We had a pregnancy scare during our time at Huachuca and even though it was a false alarm, we decided to do something about that. It was common knowledge that it was against regulations for Army doctors do any type of sterilization surgery. But with the help of my Army buddies, I found an old doctor downtown in nearby Sierra Vista who would perform the vasectomy. He was pretty popular and did that procedure only on Saturday mornings in his office.

We were a close knit group of aviators and to say we all knew each other's business was an understatement. A friend of mine told me how easy it was and that the price was $125 dollars in cash. I talked it over with Samantha and she wanted me to do it. I called and made an appointment for the following Saturday.

The doctor did the operations during his regular office hours. When I went into the office, which was in an out-of-the-way, nondescript little building; I found myself in a waiting room with 20-plus chairs and most of them were full. There were men and women of all ages there. There was a black and white Gibson television on a small corner table and several magazines scattered around. The receptionist/nurse was behind a sliding window.

As I approached she opened the window and said in a loud raspy voice, "What is your name?"

Her volume knob was turned up to the max and I'm sure people in the next county could hear her.

"I'm Nelson," I said.

Oh, yeah, you're here for a vasectomy," she yelled. "I'm Hilda. I'm the doctor's nurse."

"Yes," I said as I looked around at all the people who were staring at me.

"Okay," she said. "Take this little bottle into the bathroom there and put a sperm sample in it. Then bring it back to me. The doctor will want to make sure you need this operation before he does it."

I looked at the door she pointed to. The sign on it said Supplies/Bathroom. She pushed the little container into my hand. I obediently turned and went into the supply room as instructed. Inside the room was a tiny commode, a small corner sink, and a wall mirror about ten inches square. On the tank top of the commode was a Prevention magazine that looked like it was a hundred years old with pages frayed and worn.

I could not believe I was going to have to produce a sperm sample in that room with only that magazine to look at. Much less with a room full of people listening and knowing what I was doing in there. I knew for sure I was not the first guy to have that unusual opportunity. I was very careful to be quiet. After what seemed like forever, I was almost ready to complete the assignment.

Suddenly there was a hard rap on the door followed by Hilda's screechy voice. "How you doing in there? The doctor is almost ready for you."

I leaned near the door and whispered, "I'm having a bit of a problem getting this done."

"Yeah, well, you aren't the first one, honey," she said. "Just think about me and do it quick; you know how it's done."

So, I've got the Prevention magazine in one hand, me in the other, and I proceeded to be quick. Sure enough I got a spritz in the sample dish. I was glad as well as sad to leave the supply closet as every eye in the place was on me as I sheepishly walked back to Hilda's window.

Soon I was summoned through the door that led to the doctor's small exam room. It was barely larger than the exam table. Hilda instructed me. "Take your pants and underpants off, darling, and lay back there and put your heels in these stirrups."

She produced what looked like a 100-year-old Gillette double-edged razor and dry shaved my scrotum. It hurt like hell. Then she applied a local anesthetic. That really burned and it was all I could do not to scream.

The old doctor came in and said, "You've got some real Olympic swimmers in your sperm there, young fellow, but we're gonna put a stop to that right now. You're sure you wanna do this, right?"

"Doctor, my wife thought she was pregnant about a month ago. She's been on the pill for a couple of years. When this happened, I told her I'd start using condoms. You wanna know what she said? She said, and I quote, "You can get a vasectomy or you can start jacking off, but if you jack off you better do it in another state because I don't want your sperm within a hundred miles of me."

The doc said, "Well, I guess she told you in a way you'd understand."

"Let's get on with the cutting, doc," I said, wanting to get it done with.

I felt a tiny cut that didn't hurt. Then it felt like he reached in with his finger, pulled the cords out of the hole, cut and tied them. A couple of sutures and it was all over in about three minutes.

"Stay off your feet for a couple of days and come back in two weeks for me to remove the sutures, okay? We'll recheck your sperm then, too. We don't want any surprises, do we."

"Okay, doctor. I'll see you in two weeks."

"You give that little fellow a rest now; no sex until after you come back," Hilda said.

"Okay," I said and left as quickly as I could.

Exactly two weeks later, I went back to the doctor's office. I was pleased to see there were only a few people in the waiting room and I didn't recognize any of them.

"Let's get the sperm sample first, then we'll get those sutures out," Hilda said right on cue and loud enough for people in the next building to hear.

Again, I went into the little closet/bathroom. However, I was a little better prepared this time. I sat down and unfolded a Playboy centerfold that I'd brought with me and quickly produced a sperm sample. I returned it to Hilda and took a seat as instructed to await the outcome.

After a few minutes Hilda called out to me. "Nelson, your sperm's dead as a doornail. Come on in here and let's get those sutures out, then you can go home and have all the fun you want to."

Again the doc showed up and quickly snipped and pulled the little sutures out. When he was finished, he looked up and said, "Good luck and enjoy yourself."

After running a couple of errands, I headed home. The most important thing I did was to stop by the commissary and purchase a big steak, a couple of baking potatoes, fixings for a salad and a couple bottles of champagne. Samantha and I had planned a celebration that night with lots of romance and great sex.

Around 6:00, I was about to open the champagne and put the charcoal on when the doorbell rang. When Samantha opened the door, there must have been ten couples waiting to wish us a happy evening. Of course, their plan was to prevent any sex that night—kind of a sick joke. It was almost 4:00 in the morning when the last of them stumbled out of the house. They were successful in their plan because by that time I was so drunk I couldn't have performed if I'd wanted to.

Samantha was having great success selling real estate in Sierra Vista, the town just outside the post. We put aside a little money and Samantha was talking about finding investment property. Emma loved her school and made lots of friends in the neighborhood. Her closest girlfriends were two little girls her age that lived right next door.

The girls' father, Frank Aubrey, and his wife, Ann, had become our best friends. Frank was also a pilot assigned to the airfield detachment. He had flown medical evacuation helicopters in Nam. Coincidently, Frank was the chopper

pilot who took Jerry Thompson and me out to the Red
Cross ship the night we were shot up. Frank was about
as screwed up as I was and he was a hard drinker, too. Of
course, we never discussed the screwed up part. Samantha
told me that Ann had confided in her that Frank also had
really bad nightmares.

My drinking had taken on a new dimension. On the
days we finished early at the airfield, Frank and I and
several others would head out to the Officers' Club and
start drinking—sometimes as early as 2:00 in the afternoon.
We'd be completely drunk by 4:00.

When Frank and I had all the scotch we could handle,
we raced to our cars to see who could drive home the fast-
est. The person who got home first was the winner. One of
the rules of our game was that we had to take a different
route home each night.

One particular Friday afternoon, Frank said he
couldn't go to the club because it was his anniversary. He
and Ann were going out to dinner. I called him a chickenshit and dared him to go for a few celebratory drinks
before his date. He took the dare and we had several
drinks more than even our normal load. We left the club in
our drunken stupor, went to our cars and started the race. I
beat Frank home and stood for several minutes in my front
yard waiting for him to arrive so I could ridicule him for
being a loser. Finally, I got tired of waiting so I went into
the house and poured myself a big glass of scotch. Then I
went to bed and quickly passed out.

Several hours later Samantha awakened me and told
me the military police were at the door and wanted to talk
to me. I climbed out of bed and still half asleep and still a
little drunk went to the front door. A young sergeant told
me that Frank had an accident on his way home. He had
run a stop sign and hit a little eight-year-old girl. He had
killed her. He was in the post confinement center, and
when they went to notify Ann, she asked them to come
next door and tell me. I was paralyzed. I couldn't believe

what I was hearing. I remembered the promise I had made to my father: "No, Daddy, I will never drink that—I don't like it."

The next day I went to see Frank in the confinement center on the post. The military police let me go into his cell. We embraced for a long time, and then just stood looking at each other. Finally, I tried to tell him how sorry I was and that I felt so very responsible for what had happened. We cried for a long time and again I told him how very sorry I was. More importantly, I promised him I would never again touch a drop of alcohol. I promised Frank just as hard as I had promised my father many years earlier. Frank hugged me, stared at me and cried with me, but he never spoke a word to me during that visit. That was the last time I ever saw Frank Aubrey.

That very night I sat on my back patio for a long time holding a quart of scotch. I thought about all the events in my life that had brought me to that heartbreaking moment. I stood up and threw the bottle of scotch into the brick wall of the house. The bottle broke into a million pieces. I screamed. "Goddamn it. Goddamn it." Then I went into the house, opened another bottle and drank my fill.

Two months later, Capt. Frank Aubrey was sentenced to ten years hard labor in the military prison at Fort Leavenworth, Kansas. Four years after that, Frank was murdered when he was stabbed by another prisoner in the chow hall.

After Frank's trial, Ann took the two girls and went to live with her parents in Albuquerque, New Mexico. Samantha tried to contact her many times, but there was never any reply. Then one day, a couple of years later, when we were living in Fort Sill, Oklahoma, Samantha received an envelope post marked Albuquerque with no return address. There was no note inside just a torn out newspaper article announcing Ann Aubrey's death by suicide. When I came home that night Samantha handed it to me. We sat in silence for a long while, and then I got drunk. We never, ever uttered a word about that article.

Soon, Samantha found a fixer-upper house downtown. We could purchase it and live in it while we fixed it up to resell. We were able to get a loan to buy the house that included some money for remodeling. We supplemented the repairs with our savings and the entire project was a great success. We got lots of assistance from my friends. Deal was, they could eat all the burgers and drink all the beer they could hold in exchange for their labor. Consequently there was always an abundance of labor available.

There were both good and bad points to this arrangement. The good was I always had plenty of free labor. The bad was that I often had to put a stop to the work because the guys were too drunk to do a good job. The real challenge was to be able to skillfully figure out when that time had come.

We got the house finished pretty quickly. When it sold, I couldn't believe how much money we made. We actually made a little more than my pay for an entire year. When I called Benjamin Cain and told him about our first business venture, he said that he wasn't surprised at all. Of course, he used that as an example to reinforce the things he had told me about being in business.

"Captain, this is but a small example of being an entrepreneur," he said.

"Well, if it's always like this, I think I like it a lot," I said. "You know, sir, I think I can be good at business."

"Darn right you can," he replied. "Just remember when you're in business, you're the driver and you can make the business take you anywhere you want to go. Have you decided to stay in or get out of the Army?"

"Sir, Samantha and I have made a decision to get out and I am going into business for myself. I'm working hard on my degrees and plan to get out as soon as I get my master's degree finished."

"That's great," he said. "Glad you decided to rent your lawyers in the future instead of being one yourself."

Things changed rapidly in the Army and often for no

apparent reason. The Army brass never stopped proving to me just how stupid some of their decisions could be.

I received an alert for orders to attend, of all things, Desert Survival School. Not only was I right in the middle of courses for my degrees, but the only Theater of Operations in the Army was in was the jungle in Vietnam. If anything, why not Jungle Survival School?

Not only that, but everyone including the Pentagon's personnel officers knew I was resigning within a few months. For me to go to survival school was crazy. It was a total waste. I immediately requested an audience with my commanding officer.

I reported to Lt. Colonel Charles Mimms. "Sir, I have alert orders to Desert Survival School. I'm in the middle of two senior level college courses, and I'm getting out of the service very soon."

"So why don't you just ask your professors to let you off for two weeks?"

"That wasn't the answer I was looking for, sir."

"Well, what's your solution?" he asked. "You want the entire Army to stop for you, I guess."

"Well, sir, that isn't what I had in mind, but it's not a bad idea," I responded, showing my disgust. "Can you really arrange for that to be done for me?"

"Captain, don't be a smartass. Just because I wasn't selected for Nam duty, don't ever think I'm stupid."

"No, sir," I said sarcastically. "I don't think that's why you're stupid." I knew he wouldn't get my back-handed reply.

When a guy only outranks you by only one or even two ranks, he can't do much to hurt you, so I wasn't too concerned about what I said to Mimms. The truth was that everyone thought Mimms was a second generation inbred and he had been issued an overly generous portion of stupid. Mimms didn't let me out of going to the survival school. That would have been too logical. He did let me have a later start date. I was to start the school one week after my exams ended.

Survival school was like a lot of other Army training activities. It was mostly an exercise in being miserable. The location for the training was the Sonoran Desert in the northern part of Mexico. The survival school was a joint training exercise with a group of elite Mexican Army officers.

On the first morning, we staged at 5:00 a.m. at our airfield. I attended a short briefing with four other officers I didn't know. After the briefing, we were loaded onto a UH 1 helicopter. The other four officers were from several different installations around the country. The pilot flew us low level, south across the border 90 miles to a small Mexican Army post near the city of Hermosa. The other four officers were not aviators and two of those guys were very uncomfortable about the low-level flying. It didn't bother me at all; I was used to low-level flying. I also knew the pilot and knew he had had a tour flying slicks in Nam.

After unloading the aircraft we were introduced to the five Mexican officers who were also attending the class. They all spoke perfect English. During the next three days, we spent 18 hours a day in classroom training. About half the classes were in English and half in Spanish. Our instructors were two American and three Mexicans officers.

The classes and the course material were boring. Although the instructors tried very hard, the whole thing just dragged along. Like many of the military schools I had ever been to, it took the instructors three hours to cover thirty minutes worth of material.

During those three days of classes I gained a lot of respect for the professionalism of the Mexican officers. They were smart and motivated. They also made sure we knew they considered it an honor to train with us. I was the only gringo to have completed a tour in Nam and that fact made me something of a celebrity in the group.

Day four started at 3:00 a.m. First, each of us was issued a backpack with our survival gear and four meals of C-Rations. We were to find the rest of our own food in the desert. The equipment in each backpack consisted of a compass, poncho, canteen for water, two small plastic bags, matches, an Army survival knife, and a lot of other useless crap. I was reminded that it was an Army exercise when I opened the package of heavy string and found two fishing hooks with the string. Oh well, it might rain in the desert.

During the class we learned how to rig a poncho in order to collect condensation at night and which cacti had water in them. We learned which plants and snakes were edible and, of course, how to snare jackrabbits and desert rats. I looked forward to the gourmet meals.

We were divided into five teams, each with two men. The teams were instructed to stay separated and not link up with another team. At dawn it seemed we couldn't put off our survival exercise any longer. We were loaded onto a big Army troop carrier and off to the drop points we went.

Each team was released ten miles apart, from east to west. That meant we were spread out over a line east to west and 90 miles long. Our boundaries were a road that ran north to south 20 miles to our west; the Sea of Cortez, commonly called the Gulf of California, to our east; and the US-Mexico border 70 miles to our north. The objective of the exercise was to stay alive while navigating the desert.

The end of the course was a tiny outpost 95 miles north at the US-Mexican border. We had 12 days to get to that destination. There was no competition between teams. Everyone had the same objective. If you didn't finish successfully, and you were still alive, you'd be reassigned to the next course to try again. That was all the motivation we needed to finish.

My teammate was Captain Juan Rodriguez. Juan was a sharp, competent officer who at 30 was about the same age as me. He had been in the Army since he was 15. Juan's first assignment when he joined the Army was to attend four years of high school in Mexico City. That was followed by four years at the University of Mexico. The Mexican military put a great deal of investment into a man who expressed a desire to make the military his career.

By the time we got dropped off at our particular start point, the sun was up and the temperature was climbing fast. Temperatures in the Sonoran Desert often reached 130 degrees on a hot day. The heat was more the enemy than starvation on that exercise. Since the sun was rising from the east, I knew if I faced the sun and put out my left arm, I would be pointing to the north. I took out my compass and identified the exact direction we needed to take to get to the border.

"Did I tell you that I've taken this survival school before, about three years ago?" Juan asked.

"No, you never mentioned that," I said, surprised. "Why are you taking it again?"

"I guess my Army does illogical things, too," he said. "When my orders came, I first thought that I would try to get out of taking the school again. But I haven't seen my family for almost a year, so I changed my mind."

"I'm sure I don't understand what you're saying."

"Well, gringo," he said, smiling, "I have a wonderful surprise for you, my new friend."

I had picked up the name gringo the first day of class while jousting with the Mexicans. I actually liked it. I felt it was kind of endearing. Everyone really liked it when I referred to myself as gringo.

"Wait, don't tell me, let me guess. Someone is going to come along in a chopper and pick us up, right?" I laughed and continued, "Or is it going to be an air-conditioned limo that comes out here for us?"

"No air conditioning, but if we go south about two miles, there's a road that will take us to Baja Kino, better known as Kino Bay. Kino is my home town; it's where all my family lives. I'm only 30 miles from home. My mama is expecting me."

"So, we gonna walk to Kino, then to the border, right?"

Juan grinned and shook his head. "No, man; would I make you walk all that way? My brother is going to pick us up."

I thought about that detour a moment, I knew we'd still have plenty of days left to make our rendezvous point at the end of the course.

"Don't worry, just trust old Juan."

"Okay, you have my life in your hands," I said.

"Now you know why I didn't mind taking the school again."

I thought about the irony of that turn of events, I was going to the beach instead of going farther into the desert. We headed south and arrived at the road to Kino at about 10:30 a.m. Just like clockwork, an old pickup came rattling along the road. It looked like it was at least 20 years older than I was, and it was so rusty it looked like it had been stored for years in salt water.

"This is my brother, Roberto." Juan rushed to the driver's door. "Buenos dias, Roberto. Como esta usted, mi hermano; how are you, my brother?" Roberto spoke very little English, but that was not a problem as my Spanish was almost perfect. I had learned Spanish in Vietnam. I'd had a Hispanic tech flying with me for a full week after Larry was shot up and evacuated. With languages being easy for me, at the end of that week I was fluent. Then of course I had a refresher during the classroom portion of this school with the Mexican officers. We climbed into the cab of the truck and headed off down the dusty road to the west.

Although the area received less than ten inches of rain per year, the Sonoran desert was not just sand. There was an abundance of cacti, sage brush, low mesquite and iron-wood trees. Most all of the growth in the Sonora, looked dead, but with just a few drops of rain, it turned into a lush paradise. It was a phenomenon that had to be seen to be believed. The change was like a magic dance of time-lapse photography that ended in brilliant color. Every plant bloomed beautiful flowers.

Juan and Roberto chattered incessantly. They were both as excited as children on Christmas morning.

Soon the conversation turned to me and Roberto started asking questions. He wanted to know all about my Army career as well as my life. He told me he had wanted to go into the Army like his brother, but his hearing was really bad and he couldn't pass the physical.

We continued to exchange information about our lives and families. Roberto wanted to know how many children I had and if they were boys or girls. He told me he had been to the United States two times, once in Dallas. He liked that city, but said it was very big.

The miles passed quickly, and soon we saw Juan's village on the horizon. Kino only had a couple hundred residents, most of whom lived along the beach in small adobe blockhouses.

Most of the houses were unfinished, even though many of them were very old. I learned that poor Mexican people, like the poor in most all of Central America, built only the rooms that they needed and only if and when they could pay for the materials. In fact, it is still true that most Central Americans often buy just one or two adobe bricks at a time as they can pay for them. There were three noticeably nicer houses in the center of town. They were two stories, painted bright colors and even had adobe fences with metal gates.

Juan told me that the shrimp and fishing boat owners owned two of those houses and the third belonged to the owner of the general store. In small villages like Kino there was usually only one store. It sold everything that was needed to sustain life in the village. That meant everything from bread and groceries to truck tires, boat engine parts, building materials and clothes. When I told Juan and Roberto about the company store I grew up with they found the similarity interesting.

The nearest city was Hermosa, about 70 miles west

and connected by a dirt road. Obviously the general store did a thriving business. Upon realizing I was seeing a part of Mexico that most people never dreamed of seeing, I relaxed and took in the cacti studded countryside we were driving through.

Roberto pulled to an abrupt stop in front of a group of five houses that were clustered just a few yards from the water's edge. All the houses shared a common, sand yard with a large, thatched roof, open palapa building in the courtyard. The little compound was fenced on three sides with sticks standing about four-feet high and placed so close together they touched each other. There were no gates, just a couple of openings. Well-worn paths led from the dirt street to the palapa.

Suddenly an elderly lady with long gray hair and a mostly toothless smile came rushing from the palapa. She was barefoot and her dress looked like a multi-colored tapestry. Her hands were in the air and her voice could be heard a long way. She was screaming, "Juan! Juan!"

Juan threw the door to the truck open, jumped out, and ran toward her yelling in Spanish, "Madre, Madre. Oh, my Madre, you are so beautiful."

The homecoming was a beautiful sight. More of Juan's family started coming from inside the houses as well as from the palapa. The kids were running across the beach from the water as several arrived from the street.

I later found out that, including spouses and children, there were more than 30 people in Juan's family. He had five brothers and three sisters; most were married and had kids. The kids' ages spanned from one month old to teenagers. They were all very shy in front of me and I was sure they'd had little, if any prior contact with a gringo. During the introductions, I shook their hands and couldn't begin to remember all their names, much less who belonged with whom.

That night was something to behold. Everyone gathered under the palapa to eat, talk, and visit. The palapa is the central point where all the cooking, eating, and socializing occurs. Jullua, Juan's mother, and the other woman prepared a wonderful meal. In all the excitement, we had forgotten to have lunch and we were both starving.

The cooking was done in a large, rustic fireplace at one end of the palapa and was constructed entirely of rocks and large sea shells. The workmanship was beautiful with every stone and shell perfectly matched and laid out precisely, leaving room for an open grate on one side and a large steel grill on the other. We ate fresh fish covered with onions. Potatoes were sliced and fried and there seemed to be tons of shrimp. A big pot of black beans sat beside a stack of corn tortillas. One of Juan's sisters made a hot, spicy salad using onions, jalapeños, and a desert cucumber that look like a gourd. Cilantro was sprinkled on top of the salad as it was served. The men drank local beer that was so strong it made your toes curl, while the women and kids had Coca-Cola. Dessert was sopapillas, which is a type of puffy, fried pastry drizzled with honey.

Juan's father was a merchant seaman who came home only two or three times a year. He had come home in honor of Juan's visit as soon as he learned of it. All Juan's brothers and brothers-in-law worked on the shrimp and fishing boats. The boats worked right out of the village and when they went out, it was understood the fisherman could be away a few days or as long as a month, depending on the catch.

It was a lovely evening, and I marveled at the respect, the love, and the kindness displayed by everyone there that night. It made me feel a little sad and, for some reason, very alone. I thought a lot about Nam and no matter how much beer I drank, it seemed I couldn't keep the demons at bay.

After everyone went to bed, Juan and I took a jug of tequila, which I badly needed, and went down to the bay to drink and swim. Having had very little to whiskey for four days, I was past ready for the tequila. I knew it would top off the beer and stop my flashbacks. I wanted to talk to Juan about getting back to our survival course. Of course, that didn't happen since we both drank too much, too quickly. After a swim, we both went to sleep or passed out on the sand.

The next morning, Jullua had a big pot of coffee steaming on the fire. Juan warned me that her coffee was a bit strong. That was a major understatement as it was thick enough to qualify as syrup. There wasn't much going on around the palapa that morning so it seemed like a good time to approach Juan about returning to the survival exercise.

"Juan, how about you unroll your magic plan for me about finishing this exercise. I damn sure don't want to fail it and have to do the real thing at some later date."

"Sure, amigo, be glad to give you the plan. We're going to visit, eat, drink, and play on the beach here for the next eleven days," he said, smirking. "Then Roberto will take us north to the little town of Santa Maria. That's about ten miles from our rendezvous point at the end of the course. We'll simply hike through the desert for ten miles. By then we'll be all sweated up. Having not shaved and after crawling around in the dirt a little, we are a cinch to look like we've been on the course the whole time. We report in, we'll have completed the course, and we graduate."

He looked at me and smiled wide. "What you think, gringo? Good plan, huh?"

"Juan, my man, you're a genius."

"Yes, yes. I am proud to be your friend. You're such a fast learner."

I thought until that moment Juan was joking about not going back and covering the survival course by the book. I stood up and looked at him. "You were serious all along and I thought you were kidding me."

"Amigo, practicing misery is your phrase," he said, shaking his head. "In this case I see going strolling through the desert in 130-degree sun as just that—practicing misery."

The next few days we just hung out, drank beer and tequila, and ate way too much great food. I liked going down to the water after dark and swimming. By then the bay was calm and the air had started to cool. There were a gazillion stars in the sky and they sparkled like diamonds. Sometimes I felt like I was the only person on the planet. The only sound I could hear was the water lapping at the edge of the sand. As the nights passed, I watched the moon turn full and rise over the desert. The sight was truly magnificent.

Very early in the morning of our seventh day, Roberto took us to a beach south of the town. There was an old dock where the shrimpers and fishermen unloaded their catch. The boats had come in during the night and a swarm of men were very industriously loading fish from the boats into two large trucks. Each layer of fish was covered with ice, which was shoveled from a third truck. The entire operation was done by the men—there was no machinery.

The shrimp boats followed a different procedure. The day's catch was dehydrated by spreading it out on large plastic sheets. Juan told me they let the shrimp lay in the sun and dry for three days. Then they were packaged in large cloth bags for transport.

The best part of the entire visit was our last night at Kino Bay. A big fiesta was planned in honor of Juan and me. It was held in the town square, and I think every person who lived in town turned out for it. The women wore colorful dresses. The men were dressed in western attire and most wore white cowboy hats. There was a large mariachi band. The musicians were dressed in black outfits with lots and lots of silver buttons running down their arms and legs. The band members all wore big sombreros. There was dancing in the street and lots of great food and, of course, more than plenty to drink. The kids played and laughed. It was all like a carnival.

Using an old amplifier and microphone, the mayor of
Baja Kino called for quiet and made a speech. He called
Juan and me to come to the front of the crowd and stand
beside him. Then he started to speak more and more
rapidly while slinging his arms about. Juan had had a lot
to drink by then and he forgot I could speak Spanish. He
started to interpret and got crossed up. Next thing he was
half in Spanish and half in English. All of a sudden he
stopped and looked at me and we both burst out laughing.

"You are both wonderful and great, and you are heroes, too," the mayor said.

"Juan, this has been a wonderful experience being
here with you and your family and friends. I want to thank
you very much for allowing me to be a part of your survival course," I said, when the mayor had finished talking. "Oh. I almost forgot to tell you that Roberto has been
teaching me Spanish the entire time we've been here." I
smiled and continued, "I wanted to surprise you about my
Spanish." I could see from the look on his face that I did,
too.

"Gringo, I feel like a fool trying to talk English to you
and all along you knew Spanish," he said in Spanish.

That night I drank tequila and chased it with lots of
beer. I must have had about two bags full because the next
morning I had the worst hangover I'd ever experienced in
my life.

"Man, this is a good day to start a survival course," I
said to Juan. "I'll have to work hard just to survive myself."

"Gringo, buddy, if you do survive please keep me
with you, because I for sure am dying, too."

The rest of the plan went just as Juan said it would.
Roberto took us to Santa Maria and we struck out for the
finish line. We went into the outpost in the late afternoon
of the last day. Just before reporting in we complimented
each other on looking like we had been in the desert for a
year. We were unshaven, sweaty, and dirty.

All five teams finished the exercise successfully. Juan and I promised to stay in touch with each other, and I invited him to come visit me in Arizona. I was probably the only person who ever gained weight on the desert survival course, even after not eating any of my C-Rations. The kids in Juan's village loved them.

Back at Fort Huachuca, it was business as usual. Several days after my return I saw Mimms at the airfield. He asked me how I had made out on the survival course. I told him it was rough, but I came through it okay. He congratulated me and told me I didn't look too bad from the experience.

Just three weeks after returning from survival school, I awoke from a horrible nightmare with severe pains in my chest. I was having trouble breathing. Samantha immediately phoned the post hospital and an ambulance quickly arrived. By the time I got to the emergency room, I was throwing up and had terrible, crushing pains in my chest. After several hours in the emergency room, and several tests later, the consensus was that I had suffered a mild heart attack.

The next day I felt much better, but I was very weak. I felt a lot better physically than I did emotionally. Emotionally I was pissed; I couldn't believe I'd lived through Vietnam only to come home and have a fucking heart attack. I was so very angry and I felt cheated. The thought of never flying again was totally devastating.

During the next week in the hospital, the doctors administered every test known to man. All the tests results were negative and the final analysis was that I had eaten something I shouldn't have. I didn't tell them about the thousand pounds of spicy Mexican food I had eaten at Juan's home. I was released from the hospital and the next day I reported to the flight surgeon to get back on flight status.

Captain Karl A. Kent, MD, better known as KA, a good old boy from North Georgia, was my flight surgeon.

Our relationship went all the way back to early Nam. KA told me he would release me back to flight duty, but he wanted to have me answer a couple of questions first. He went on to ask me if I ever had any nightmares about Nam or if I ever had flashbacks and intrusive thoughts. When I asked what he meant by intrusive thoughts, he told me that meant uninvited thoughts about Nam.

I moved my eyes up and to the right as if I was thinking about what he had asked. Then I lied. "No, not at all. Why do you ask that?"

"A lot of you guys seem to be having a tough time of it, mentally," he said.

"Damn, KA, you don't think I'm a psych case, do you?" I asked, laughing.

KA answered. "Truthfully, I don't think anything about it; I know all you damn Mohawk Jocks are lunatics."

He gave me a form that he marked "return to flight status." I left his office and started back flying the next afternoon.

In no time I finished both my bachelor's and master's degrees. Samantha and I decided I would resign then and start a business right there in Sierra Vista. There was a good opportunity for me to start a construction company since Samantha's real estate sales were strong. She would sell the houses as I built them. Seemed like an excellent plan.

On May 31, 1971, which was my birthday, I took my letter of resignation to the personnel office and had it receipted into channels. All that was left to do was wait for my release orders.

Chapter 7
I Plan to Resign, But the Government Has Other Plans

"Major, your orders are at personnel, but you'll have to wait until Tuesday. When they called they said they're all leaving early for the three-day Labor Day weekend," the operations sergeant said.

"Damn! Damn! I've been waiting since May for those orders. Don't they know how bad I want to get out of this Army?" I asked, shaking my head.

I had submitted my letter of resignation. All I had to do was wait it out as it went through channels. By the Fourth of July I was starting to get antsy, imagining something had gone wrong. After returning from a late afternoon flight just before Labor Day, I was in debriefing when the operations sergeant entered the room and gave me that word.

"Well, if you've waited this long, you'll probably make it through the weekend," the sergeant said. "Shit, it ain't like personnel would ever be considerate of the troops. I think they're all Communists anyway."

"You got that right, Sarge, but I won't be puttin' up with it much longer. I'm like out of here. I'm a short, short-timer."

I called Samantha to tell her what had happened. "Hey, honey, my discharge orders came in, but I didn't get to personnel in time to pick them up. Guess who their first customer will be on Tuesday morning."

"I guess I hope it's you," she said half-heartedly. "Let's go to Dominick's Steak House for dinner and celebrate, okay?"

"You got it. I'll be home in an hour," I said and hung up.

Dinner was great. Since Dominick's was the best steak house in southwest Arizona. we could always count on a great meal. I didn't appreciate it a much as I could have as I drank a few scotches and a couple bottles of wine. Samantha was pretty cool to me the entire weekend, so I just kept up the drinking till Monday night.

When I rolled out of bed Tuesday morning, my feet hardly hit the floor. I was out the door to the personnel office.

"You want coffee," asked the personnel officer who managed my record?"

"Hell no, I just want my discharge orders and the date I'm getting out."

"Man, you're not going to like this," he said, shaking is head. "I'll make it quick. You don't have any discharge orders and you ain't getting out. You're reassigned to Fort Sill, Oklahoma. Your slot there is VIP Flight Detachment Commander. You gotta get there by the fifteenth of this month."

"Big joke, fella, but this shit's not funny, " I said. "Come on now, let me have my orders."

"Look, man, I was all over this thing on Friday," he said firmly, raising his voice a little. "I talked to everybody all the way up to the people in officer management at the Department of the Army in the Pentagon. When you accepted the field commission in Vietnam and you accepted promotion into the regular officer corps from being a warrant officer, you incurred an additional five-year commitment. And the Pentagon isn't at all interested in letting you out of it. Your new discharge date is August 1973."

"But I didn't agree to any extension. I didn't sign anything and no one told me about any extension," I said, protesting vehemently.

He moved around the desk and shook his head in disgust. "You know and I know this is a royal screw job, but there's nothing anybody can do. You just gotta go to Fort Sill and serve it out."

I got to the airfield and called Samantha. When I told her what was happening she was pissed, too. Although she didn't really want me to get out, she knew what was happening was unfair. As the day went on, I became more and more pissed off. On the way home I was still so angry I could hardly control myself. I stopped and bought a half gallon of scotch and had a couple of good belts in the parking lot before I continued home.

When I went into the house Samantha was waiting for me. I poured a big glass of scotch on ice and sat down to discuss the situation with her.

"I can't believe that I can't get out of the goddamn Army. When I took that promotion in Nam I took on a five-year commitment I knew nothing about until today," I explained. "I know this isn't a big deal to you because you don't want me to get out of the goddamn Army anyway."

She didn't cut me any slack. "You bet your ass I don't want you to get out. I told you I'll support you doing it, but I think it's the wrong thing to do. You're just now getting over the hard years and finishing your education. You know you're set for a high rank if you stick it out."

"I don't want a high rank, I want out of the Army," I said, raising my voice. "Can't you imagine what it's like working for an organization you have no trust in. I love my job, but I hate the fucking Army. Every person in the government is a liar. I don't want to be part of it. I don't want anything to do with it."

"Well, why don't you stick around so you can make a difference?"

"Don't forget, it's my goddamn life."

"It's my life, too, you know," she yelled.

I took another drink from my glass and threw it across the room. It hit the brick fireplace and shattered. I screamed right back at Samantha. "I don't want to hear anymore of your shit. It doesn't make any difference what you want or what I want either. I'm stuck. I can't get out."

"Nelson, let's just see what the next couple of years

bring." she said, trying to be calm and calm me down as well. "Just take it easy. This can be a good thing; you can use the time to finish your PhD."

I left the room, went into the kitchen and poured another drink and got myself under control. When I went back into the den I said, "You win, Samantha. "I'll be a good little soldier. We'll go to Fort Sill and I'll fly my airplanes and I'll study for my PhD."

"Please don't be condescending. I'm trying to support you here."

We soon hatched a plan of action. Samantha was to stay behind with Emma and sell the house, and then follow me to Fort Sill. I didn't like the plan, but there seemed no other way to do it. I thought at least I could drink all the whiskey I wanted to while I was living alone in Oklahoma. My resentment and anger about the entire situation deepened though.

The night before I was to begin driving to Fort Sill, I visited the Officers' Club. Of course, I inhaled all the scotch I could hold. As I got in the car to go home, I thought about Frank and my emotions sank like a rock. I needed to feel better, so I decided to stop off at a local strip joint before going home.

When I entered and sat down at the bar, which was also the dance floor, there was a tall goddess with long, brown hair dancing. She was finishing her routine wearing only very red, very high heels and very little else. She worked her routine over in front of me and when she bent over, I inserted a ten-spot between her breasts. She would hold them together with her arms while she danced around the bar collecting her reward money. Tradition was to dispense only one dollar bills to the girls, so when I gave her a ten she made eye contact with me and gave me a glowing smile. She blew me a kiss and mouthed the words, "I love you."

During her routine she took it all off and her dance was particularly seductive each time she got close to me.

When she finished her routine she put on a G-string and showed up beside me at the bar. As she sat inches from me with her bare breasts almost touching me, I reaffirmed just how luscious she was. I figured her to be about 21.

"I'm Vickie, flyboy. What's your name?"

"Nelson. I wanna tell you that you're one gorgeous creature. You wanna get married?"

"Yeah, sure, but just for a little while," she said, chuckling.

"Vickie, you may have to lay down and let me be sure I love you first."

"Oh, have no doubt—you'll love me, honey."

"Yeah, so where you from, Vickie the dancer?"

"Tucson. You wouldn't be going that way would you?"

I threw down another scotch and felt Vickie's hand on my thigh. She moved around on her bar stool so her legs were touching mine and said, "I'm getting off at 2:00 and I lost my ride home. The girl I rode down with got sick earlier and she went home and left me. I knew some white knight like you would come in and rescue my little damsel self."

"Hell, honey, its 70 miles to Tucson," I said.

"That's okay; I'll drive your car for you."

"Like hell."

"I don't have any place to stay down here and I really need to get home," she said. "Tomorrow night I'm going to drive my own car down."

Another drink showed up. I sipped it and said, "I'm way too drunk to drive you to Tucson tonight, but I do have enough for a motel room."

"You got it, Nelson. When I get off we'll see if a fly boy can fly me to the moon. How about that?"

"Works for me, baby."

"Okay, Nelson, I gotta go hustle up a couple of table dances. I'll see you when I dance again."

Vickie gave my leg a firm squeeze. She stood up, came

close and pushed her breasts on my shoulder. Then she bent over, gave me a kiss on the cheek, and whispered, "We might not get to the moon, but we'll damn sure get to heaven."

Suddenly I felt someone rubbing an icy cold, wet rag over the back of my neck. I jerked my head up and saw Samantha glaring down at me. I was in a booth in the strip joint. There were several other people watching, none of whom was Vickie. The party was over and the strip joint was closed. I was passed out and when they couldn't wake me they called the post duty officer who called Samantha. It was not a good practice for a strip club to call the police when a patron was incapacitated. Of course, it was also less than terrific for them to call your wife.

"Looks like you've been having a big going-away celebration," Samantha said, smirking.

"Actually I just stopped to say goodbye to one of the guys from the airfield."

"Oh yeah, when did Vickie start flying for the Army?"

Samantha didn't say a word nor did I while she drove me home. The next day she took me back to get my car and she was still pretty chilly. When I tried to apologize she very coldly said, "Just remember this, I know you justified fucking around on me in Vietnam because you thought you'd never get back, but if I ever catch you again, we're finished; no second chance."

I didn't reply. Late that afternoon I left to drive the more than 800 miles to Fort Sill. When I pulled into a road-side motel in New Mexico about midnight, I suddenly realized I didn't have anything to drink with me and the bars were closed. I checked in, went to my room, took a shower and sat down to watch TV for a few minutes while I tried to get through the night without a drink.

I cussed myself for not having any whiskey. After the fiasco the night before at the strip club, perhaps it was best that I didn't. I realized how tired I was and laid my head back on the chair and drifted off. Just as I passed through that stage between awake and asleep, a roaring nightmare hit me.

Try as I might I couldn't break out of the cockpit. I couldn't get to Jerry. I couldn't do anything. I was paralyzed and screaming as the plane was diving straight down to the jungle. When I finally came to, I was soaking wet with sweat. I was flailing my arms and yelling. I knocked over the lamp on the table next to me and it broke on the wall. I realized I was screaming, "No, no, no," when I heard the resident in the next room pounding on the wall.

I just sat on the bed in a daze until it was light outside. As I left my room, I decided the first thing I should do was find a drink. I soon purchased a quart of scotch and sipped on it all the way to Fort Sill. On the road that day I had a long time to think about where I was in life and where I was headed. It seemed like a good time to take inventory. Taking my own inventory was a very important lesson that Samuel Goodman taught me.

I was 33 years old. I had finished a master's degree and had started working on my PhD. I was headed for a new assignment that could be great. As the commanding officer of a VIP Flight Detachment, I would mostly be my own boss. That was a nice feeling. I had always been working directly under someone else's thumb since joining the Army. Like Samantha said, I was through the hardest years and I did have to wait it out. I decided I'd adjust my attitude and make the best of the time left.

Life at Fort Sill was good. I had plenty of time to study. As commanding officer, I could pick and choose what flights I wanted and assign the rest. The airplanes were well-equipped, twin engine Beechcraft. The maintenance crew chiefs and the pilots I had were all competent. My first sergeant was a 22 year veteran and he ran a tight ship. He actually made my job easy because he took care of all the daily bullshit.

Our mission was to fly high-ranking officers all over the country as well as into Central and South America.

Sometimes the flights only lasted a day and sometimes they lasted as long as a week. This was a cherry assignment.

Samantha and Emma arrived a few months after I got there. Samantha soon found a house downtown in Lawton, which was the town just outside the post. Samantha went to work in a local real estate company and that fall Emma started school. Somehow I should have figured things were going too smoothly and it was all about to change.

One morning the first sergeant informed me that I needed to get over to personnel because I had orders waiting.

"Orders? Orders for what?" I asked.

"Hell, I don't know, sir. They just called and said you had orders waiting and for you to go over there."

When I got to personnel, the personnel officer, who was a lieutenant colonel, had me come into his office. "Congratulations, you are officially promoted to Lieutenant Colonel."

"The hell I am," I replied. "I just got promoted a little over a year ago."

I frowned, jerked my head no and continued, "Sir, excuse my blunt words, but I don't want a fucking promotion. As a matter of fact, I refuse it. I won't accept a promotion because I don't want any more obligation. I accepted one promotion in Vietnam and I got extended five goddamn years."

"Yes, you did, but only a promotion from warrant officer to regular officer carries an additional time commitment. Once you're a regular officer, you can be promoted without any additional obligation."

"I don't want it anyway," I said.

"I never had anybody refuse a promotion before. I don't even know if you can refuse it."

"Well, we better find out," I said, firmly.

"Okay. It's gonna take me a few days to check this all out," he said. "You'll have to give me until next week to research the regulations."

"Sure, just research all you want to, but I don't intend to accept the promotion. You see, I don't trust the fucking Army. I'm really being screwed around here."

The minute I got to work the next day, I received a call from the office of the post commander. It seemed Major General George Hale wanted to see me in his office at 1:00 that afternoon.

I arrived precisely at 1:00 and entered Hale's outer office. Major Ben Ally, the post adjutant, who was also Hale's deputy post commander, was waiting there for me. Command Sergeant Major Chuck Waters was coming out of the general's office. He said the general has a quick call to make, and then he'll bring us right in. We chatted about nothing and the Sergeant Major told a couple of jokes. He was a very funny man and everyone who knew him confirmed that. In fact, he frequently had some stand up comedy appearances in the area. When he was introduced, he always stood at the mike and said "Waters up, don't ya'll get wet out there."

"Major, oh, I mean Colonel, congratulations on your promotion," Waters said." I heard that you're playing the fool and trying to screw with the system. But, you can't refuse a promotion, it's against the regulations."

"Against the regulations or not, I don't want it."

The Major chimed in. "It's probably best if you take the promotion gracefully, Bennett. Else, they're just gonna ram it down your throat."

Just then the general's door opened, and he waved us into his office. "Come in gentlemen, have a seat."

The office was large and the furniture was luxurious. The high back chairs were made of rolled red leather, and the walls of the room were paneled with rich cherry wood. One entire wall was lined with bookcases built with glass doors and backlighting. The walls were covered with what I called "ego hangings," or decorations, awards, pictures and "atta boy" letters the general had received over the years during his career.

We sounded like a well-rehearsed choir when we simultaneously responded, "Yes, sir."

The general moved to his desk and sat on the corner closest to us. I counted seven rows of medals on the general's chest. He was also wearing master aviator wings, which indicated that he had logged in over two thousand flying hours.

He was a large man, over six feet tall, and his hair was nearly all gray. I knew he had flown combat in Korea and Vietnam. That alone commanded great respect. I knew he was a squared-away commander — tough, but always fair.

The General said. "Well, colonel, let me ask, do you think we have enough horsepower in this room or what?" He looked at me and chuckled.

I smiled and replied, "I believe so, sir. I'm flattered that I deserve such a show of power."

We all laughed. The general continued, "I can pussyfoot around this thing and we can be here all afternoon or I can come straight at you, colonel, and tell you how it is and how it's going to be. I think I'll just take the direct approach. That okay with you?"

"Yes, sir, I prefer it"

He stood up and moved around behind his desk. Still standing, he turned to face me squarely and said. "You're a wonder boy, Nelson, an Army poster child. You're 33 years old, you've earned two master's degrees and you're well along to completing a PhD. You've flown missions the equivalent of three-and-a-half combat tours. You're one of the most highly-decorated, if not the most highly-decorated pilot to come out of Vietnam. You've earned the Distinguished Flying Cross and two Bronze Stars for Valor, 34 Combat Air Medals and a Presidential Unit Citation. You are blessed, or cursed, I'm not sure which, with a very, very high IQ, which as you know, is rare in the Army. In fact, it may be there has never been a soldier with an IQ as high as yours." He laughed and continued, "Your accelerated promotions are not gimmies; you've earned each and

every one." Hale stood back on his heals, stood porker
erect and stared squarely into my eyes. I didn't know
until yesterday, when Major Alley briefed me, that you
never took a day of leave time to attend college. You did it
nights and weekends. Now, I ask you, if you had a soldier
working for you who had a record like yours, would you
let him get away from you? Hell, no, you wouldn't and
neither is the Army going to let you get away. Now whatta
you think about that?"

I didn't have a damn clue as to what I was going to
say to the General. "Sir, I am truly humbled by the flattering things you say—"

He cut me off short.

Suddenly it was like he was another person; he
slammed both hands down on the desk top and almost
screaming said, "I don't give a shit that you're flattered—
flattered your ass. Hear this; you are promoted to Lieutenant Colonel and that's the way it is. You got that?"

I had been in the Army long enough to know when I
had lost a battle. There's an old Army saying, you argue to
the point of decision, then when all are on the same side,
you go with it. I said, "Yes, sir. Thank you, sir."

He sat down in his chair and, with a big, cool, smile on
his face asked, "Now that wasn't so hard, was it?"

The sergeant major felt he had to say something, so he
stupidly added, "Just totally painless."

"I think I made a pretty good speech about your past
career," Hale said. "What we need now is a close look at
your future career."

"I'm not sure I understand, sir. I really want out of the
Army, but I have no choice." I said.

"In the end you've made the right decision. I want you
to go to DC with me and let the powers in the Pentagon
look into their crystal ball and tell you what they see for
your future. After that, if you still wanna get out, come
August '73, you're free to go."

I felt like I'd been in a pressure cooker, but I wasn't

totally stupid. I realized I had no choice; that made my decision easy. Not saying I liked it at all, but...

"Yes, sir," I said.

The general relaxed in his chair and said, "I've got a meeting at the Pentagon next Wednesday, and I want you to fly up with me. Assign a couple of your best pilots to fly us. Naturally, I want you to wear your Class A uniform and be sure to wear all your metals and shit. I'll make sure the appropriate hierarchy is in place to brief you. I'll see that my meeting ends early enough so I can be there."

"Yes, sir. I saw your flight on the schedule and I'll be ready. If I remember, we'll be staying overnight."

"That's right. I've got an early meeting on the budget. These days you almost have to give a congressman a blow job to get an approbation approved for anything. Since the president decided to shut off Vietnam, they shut the purse strings as tight as a virgin's vagina."

Hale got up and moved toward the door, ushering us out. "Okay, I guess this meeting is over. Thank you all for coming and have a nice afternoon," he said.

We all stood, saluted the general and started for the door. Just before I got through the door the general said, "Colonel, I'd like for you to bring a copy of that Aviation Digest article you wrote. I've heard a lot about it, but I haven't taken the time to read it. I'll read it on the way up."

"Yes, sir. I'll be sure to bring a copy for you."

The whole thing took about ten minutes. When we were leaving the building, the sergeant major pulled my new rank insignia out of his pocket and handed it to me.

I looked at it in my opened palm and said, "Sergeant-Major, how did you know I was gonna accept the promotion?"

He smiled and responded, "Sir, I've seen General Hale at work before. He's very convincing isn't he?"

"Yeah."

Over that weekend, I was off for three days and I had

time to think about what was happening in Vietnam, and why I had written the article that the general had mentioned.

On Saturday, I worked around the house. I cut the grass, drank some scotch, washed the car, drank more scotch, watched a football game on TV, and drank a lot more scotch. By the time Samantha got home from work, I was totally wasted. I went into the bedroom with a bottle, took two big slugs off it, and passed out on the bed. Early the next morning, I got a mandate from Samantha that we needed to talk. I, for sure, knew what she wanted to talk about. "How about this afternoon after church?" I asked.

Samantha poured each of us a fresh cup of coffee and said, "No, I don't want us to go to church. I want to talk about this problem; right now, it's very serious, don't you realize that?"

I opened the cabinet door, took down the bottle of scotch, and started to pour a generous shot into my coffee. Samantha got up from the kitchen table, walked over to me and abruptly grabbed the scotch. "You shithead jerk; don't you know you're killing yourself with this poison? You've got to stop drinking," she said.

I wanted to fight back. I wanted to scream. I wanted to take the scotch back, but I didn't do any of those things. "Samantha, you have what you want out of this, I'm stuck in the Army. Now, I've also made an attempt to stop drinking or at least slow it down," I said very deliberately.

"I'm just so worried about you, Nelson. The drinking and the nightmares seem to both be getting worse. This is becoming a huge problem for me and for us. I wish you'd reconsider seeing a private therapist."

"Okay, your damn pressure doesn't help it. Just leave it alone. I'll work it out," I said.

Samantha sent me a somewhat veiled threat, but a real one just the same. "I don't know how much longer I can put up with living this way."

"I'll work it out," I said. I took the scotch bottle back and filled my coffee cup.

The entire weekend was miserable. I just sat around in a drunken stupor. Samantha and Emma stayed away from the house most of the weekend. When they did come home, I was either crashed on the sofa or on the bed. Neither of them had anything to say to me, which was fine with me — that made it easier.

I was all too ready to get back to work on Tuesday. Most of the day was spent pushing the mound of paper called admin trash. So help me, 99.9% of everything that came across my desk was total bullshit. Once, for a 15-day period, I took every piece of distribution that came to my inbox, put it in my briefcase, then took the briefcase out and emptied it in a box in the trunk of my car. I never had one single word mentioned about even one piece of it.

Wednesday, Pentagon day, was a beautiful day full of sunshine. All went as scheduled, and we were wheels up at precisely 6:00 a.m. General Hale was alone; there were no aides accompanying him. It was just the two of us and a steward in the cabin. We settled into the big, comfortable, executive leather chairs. We were facing each other with a low table between us.

"Sir, I brought you a copy of the Digest with my article in it," I said as I opened my briefcase which was on the seat beside me. "I also brought my entire doctoral thesis, less a few strike-outs to declassify it somewhat. "All my research, facts and figures, in the thesis are as accurate as I can possibly make them. Sir, the facts support my thesis that we should take the Mohawk to Central America. Hell, it'll be a waste to mothball the aircraft."

Hale reached over, took the two folders the table and put them on the seat beside him. He loosened his tie and put his feet on the table. "Might as well make ourselves comfortable."

As General Hale relaxed and focused on the Digest article, I thought about the facts that led me to develop the concept and write about it.

In 1972, the Vietnam War was winding down fast. We had started pulling troops and units out of the war and abandoning the South Vietnamese people. Those of us who had been there, and those who were still there, knew we were leaving the South Vietnamese exposed. It was inevitable that they would be taken over by the Communist North, and it would happen almost immediately.

The end result was total failure. All the years of fighting against the aggression of Communism was for nothing. All the fifty-five thousand plus lives and the hundreds of thousands of maimed and injured were for nothing. Fifty-five thousand will fill most college football stadiums and the hundreds of thousands of injured are more than live in most cities. Still all the pacifists in the United States and abroad wanted us to do just that—give up, quit, and go home.

The president and the Congress just wanted the war to go away, regardless of the cost, even though the currency was paid in human capital. "Just get us the hell out and get the American people off our backs." This and others like it were comments taken from released White House tapes years later.

Make no mistake about it, Vietnam was a war that could have been won in any one-month long period had it been turned over to the military commanders in the field. It was, however, the only war in history that had been run by three presidents from the Oval Office; none of whom had ever spent even one day in the military. They never allowed more than a limited war to be conducted against the Communists.

Chapter 8
Pentagon Duty:
What a Bizarre Twist!

I was in a swimming pool completely naked. There was a bright, full moon set against the ink black sky. The temperature was warm and the water just a little warmer. A perfect night by any standards. I looked around and determined I was the only person there. My uniform was lying on the back of a lounge chair. The large deck led to a long row of sliding glass doors and into the rooms of the motel. On the other side of the pool, there were gas lamps lining the edges of a beautifully manicured lawn. There was only one problem with this perfect night—I had no idea where I was.

I climbed out of the pool, picked up my uniform and walked into the little bathhouse. I used paper towels to dry off. No matter how hard I tried to concentrate, the only thing I remembered was sitting at a bar after finishing work on Friday. It was my second week working in the Pentagon.

I put my hand in the pocket of my pants and found a key to one of the rooms. I went to the door and inserted the key slowly and quietly. I turned the key, then the knob. The light was on, the TV was blaring, and a black preacher with a sweaty face was cautioning, "We all need to praise the Lord."

I thought about the preacher back home as I walked over to the TV and turned it off. Then I heard, "What's wrong, honey babe? Don't you like big, black preachers? I've heard that guy before, he's a pisser."

I didn't recognize the voice. And when a young blond girl walked out of the bathroom buttoning her blouse, I didn't say a word. Try as I might, I didn't recognize her.

She picked up her purse, walked to the door, opened it, and as she stepped outside she said, "That was terrific; hope we meet again. I have to run, now. I've got a long ways to go and I have to figure out what I'm going to tell my old man. Bye now."

I never saw her again and I have no idea who she was or where she came from.

The clock radio by the bed read 3:55 a.m. Sunday morning. I'd had blackout drunks before, but they were rare. This was my third in the ten days I'd been in DC. My commitment to Samantha, to myself, to my dead father, and to God had lasted less than a week. I was so remorseful, it was unbelievable. I hated myself. Maybe I'd never be able to quit drinking.

I had come to my new job only days after my Pentagon interview. As usual Samantha stayed behind at Fort Sill to sell our house. She said it might take her a few months because the real estate market was slow. The military was phasing down Nam, and all the services were releasing large numbers of troops. This was producing a glut of houses for sale around every base in the country. I had rented a small efficiency apartment in a motel close to the Pentagon in DC.

My biggest concerns were how I was going to tell Samantha I was drinking again and what she was going to do with the information. I was going to have to handle that, but at that moment I needed to get my ass in a clean uniform and get to work by 6:00.

The work days were long—twelve or more hours each day and we went six and sometimes seven days a week. I soon had a team assembled to build the action plan I needed before our mission could go forward. Over the next few months, we put together a good framework. First, we formalized an estimated need for funds—in civilian terms, a budget. We also had to create a staffing guide listing the specialties, capabilities, and job skills each soldier had to possess. The final piece of the plan was how best to present the concept to our allied friends and which country to approach first. Each segment of the plan had to be thoroughly researched. The appendix to the plan pertained to the what-if games.

The what-if games were just that. Each tiny segment of an action plan is dissected and the team then asked, "What if this happened?" and "What if that happened?" Not all, but every possible eventuality was covered and planned for, and then logged into an appendix to the main document. Then, when the what-ifs were properly projected, the plan provided for a course of action regardless of what happened during its implementation.

I had come to Washington in the summer of 1972 and by the time all the planning was complete, it was almost Thanksgiving. My drinking was advancing and was now a nightly occurrence. If I didn't get knock-out drunk, the demons came roaring in. I had been back to Fort Sill for a weekend only twice during that time. On both occasions, I was able to refrain from drinking and I still had not told Samantha that I'd been unable to quit. I felt horrible about drinking, and I felt even worse because I hadn't told her. I wondered if the reason she didn't ask me about it was because she trusted me to keep my word, or maybe she just didn't want to know the answer.

Finally the finishing touches were put on what had come to be called "The America's Communist Insurgency Resistance Program." Of course, the Army had to have an acronym for everything so that one was known as TA-CIRP.

It was nearing time for me to present TA-CIRP to the Joint Chiefs of Staff. The dog-and-pony show was originally planned for mid-January, but after General Barfield saw the final document, he secured us a spot on the Joint Chiefs' calendar for December. I assumed that General Barfield would be making the presentation. I prepared a full mock-up for him to study.

I discovered my error when I phoned General Barfield

to tell him I had his study copy ready and to arrange an appointment to deliver it to him. I had decided the entire presentation should be presented on 35mm slides. They looked much more professional than the traditional overheads that were normally used in briefings.

When General Barfield came on the line, I explained my call and he let me know the error of my thinking. "What the fuck are you talking about? You have the full TA-CIRP presentation ready for me?"

"Yes, sir. I thought you'd like plenty of time to look it over and prepare your presentation."

Barfield had a good laugh and said, "You gotta be shittin' me, Nelson. I'm not going to conduct this briefing. This is your show all the way. I sure don't need the credibility; this is all about you, colonel. I know you'll make me proud."

He caught me totally by surprise. I had no idea he would give away the credit.

"General, I'm fully prepared to conduct this briefing. I didn't expect you to want me to do it, but I assure you, I won't embarrass you." Then I laughed.

"Hell, I know you won't fuck this up, it's your baby," he said. "Now you pack your shit and go home to Oklahoma for Thanksgiving. You've been working too hard. Have a great little vacation and relax. I'll see you back here next week."

I did as instructed and took a four-day weekend over Thanksgiving. Catching an early hop out of Andrews Wednesday afternoon and arriving at Sill before dark; the weather was brisk and windy. Samantha picked me up at the airfield on the post and we went to the Officers' Club for dinner. I knew that would put my sobriety in danger, but I figured I could handle it.

"I have something exciting to tell you," Samantha said just about the time we were seated in the dining room. "We have a contract on the house. We're getting full price and the buyer wants to close in February."

"Gosh, that's about wonderful," I said. "When I get back to Washington I'll apply for quarters for us at Fort Myer. The houses are terrific and it's close to the Pentagon."

Samantha said, "Nelson, I may not want to work there for a while. I may take some time off. Do you know how long we'll be stationed there?"

"Honey, I don't know, and I can't tell you where we'll be next after that. I have a briefing coming up later in December, and I'll be able to tell you more after it happens."

"Okay, that's good enough for me." She paused, and then said, "For now. I can handle anything just so long as you're not drinking."

The holiday was uneventful until Sunday morning. Samantha and Emma went to church, and I took that opportunity to drive out to the Officers' Club. There was no liquor in the house and I wanted a drink real bad. My plan was to have a couple of quick ones and be back home before the end of church.

The club was practically empty. There were a couple of female officers far down the bar from me. The bartender recognized me and quickly set two double scotches on the bar in front of me. He remembered I never ordered one at a time. I took a big, long drink, closed my eyes and savored the warm feeling as the scotch went down to my gut. I really needed that drink.

I was working on my second double when someone tapped me on the shoulder. I turned my head and an open hand come at me from nowhere. The slap was so hard it almost knocked me off the bar stool. It took me a long moment to shake it off, and when I did, all I could see was Samantha standing glaring at me. "You son of a bitch," she said. Emma was standing just behind her.

"You are a good for nothing, lying bastard." She spun around, took Emma by the hand and walked out of the club.

I composed myself, then quickly got up and followed

them out to the parking lot. I caught up to her just as they reached Samantha's car.

"How did you know I was here?" I asked.

"I didn't until I came over to get my coat after church. I left it when we ate dinner Wednesday night," she said. She raised her voice as she continued, "It's not me who has the explaining to do, asshole—it's you."

"Look, can we talk about this at home and not here in the parking lot? I think you've embarrassed me enough, here," I said.

"Oh, you poor, pitiful, embarrassed thing. We don't have any talking to do. You just pack the rest of your shit and go the hell back to your little Pentagon and play with your little war."

Now I was getting pissed. "If you don't stop screaming in this parking lot, I may do just that and never come back."

"Good, that's perfect. That's just what we agreed to if you started drinking again. What about all the promises? You never stopped, did you? You've been drinking the entire time you've been in DC, haven't you? I don't think you can quit drinking. Besides that, I don't think you even want to. You're too stupid to stop. Fine, just go ahead and kill yourself or maybe you'll be like Frank and kill somebody else when you're drunk in your car."

That one hurt, but I shook my head and screamed back. "That's it. It's over. I'm out of here."

I turned and walked to my car and left. I was much too mad to be even close to rational and besides, my face hurt like hell. I knew that before dark it was going to be a shiner and it was. I drove off the post, stopped at the first bar, and started working on double scotches. I went through many different emotions and many thoughts that afternoon, all of which were negative and depressing.

I felt so remorseful I didn't know if I would ever be able to make it right with Samantha. I hated lying to her and I hated lying to myself, too. I was feeling very angry with myself and I was also angry with Samantha. No matter how mad she was, she shouldn't have made a scene in the Officers' Club; there was no excuse for her actions. I sat there and felt sorry for myself until late afternoon. I couldn't do what I wanted to do, which was get falling down drunk. I had to catch a return flight at 4:30 in the morning. I sat there and pushed the limit though, and then I drove home.

Of course, driving was a stupid thing, but I thought I could handle it. When I went in, Samantha wasn't in sight. I called out for her, then for Emma — no answer. I went through the kitchen to the garage door and opened it — no car. Hell, there was no telling where she was. That was probably a good thing. Nothing good would have happened had she been home.

Samantha had two distinct character traits. First, she had an extremely well-developed sense of humor. She also had the most violent temper of any woman I had ever known. She was slow to boil, but when she did, everyone in her path did well to take cover. She screamed. She threw anything she could get her hands on. Her conduct was unbecoming an officer's wife. After I confirmed she wasn't home, I also confirmed there was no whiskey in the house. I went to the wet bar, opened the doors, and then slammed them shut. I sat down on the sofa and went to sleep.

I caught my flight the next morning, but didn't feel too great. The pilots were too polite to ask about my black eye, but everyone else in the entire Pentagon did. "I slipped in the shower." The only person I told the truth to was John. I told him about the entire weekend, the Officers Club, and all the rest. His reply was, "You really fucked up, old buddy. You know, you make that woman mad enough and she might kill your ass."

During the next two weeks, I got drunk every night, but I was at work every morning by 6:00. I was in my office on the Friday afternoon before the briefing on Tuesday when I was told that the Secretary of State would be attending.

"Nothing like a little pressure to make a guy have a drink." I knew the speaker was John Mills even before he rounded the corner into my office. "It's Friday, man, let's go out and celebrate your success."

"John, that's a great fucking idea. You must be one of the most intellectual thinkers of our time. The only problem is, I haven't been successful, yet. However, I guess we could drink away my sorrow in advance, just in case I fail with the Joint Chiefs."

John gave me a giant smile. "Don't worry, my man, the fix is in. Just don't tell Barfield I told you, but enough of what you're going to say has been leaked even up to the Prez. It's a done deal; just deliver your little show without pissing your pants in front of them and you got it. Understand?"

I locked up my secret briefing files, gave John a big smile and said, "Where you wanna go, my man?"

"How about we take the shuttle across the river to Bolling AFB, I heard they graduated a large class of intelligence analysts today," he said. "Usually those classes have a high percentage of young female lieutenants in them. Most of those gals probably haven't had a good screwing since the course started. I feel duty bound to try and help as many as we can with that problem. After a tough class like that, they need to feel loved."

"Like I said, John, you're a true deep and intellectual thinker and you're an honor to your country."

We stopped by the locker room—both of us kept a change of civvies there—and then we headed to catch the bus.

The shuttle bus ride took us about 20 minutes. As soon as we left the parking lot I asked John to tell me about his call to Samantha. I had asked him to give her a call and see how she was doing.

John said, "Nelson, Samantha loves you very much, but I don't think she's coming to DC. That may not matter because General Barfield told me you were going to be assigned to command the implementation of TA-CIRP. He also says that the great generals' grapevine in the sky tells him the program is going to be moved on immediately — like very immediately. Twenty-three Mohawk aircraft are setting on the deck of an aircraft carrier on their way back to the States as we speak."

"John, you know I want this command, but if it means giving up my family, I don't think I'm willing to do that."

"Look, Samantha doesn't grasp functional alcoholism," he said. "You and I know we're both functioning alcoholics. The service is full of us. We drink much too much, and we do it much too often, then we get up and go to work and outperform everyone else around us. Alcohol is our shut-down switch. It's been going on like this since the Roman soldiers and even before that."

"John, I don't think I've ever heard it put exactly like that, but you know, you're 100% right on."

"About Samantha, I've talked to her until she almost won't take my calls, either," John said. "I've explained everything I just said to you. I've told her what little I can about what's going on with the Mohawk. Of course, I couldn't tell her very much about TA-CIRP, but I did touch on it."

"John, she's got the house sold in Oklahoma and she's going to have to move somewhere. What's she saying she's going to do? Buy another one?" I asked.

"No, she's going to move to Austin, Texas. Samantha says she and a gal named Janice are going to move to Austin and open their own company. They have both been very successful. Janice's husband got a transfer to a liaison officer's job at Bertstrom AFB there at Austin."

"Oh shit, John. That's fucked up."

"Well, good buddy, you can always quit drinking and maybe she'll eventually take you back."

"Shit, I'm fucked. John. I don't think I can quit. God knows I've tried. I can stop for a little while, but I just can't quit. John, do you think you can quit drinking whiskey?"

"No," he said, quickly. "I don't even want to."

"It's kind of a pathetic situation," I said. "There are thousands of us, maybe tens of thousands of us in the military who need professional help. From all I can read, there's a fairly high recovery rate with addiction where long-term care is involved. I've read about a 12-step program that Alcoholics Anonymous practices. The Catch-22 is that we, those of us in the military can't avail ourselves of anything like that. It's a real shame. The moment we uttered a word about it, we'd be out of the service and sitting on a street corner."

John squinted his eyes, shook his head and said, "I hadn't thought of it that way, but you're right. What you're saying is fact."

"Hell, John, the military is the only place in the world where the hierarchy knows about the alcohol abuse. The damn system is full of it. But they close their eyes to it because just as many of the brass are alkies, too. The end result is that as long as an individual performs at an acceptable level, no one makes a wave."

"I don't see anything changing, do you, Nelson?"

"No, I don't. Over the years, alcohol use and abuse has become a fabric of our military. I see no end in sight to it, either." I ended the conversation.

By then the shuttle was pulling up to the Bolling Officers' Club.

John said, "Neither of us can see an end, but we can see a great beginning. The beginning of a great night of partying and, if we're lucky, we'll get laid. Come on, let's go."

As we stepped off the bus, John asked the driver, "What time is the last shuttle back to the Pentagon tonight?"

"Sir, buses run every hour on the hour until zero three hundred in the morning,"

As we entered the door to the club John said, "Good buddy, we got nine hours to catch a kitty in here. Surely to goodness, we'll be able to do that."

The club looked very stately in its setting on the east bank of the Potomac River. It was designed and built to take full advantage of the views to the west across the river. I had never been to Bolling and when we entered the bar, I was impressed. We were facing a wall of glass that was at least a 150 feet long and over 20 feet high. The panorama of all the buildings and the lights of DC across the river made it a breathtaking sight. The Washington Monument, which was lit with floodlights, punctuated the entire picture and made it even more beautiful. There was a large, kidney-shaped bar in the middle of the giant room. It took half dozen bartenders to man it and they had to hustle to keep up. Although it was early, the Friday night celebration was in high gear and the bar was already crowded.

John looked at the room then looked back at me and smiled. "What'd I tell you amigo, is this a meat house or what. And lot's of it's pure prime, too!"

"John, all I want right now is about a quart of Johnny Walker Red."

"Okay, good buddy," he said. "Let's get a drink and find a good spot to hold interviews. In fact, I've got a great idea. You go find us a place and I'll get the drinks."

"There's an empty stand-up table over by the window. You see it?" I pointed. "I'll be over there. Remember, I'm going to die of thirst if you don't hurry it up"

John soon came back holding a tray with four double scotches on it. We talked a lot about Samantha and her plan to move to Austin. I had kind of gotten my mind around the idea by then and was starting to realize it was probably the best thing for her to do. At least she and Emma could have some stability. It looked like I could be going somewhere south of the border and no telling for how long. I didn't know what the living conditions would be or if there would be schools for Emma.

Most of the people in the bar had changed into civvies, too. The place was alive with young female officers and it looked as if they were the ones having a problem because there weren't nearly enough men to go around. What a shame! John made several reconnaissance missions into the crowd and each time came back with two young ladies. A couple of times I was very tempted to give into my male urge, but I resorted to loading up on the scotch instead.

Around midnight John finally found the girl of his dreams and apparently was able to negotiate a mutually agreeable understanding. He left with her. As the night wore on, I had a couple of walkups who were quite obvious about their needs, but I continued to break the rule of Samuel Goodman and I passed on the kitty.

Truth was, I was too drunk to function by then and at 2:00 I caught the shuttle back to the Pentagon and took a taxi to my motel.

Briefing day finally came around. The room was set up like a theater. I stood on stage behind a lectern and used a remote control to advance the slides that were shown on a large suspended screen, that gave me the freedom to move around the stage. General Barfield came to the stage from his front row seat and introduced me. He was so flattering that he embarrassed me.

"I'm sure you all have read the brief on this soldier's career. He is highly-decorated, extremely well-educated, and he speaks nine languages fluently. He is, without a doubt, the finest young officer I have ever known and had the pleasure to work with. Please give him your strict attention here today. He has a valuable concept to deliver to you."

When he turned the briefing over to me, I briskly moved to center stage, came to attention and executed a snappy salute to my audience. I then stood stick-still at attention for what seemed like several minutes. It was, in fact, only about one minute. I could see people in the audience starting to squirm and look at each other. The silence was screaming. I advanced my first slide. It had one word on it in big, red letters on a black background. ALARM.

Then I spoke.

"Mister Secretary, Joint Chiefs, gentlemen and ladies, thank you very much for allowing me the opportunity to be here today," I said. "Alarm. The alarm is ringing. It must be considered a wake-up call. Last night, right on this continent, somewhere south of our border, one or more small groups of Communist insurgents came ashore. This event is not an isolated, one-time thing. On the contrary, this is a regular, well thought out, planned assault. The mission of these men is to covertly and, over time, create any disruption they can to local governments. They use many techniques to accomplish their mission including recruiting locals to increase their numbers for their cause. They infiltrate local populations in an effort to breed unrest. What can be done to counter this movement?

"Of course all of us know our military is forbidden by law to take action against these insurgents in any of our allied countries without that specific country's approval. That approval must come in the form of treaties. In this case, the nature of such treaties must be classified and kept top secret."

I continued narrating the rest of the 51 slides. During my briefing, I was specific about each point of my action plan. I spelled out every aspect including staffing, equipment needs, estimated cost data, and timelines for each accomplishment. Forty minutes later, I had presented a highly intelligent and very clearly worded picture to counter this invasion.

It was then time for Q&A. At that point, General Barfield came to the stage again to moderate. "Gentlemen, one week ago, each of you was given a pre-presentation copy of what you have just seen and heard here today. As you have seen, the lieutenant colonel has covered every eventuality and has laid out a step-by-step plan. We will now entertain any questions you may have."

Without a pause, the Secretary of Defense stood and asked. "What country first and how soon can you move on this, colonel?"

My reply was. "Sir, I believe our state department staff through our ambassador to Guatemala has been well-received there regarding this concept and I recommend that be our first location. Did I answer your question, sir?"

"Yes, colonel, you did, and I want you to immediately become Commanding Officer of TA-CIRP. I also want you to send directly to me a regular event report in addition to your normal chain of command."

Assuming you are successful in negotiating this first treaty, your estimate of a year to operation is too long. You will have to make it happen. I very much want to be able to give the president positive and quicktime reports on this project. TA-CIRP can turn out to be a diamond in our party's crown. And, colonel, I believe you are the man who can best produce that diamond. I'm counting on you to do that and in record time."

I replied with a salute and said. "I believe I can do it, sir"

Wow! This was like a fairy tale. The meeting was over.

Chapter 9
I Want No More Stars

I thought the wind shear was going to rip the wings off the VIP Saber Jet as we lifted off the runway at Bergstrom Air Force base. I was in the jump seat behind the pilot in the cockpit and complimented him on his professional handling of the aircraft. He was trying to beat a threatening thunderstorm coming in from the west. It had just started to rain and almost immediately, the wind went from light to 60 knots.

He quickly turned southeast and put the storm on our tail. We could have been delayed several hours if he'd hesitated. I had caught a hop that had stopped to pick me up on its circuit of shuttling paper and a few people to embassies around the world. I thought, what a waste of money to fly this, or any airplane around the globe daily, to pick up and deliver mostly non-essential paperwork to and from the over 120 embassies we maintain in that many different countries. It took hundreds of thousands of dollars and hundreds of man-hours to support this mission. It could all be done via commercial airliner for a pittance of that, but no, this was the great United States of America.

I left feeling a great sense of loss. I knew I'd just finished drinking away my wife and family and I had no reason to expect I'd ever get them back.

Samantha and Emma had moved to Austin and I stopped off on my way to Guatemala to visit Emma. I was now the commander of TA-CIRP and was to put Base One somewhere outside Guatemala City.

As I drove up the driveway, Samantha was backing out of the garage. I walked up to her car window and she said, "I would appreciate it if you would get a motel room and not stay here at the house. I really don't want you staying here."

"Hell, that's just fine with me," I replied, just as sternly as she had spoken. "Why don't you just give me a call at Holiday Inn if you want to talk. I'm coming over this afternoon to visit with Emma."

Being at a motel at least gave me the opportunity to drink at night without interruption. I gave Emma a call after school and told her I was on my way over. When I got to the house, Samantha had what few things I had left there packed and ready to move. I told her to give it all to charity. I didn't want any of it.

I knew full well Samantha wasn't going to call me. She was too damn stubborn to do that. After two days, I called her office and asked for a peace negotiation meeting. I didn't suspect it would work, but I immediately launched into suggesting that she might really enjoy a few years of an opulent lifestyle. That's what she'd have if she was living with me on the embassy grounds in Guatemala City.

Samantha was having nothing to do with it. She was polite but very firm. "I'm sure the lifestyle would be nice, but I can never trust you again, Nelson. Consequently, I'll not put myself in a position where I have to. I'm at the height of my game in real estate or very close to it."

"Then you plan to divorce me?"

"No, Nelson, I have no need for a divorce, and I'm sure it would be very harmful to your career," she said. "I have no desire to hurt you, so unless you want to pursue a divorce, there's no need for it at this time."

"Are you saying that you don't want a separation, either?"

"A separation in our living arrangements, yes. Legally, I don't care."

I exhaled and said, "Well I guess you have to do what you feel is best for you and Emma. God, I hate it. I'm so very sorry."

"I know you are, and I know you've tried, but you can't quit drinking. I do appreciate that you're not drinking while you're here," she said. "I moved here to Austin to open a real estate company. You go on with your career. As far as I'm concerned, we don't need to make any announcements to anyone other than that."

I arrived in Guatemala City as my own advance party. After a couple days settling in, I went to see the United States ambassador in his office at the embassy compound. Things were moving fast. It was just a month after my presentation to the Joint Chiefs. I was in residence in the embassy with a mission to coordinate our first covert Mohawk base.

Our state department people had done all the run-up work for a treaty agreement and they'd done it in quick time. I selected Guatemala because of its strategic location. From an airfield there, missions could be launched south all the way to the Panama Canal as well as north through Mexico to the southern border of the U.S. We could run surveillance missions on both the Atlantic coast and the Caribbean to the east. The TA-CIRP treaty agreements were not difficult since every country involved had everything to gain and nothing to lose. It wouldn't even cost them anything; it was a freebie for them all the way.

The ambassador, Franklin Mundy, was a career diplomat. I had done some schooling on him before I left DC. An ambassador was like a supreme commander of his turf. Mundy was 54 years old and didn't have a wife at that time, although he'd been married three times. It seemed every time he finished an overseas assignment, he went back to DC and traded the old model in for a new one.

Mundy certainly fit the mold of a senior dignitary in every way. He was very formal, guarded, and precise. When I met him, he gave me a strong handshake with burning eye contact and invited me to sit. He started his briefing, talking about the fact that I was in dress uniform.

"I'm very impressed with your rank, colonel, and with your achievements, which are attested to by the decorations on your chest," he said. "Here, though, we do not wear uniforms at all. Well, of course the Marines do when they're on duty at the gate. The uniform calls attention when we're outside the compound and you're going to be outside the compound quite a bit. Attention is something we don't want here. It's better if the American staff is as inconspicuous as possible; it's just easier that way."

"Ambassador Mundy, you have no idea what a pleasure it's going to be to work in civilian clothes. I love it."

"Good, I didn't think that would be a problem for you. It's pretty quiet here in Guatemala right now; however, you can get into trouble if you stray into some back areas of the city. Your driver will know where not to take you and you should pay attention to his warnings."

"Okay by me, sir. I don't know why I'd need to stray into those areas anyway."

"Good. By the way, we're all set for a treaty-signing agreement tomorrow afternoon at the president's office in the capitol. I'll be doing the signing for us, of course. It's all set up," he said. "You'll find that most all of your requirements here will be taken care of by my staff. If you do need anything, anything at all, please voice your request to one of my staff. I have over 250 staff members here and most are seasoned pros."

"I've heard that you run a professional operation, sir, and I congratulate you on that."

"Yeah, well I don't know who told you that, but we try hard. Most people don't have any inkling of how much work goes on in a foreign embassy," he said. "We're not just here to help out stranded tourists. There's millions of dollars of commerce that goes on between countries — hundreds of import and export contracts. Managing the millions in foreign aid alone requires several dozen staff specialists. We don't only give these countries the aid money, we monitor where and how they use it. And we're always officiating at some sort of function for visiting dignitaries. Hell, half of Congress comes through for three or more days every year. The length of their stay depends on how much shopping their wives want to do or how much golf they want to play."

Mundy continued, "When these guys come without their wives, they stay as long as they can stand up to the nightly activities in Boys Town. We've got a great Boys Town here in Guatemala City, one of the best I've seen, and I've seen a few in my time. You'll enjoy it."

I decided that it wasn't necessary to tell the ambassador that I had already experienced their Boys Town, so I didn't respond at all. He ended his briefing by walking me to my new office where he introduced me to Mary Lee Ames. Mary Lee would become very important in my life in more than one way.

"Mary Lee here has been working at this embassy for eleven years," the ambassador said. "In that time she's seen the overthrow of four different governments. Until a few years ago, there was major unrest among the indigenous people in Guatemala. I'm not telling you anything you don't already know. That's why you're here — to try to prevent some of that unrest in the future, right?"

"Yes, sir. I hope I can be of assistance in that direction, not only here, but all through the Americas. Assuming we make this first TA-CIRP program work, we can continue all the way through South America."

"Okay, I'm on to my next appointment," he said as he walked away. "I leave you in good hands."

Mary Lee was the most intelligent and the most competent secretary I have ever had. During the next four years, she and I became the best of friends. Although her title was secretary, she was more like an assistant. In her mid-30s, she started working at the state department right out of college. She soon moved to the diplomatic corps and then here. She was extremely attractive and took great pains to keep herself that way. She worked out for an hour every morning, six times a week. She always chose the healthiest meals from the menu in the embassy dining room. Mary Lee had impeccable taste in clothes. I learned she made several trips a year back to the States to select her wardrobe from the finest fashions.

Living in an embassy was like living in a fairy tale. I had quarters that rivaled the finest apartments in New York City. Domestic help came in daily to prepare meals — anything that I wanted — or I could eat in the embassy's main dining room. There was also a 24-hour coffee shop that was a very good restaurant in itself. The domestics on the compound were local Guatemalans, and they cooked, cleaned, washed, and shopped. They did whatever it took to run a residence.

My apartment was a ground floor unit with glass doors leading to a large patio in the back. The setting was idyllic; there were palm trees, flowering shrubs and perfectly manicured green lawns. The entire compound was beautifully maintained.

Embassies, like military bases, had very tight security provided by the Marines. The Marines selected for embassy security were the best and the brightest. The assignments were greatly sought after because of the lavish living conditions. The compounds had every conceivable service and facility available including a movie theater, commissary grocery store, and retail store providing everything from clothing to appliances, as well as medical facilities and a chapel. There was even an English school for the children. The plan was to provide all the necessities and luxuries so no one would ever have to leave the compound. The people who lived at the embassy lived like royalty.

After the treaty-signing ceremony, I was introduced to my Guatemalan liaison. Rodrigo Emanuel was a tall, good-looking, one-star general in the Guatemalan Army. Rodrigo had been educated at Harvard and he spoke perfect English with no detectable accent. He was a staunch Catholic married to a beautiful woman. They had two young sons. Rodrigo's father was the Secretary of Defense, a cabinet level appointee who answered directly to the president of the country. I knew immediately that Rodrigo was going to be a team member who would make my life much, much easier.

The first thing we had to do was find the place to install a base. Using the embassy helicopter, which was operated by CIA operatives, Rodrigo and I located a perfect spot of land in a mountainous jungle area. The spot had good approaches for landing and was located in a national park about one hundred miles southwest of Guatemala City.

Then the work began. Building Base A on a mountain ridge line with a mile and a half of runway in the middle of a jungle with no access roads and no utilities was more than a bit of a challenge. I had several teams of Army Corps of Engineers assigned. These guys were pros at this and the start-up moved rapidly.

Every single nut, bolt, and screw had to be flown in. Building materials, runway and ramp parking areas all came initially by helicopter, then later by Air Force transport. First came the bulldozers slung under helicopters. In short order, they had pushed back the jungle and created a crude gravel runway that set the program in motion. Once the runway improved to accommodate larger transport aircraft, things really started cooking.

The little city, appropriately called Base A, was swarming with workers. Many of these folks were U.S. and Guatemalan military, although most were local Indians of Mayan descent. Work continued around the clock. My target was to be ready for staffing and Mohawks in 14 months.

My drinking had slacked off somewhat because there just wasn't enough time for it. I still drank almost every night, but didn't get knocked out as often as I used to. Nothing had changed to reduce the nightmares, however. All too often, on the nights I didn't drink or drank very little, the demons would come. I stayed at the site about two-thirds of the time and then rotated back to the embassy. Hell, it was like going on a luxury vacation when I returned to my office and condo.

During a period when we were running far ahead of schedule, I had a radio call at the base from Mary Lee. She said, "We received a call from General Barfield's office and they're requesting a formal update briefing next month."

"Mary Lee, that's not a problem at all. Preparing a briefing will give me a chance to fully appraise where we are in the construction."

"A month? They've certainly given us ample time to get a first class briefing ready for them," she said.

Two weeks before the briefing, I left the base and went back to my office. Mary Lee and I worked every day. I had my briefing all ready to go several days early. The night before I was leaving for the Pentagon, Mary Lee and I put a couple of last minute updates in and when we finished, I asked, "Mary Lee would you like to come by my place for a drink?"

"Sure I'd love it," she said. "I'm a martini drinker. Do you have the makings for a good one?"

"Yes, just so happens I do."

As we walked into my condo Mary Lee said, "I've been waiting months to see how you live. We don't have many eligible bachelors around here, you know."

"Just for clarification's sake, I'm technically not a bachelor; I just don't have an operating wife. My wife and I agreed on a forever separation. Neither of us would gain anything by getting a divorce at this time and it could be hard on my career."

I made Mary Lee a martini and poured myself a large scotch. As I handed it to her, she caught me totally off guard when she said, "Well, if that situation makes you eligible, I'd like to apply for that position. On a part-time basis, of course"

We laughed and I soon poured myself another scotch and refilled Mary Lee's martini. "Would you like a little mood music?" I asked.

Catching me off guard again, she said, "Mood music would be nice, but actually I'm already in the mood."

I knew then it was going to be a nice evening, as it suddenly occurred to me that I was going to get screwed. It seemed like a long time since I had been with an American woman. Oh, I had had lots of sex while I was in Guatemala, Rodrigo and I were regulars at that nice Boys Town the ambassador had told me about.

Mary Lee wasn't an accomplished lover, but it wasn't because she didn't try hard. The one thing she did have was super stamina. Thank God for all that nice gym equipment. That night was the first of many times we made love in my apartment over the next three years. We became an item at the embassy and we never tried to hide it. During that time Mary Lee's sexual skills improved tremendously and she actually became quite good. She was an eager student and she liked it when I gave instruction. Her conversation was kind of exciting, as she was so totally uninhibited.

That first night, she stayed at my place and the next morning, she had coffee ready early. We made love again and I was off to brief the brass with a special smile on my face.

I found pleasing and surprising news when I arrived at John Mill's office. John was now General John Mills. Major General Ronald Barfield was a three-star. Well deserved for both, I thought. The biggest surprise was waiting for me after the briefing.

The Pentagon briefing went well and everyone was impressed with the progress of the mission. I had the appearance of Base A well-documented with pictures and felt like a proud new father as I went through the briefing; hell, I knew every nail in the place. In my closing, I hung it all out there when I said, "Gentlemen, Base A will be operational in 60 days."

As we exited the briefing room, John put his arm around my shoulder and said, "We're having a small reception in Barfield's office this afternoon around 4:00. He wants you to stop by. You're not going back tonight anyway, are you?"

"No, I'm going to fly to Austin tomorrow and visit

Emma for a few days. Man, can you believe she's 12 years old?"

"Yeah, I know it," John said. "I talk to Samantha from time to time. She says she's doing well in her new business. They've opened several new offices and she's planning more."

As we came to the senior officers' dining room I said, "I talk to Samantha, too, every few weeks and she also told me how well she's doing. She's always distant, but civil to me. I'm going to peel off here for a coffee, you want one?"

"No, thanks. I'll see you at 4:00."

I arrived at the general's office promptly at 4:00. All the food and trimmings for a reception were in place in his outer office. John was giving final instructions to several stewards in white coats who were there to make drinks and serve food. None of the other guests had arrived.

"Am I early, John? Didn't you say 4:00?"

"Yes, I did, and you're right on time. Come on into the general's office; we're waiting for you. The general has something he wants to tell you. We've been keeping this a big surprise."

I knew the general was excited about the status of Base A; He considered both TA-CIRP and Base A his own creations. What waited for me was a biggie to say the least.

I followed John into Barfield's office. The general got up from his desk and we saluted each other. I thought no one had arrived, but the office was full of big brass. There were several civilians I didn't recognize and Barfield's desk was usually piled high with papers, files and documents. This time, his desk was absolutely clean, except for three thick, buff-colored folders. Each had "Cryptic Secret" stamped on it in large white letters.

At that instant, I didn't have a clue what to expect. My distrust for the Army roared through my mind like a sonic jet. Hell, I could be getting assigned to Zibuskeria or some other unknown place. I stood thinking it couldn't be all bad, though, because the Army was making such a big deal about it.

The general very deliberately looked down at the three files. He seemed to pause for a long time before he picked up the first folder. He called the room to attention, opened the file and read. "By direction of Gerald Ford, President of the United States, in executive order, you are, effective immediately, hereby promoted to the rank of Full Bird Colonel."

I started to speak, but the general put his hand up to stop me. He started to read from the second folder. "By the direction of Gerald Ford, President of the United States of America, in executive order, effective immediately, you are hereby promoted to Brigadier General, one star." I was shaking my head in disbelief. Could this be a joke they were playing on me?

Now, as if all this wasn't enough, what was to come took me a minute to get my mind around.

Barfield spoke again. This time he didn't even open the third folder. "Effective immediately, by direction of the Chief of Staff of the United States, you are assigned until further notice to the full operational control of the Central Intelligence Agency."

He snapped a salute, stuck his hand out to shake mine, and said, "Congratulations, general. Now you may speak."

I had no idea what I said to him.

It seemed the Guatemalan government decided they had some serious misgivings about a general in the United States Army running a United States covert base in their country. So they approached the State Department and, voila, they had no problem at all with a covert CIA operation.

The announcements were followed by handshakes, smiles and congratulations all around. The celebration began. Predictably, I was well on the way to having to much to drink when John pulled me aside and brought me up short. I cooled it until the party was over. That night in my room I poured it on and got myself a double snoot full of drunk.

I went to Austin, rented a car at the airport and drove to Samantha's new house. This time, I noted the extent of its opulence. The house was quite impressive and in a beautiful area of town. Samantha wasn't home from work, but Emma, who was home with the housekeeper, was ready to go. It was late afternoon, so we decided to go to dinner then to a movie. During dinner I resisted having a drink, although I sure wanted one – a few, actually. Emma never stopped chattering. She had so many things to tell me, she said she couldn't think of all of them.

When I went away she was a little girl; just over a year later, she was a young woman and a beautiful one, too. She had the poise of a lady, her conversational skills were terrific and her intelligence was that of a much older person. I knew Samantha deserved all the credit; she was a great role model. I regretted not having been there for Emma, but I was powerless to beat my problem with alcohol. It was probably best that I was gone for so long.

Much to my displeasure, after the movie, when I asked Emma what she wanted to do, she said, "Dad, I want to go to your motel and watch movies all night like we used to."

That meant the end of my drinking opportunity for that night. I thought of trying to hide a few drinks, but knew that I couldn't. Anyway it was good that I didn't have one stashed in my travel bag or I would have screwed up for sure.

We stopped to pick up Emma's things. Samantha was home then. She was, as always, cool but nice. I asked if she would like to go to breakfast the next morning before I left. She accepted and told me to bring Emma home early. She said the housekeeper would be up and we could go for an early breakfast, but that she had an appointment at 10:00 at her office. I sensed that was a self-protection thing so she could get away more quickly if the breakfast didn't go well.

The next morning at breakfast, we just made casual chit chat. I didn't know why I didn't want to tell her about my promotions, and I couldn't tell her about the CIA assignment. When we got back to her house, Samantha opened her door and started to get out of the car. I put my hand on her arm and she looked at me. "Samantha, are you happy?" I asked.

She continued looking directly at me and said, "As much as I can be, Nelson."

I drove away with a hole in my gut, an ache in my heart, and a blanket of guilt like I had never felt before. What a fucked up mess I had created. If only we weren't separated by a sea of alcohol. I stopped at the first liquor store and had to wait a long ten minutes for it to open.

On the way back to Guatemala that night, I realized that I'd stuck my neck way out by telling the brass I'd have Base A up and running in 60 days. I had to redouble my efforts in order to do that.

I spent my first night back with Mary Lee, acting as if everything in my world was great. She had no idea of the pain I was in and she still didn't realize my overindulgence. After we made love and she was asleep, I had a few minutes inventory and a pity party. I thought about Samantha and Emma until it was just to painful to contemplate. Focusing on what it was going to be like to finish Base A on such a short fuse made for much less stressful thinking even considering I had more chain than I could swim with. I figured it was about time God lightened up a little. I had several more big drinks and finally went to sleep on the sofa.

Next morning, Mary Lee brought me coffee and said, "Nelson, I have something real important to talk to you about, so get ready."

Oh, goddamn. I thought about two marriages ago when Janice told me she was pregnant. Mary Lee climbed back on the bed facing me and crossed her legs under herself.

My reply was a bit rough. "Mary Lee, I've got more on my mind right now than I can deal with. Please, can it wait a bit? I'm in a dead run to get out to the base. I told you last night I'd made a commitment to a quick finish out there."

She ignored my words and looked into my eyes and said, "Nelson, I think I love you; in fact, I know I'm in love with you."

I didn't reply at all. I was thinking, Oh, shit, damn, hell. Goddamn it! I didn't want to hear that either, though it was better than "I'm pregnant." Anyway, I couldn't deal with it then because I had to get back to work.

When the helicopter dropped me off on the tarmac at Base A, Rodrigo was waiting for me. The word of my promotion had preceded me.

"Congratulations, from me, my father, and the president," he said.

"Thank you and them very much," I said. "Come on into my office and I'll tell you about the briefing in Washington. We've got Mohawks coming in here in two months."

Little did I know that my world was getting ready to shake again. This time it almost cost me my career and the TA-CIRP program.

We were on a critical time line and I had asked John Mills to get us in front of the House Intelligence Committee to start the ball rolling on funding for the next base. Just three weeks later I was back in Washington. The hearing went very well and I left feeling good.

Shortly after I got back from the hearings though, Gen. John Mills called and pissed me off. "John, you tell Barfield he can take this whole goddamn operation and stick it up his ass."

"Hey, slow it down a bit, just cool off. General Barfield's hands are tied on this. Hell, he knows it's not the best way to go but some damn congressional committee is pulling the strings."

"Look, John. If you remember, when I took this job I was told I was going to be pulling the strings."

John raised his voice. He was obviously irritated. "Listen, we know this isn't about turf on your part. Nobody up here thought this was going to happen. But it's happened. Now, let's suck it up and go on."

"Yeah, yeah. I know we have to think about the greater good, right John? Well let me tell you, this ain't about turf or power, dude, this is about doing this the smart and easy way or doing it the dumb and hard way."

Base A was soon operational and I had made the 60-day window I had committed to. In fact, we did it in 47 days. On November 13, 1976 at 3:14 in the morning, I launched our first mission. I was in the pilot's seat and my senior master sergeant, Sammy James Watts, across from me in the system operator's seat. He, like me, was a Vietnam veteran.

I pushed away the picture in my head of Jerry bleeding in that seat the night we were hit. What a waste, I thought, as unbelievable rage surged through me knowing all the while there was nothing that could done about it now.

Dragging myself back into the present moment, I was able to push the intrusive thoughts away and begin to enjoy my current situation: The culmination of all my dreams! It had taken seven long years from my first concept to fruition. Maybe I was a hero after all. I smiled and continued into the mission.

We took off west to the Atlantic coastline and the town of Ocos, which was at the corner of Guatemala and Mexico. There we turned south and let down to fifty feet above the trees. It was two hundred sixty miles of coastline south to El Salvador. Although there were agreements in place with both those countries to run search missions, I had decided we would work the coast line one country at a time.

Watts and I had chit chatted along the way and we were one hundred twenty miles south of Ocos when he said, "We got Iztapa coming up in zero three minutes, sir. You want to pull up and cross over it?"

"No, let's stay down here and just turn 45 degrees out to sea until we're south of town and then resume flying the coast line. I don't want to advertise our presence."

"General, you got it," Watts said. "Come left to a heading of 227 degrees now. Shit, sir, I mean right — right, not left."

"I know what you meant, Watts. What's the matter, all those Guatemalan women addled your brain?"

"Oh, yeah, that's probably what's wrong. Them gals love us black boys."

"I think what they love is our green money. They could give a shit if we were black or green or if we had stripes."

"Shit, sir, you hurt my feelings. All along I thought it was my charm and good looks and of course the size of my tool that made them get after me the way they did."

"Watts, most likely it's the money."

"They sure ain't like the Nam women, though. These gals can love mighty good. They don't just lay there looking at the ceiling. They fight back; they meet you on every stroke."

"I laughed in my helmet and said, "Watts, you ever think maybe they were just trying to get out from under your big, black ass?"

Watts roared with laughter. "Nah, I'm sure they love me. You can come left now to one seven zero to re-intercept the coast line; we're clear of Izpata. It's 40 miles to Monterrico."

"Coming left to 170, now," I said.

The lights of Monterrico were coming up and, although I had never flown over that city, I could tell from the glow it was quite a large metropolitan city. Intelligence passed onto us from Rodrigo and his staff told us there was an active cell of insurgents operating from that city. Again, I turned out to sea then back to the beach south of town. The sun was starting to come up over the mountain range to our east as we intercepted the coastline.

We found no activity that night, but we soon would.

"You know, sir, this duty is a sin—flying here in Central America with no anti-aircraft guns trying to kill us. Seems kind of unreal, don't it?" Watts chuckled, turned his head toward me and popped a big smile.

"Watts," I said. "Keep your mouth shut, the reflection off your white teeth is gonna give us away."

Sammy grinned even wider and said, "It's gonna be light in a few minutes anyway. We're right on time with only 30 miles to Salvador."

I chuckled this time and responded, "Of course, we're right on time. You're flying with the best Mohawk pilot the Army ever had."

"Truth is, sir, you're the smoothest on them controls I ever saw."

"Well, thank you, Sergeant.

Watts and I completed our mission, climbed to 15,000 feet and headed home. When we landed, I went to the operations building and debriefed with the intel guys—an Army major, two CIA staff, and three Guatemalan officers. Our total staff at Base A was 116. About half were U.S. Army, and the rest were Guatemalan military except for a few CIA communications specialists. Every person on the base had at least a low-level security clearance.

I had been at Base A for three weeks without sex. I was feeling the need, and I wanted to make love to Mary Lee; I just didn't want to feel love for her. I caught the chopper back to the embassy, climbed off, and went directly to my office.

Mary Lee met me as I arrived at the embassy helipad. "How's it going out there and what's going on with John Mills?" she asked. "When I called up there with our staffing report for Base A, he asked me if you had cooled off yet. I didn't know what he was talking about and told him I hadn't seen you in two weeks. He said to give you a message."

"Yeah, what's the message?"

"He said to remind you that it's for the greater good. What the hell is he talking about anyway?"

I kissed her on the cheek, smacked her on the fanny and said, "I'll tell you later. I have to get over to Rodrigo's father's office for a briefing. Let them know we've completed our first missions and things are going well. He already knows it, of course. Rodrigo's told him by now. I'm going over there to tell him face-to-face to make it official."

"You don't have to go to the capitol. I've already sent an official communiqué about the missions and the status report," she said. "Secretary of Defense Armando Emanuel called here an hour ago and said to congratulate you on a job well done."

Mary Lee was very obviously displeased when I said. "I'll tell you later." She shook her head and said, "Come on, Nelson, you know I can't stand not knowing something. Besides. if it's something official, I'm supposed to know."

When we got into my office I reached out and pulled Mary Lee close to me, put my arms around her, and hugged her tight. Then I gave her a long kiss.

"You are some special woman, girl," I said.

"Okay, I know that. Now, for the last time, will you please tell me what the hell is going on in Washington?"

I went behind the desk and sat down. Mary Lee sat in front of the desk in a big, blue, rolled leather chair. She crossed her legs and leaned forward as if she didn't want to miss anything. I told her about John's phone call notifying me that the House Defense Appropriations Committee had approved funding for the next base, but they wanted to put the goddamn thing in Chile.

"Mary Lee, you know most of this," I said. "When I was in Washington last month and testified before the

Appropriations Committee in a closed door session, I
told them we were ready for funding for Base B and that
I wanted to put it in the southern part of Columbia near
the Venezuelan border. My reasoning for that was that it's
reachable from Base A for logistical support. It's a logical
step out and the two could share re-supply flights.

"We have two re-supply Air Force Star-lifter cargo
planes a week coming in now. If we put this damn Base in
Chile, that's the other end of our planned four locations,
it's a 5,000-mile flight from the States that will require
individual flight support. That's just damn stupid. Why go
as far away as possible and stretch the supply chain that
long."

"I thought your testimony went well up there," Mary
Lee said.

"It did. They were all in favor just as I proposed it, no
changes. Every one of them was grinning like a cat, just
as if each of them was the owner of the entire program.
John Mills and General Barfield had done a great job of
softening them up. Fact is, at the close of the hearing, they
ended by saying the funding would be forthcoming and it
wouldn't be long."

Mary Lee leaned back in the chair, shook her head and
asked, "What could possibly have gone wrong?"

"Hell, I don't know what went wrong, but it's my rep-
utation on the line here. If I fuck this up, and I very likely
could if I do what they're saying, I'll get flushed and quick.
The biggest problem is the drain on funds and logistical
support at that distance."

"What choice do you have? If you can only get funding for a Chile base, there's nothing else to do, is there?
We're talking seven million bucks here; it's not like its big
money," Mary Lee said and laughed.

"Damn it, I just might be ready to hang it up anyway,"
I said, smirking. "I've got my 20-plus; I'll have a good pen-
sion and no hassle."

Mary Lee stood up, moved to the end of my desk and

said, "God, Nelson, you don't mean that, do you?"

Now I stood. "I had hoped to finish TA-CIRP, but I'm not going to be a party to doing something we can never support. That's exactly what I'll be doing in Chile. We'll end up so far over budget, it'll all go down the drain."

"Do what you gotta do, but it'll be a tragedy for you to quit the service now," Mary Lee said. "You've got three more stars waiting for you, don't forget."

"Right now I'm too pissed to think about it. Let me cool off a day or two then we'll see what it looks like. Incidentally, I'm ready for some mad, passionate sex tonight. That meet with your approval?"

Mary Lee came close and kissed me on the cheek. "Gee, I thought maybe you had gone celibate on me, it's been so long," she said. She turned and headed for the door. "I can be through a little early here. I'll stop at the commissary and pick up a couple of filets we can cook on the grill tonight. I'll pamper you. Let me handle all of it. You just try to relax, you're gonna need your energy."

I really wanted to relax, but I couldn't get TA-CIRP off my mind. "I think I'll go over to the apartment and have a drink or six," I said.

"Well, don't overdo it, big man. You still have a big job to do on me, remember?"

Everything about the entire program had worked slick. I refused to let it go into a dead end. As it turned out, this hiccup was a good thing. I soon came to the conclusion that there might well be a way to turn that mess around and make a winner out of it. What happened next ended up putting us almost a year ahead of our master plan.

I took another trip to Washington and made the rounds. I wanted to know it there was any chance the Chile thing wasn't set in stone, but it was. Seems the president had just appointed a new ambassador to Chile and he wanted him to have credit for immediately bringing in our services, in the form of Base B. One thing I learned from that was that there was always somebody higher up than you to pull the strings, no matter what the issue.

General Barfield had been in the Army over 30 years and he had seen it all. He was as frustrated as I was. He, too, had a lot to lose if TA-CIRP went down. He decided it was time for us to go to Langley and talk to the CIA super spooks to investigate an alternate route to the money. Barfield knew every person in Washington, and most of them by first name.

Over the period of several days, we worked our way up to an off-the-record meeting with the director of the CIA. Most people think the President of the United States is the most powerful man in the world — wrong. It's really the director of the Central Intelligence Agency. If something came along he didn't like or some politician didn't like the program he was running, he simply made it blacker and sent it deeper underground. That's exactly what he did with the TA-CIRP program.

I left Washington with ample funding, more than I needed in fact, to build both bases simultaneously. Once we got the channel for funding figured out, we were off and running. For the first time in my career I had more than sufficient funding. The next three years were far and away the most satisfying of my career. I continued to live in the embassy in Guatemala. As the command grew and we expanded, our responsibilities grew as well.

I helped Mary Lee get promoted to executive assistant, and she was given two secretaries to support her responsibilities, which were many. One of the gals had been a security analyst who came out of school at Bolling. I wondered if the place was still a meat house like it used to be, but I decided I should never ask her.

Our missions by then were producing big results. It was soon obvious there were many more bad guys coming ashore than anyone first thought. TI-CIRP didn't get them all by any means, but we got a bunch. During the four-plus years I ran the intercept command, all four TA-CIRP bases were finished and functioning well. We were credited with

helping eleven different Central and South American countries capture or kill over 1,700 Communist insurgents, all
of whom our Mohawks had located in the jungles.

I completed my PhD at the University of Guatemala
and was promoted to a two-star major general. Mary Lee
completed her master's degree. Rodrigo Emanuel was promoted to Secretary of Defense for Guatemala. His father
retired and moved to, of all places, Houston, Texas. General Barfield retired as a three-star and John Mills was given
another star. He was still my boss at the Pentagon.

I continued to drink heavily almost every night. All
too frequently, when I couldn't get to the whiskey at night,
I had a roaring nightmare. Jerry and I were still in the cockpit screaming straight down into the jungle of Vietnam. We
were going to crash and burn.

I had started drinking a few at lunch, if I could sneak
them in. On most of my days off I was screwed up by early
afternoon. Mary Lee never again said she loved me.

I visited Emma periodically during that time and
enjoyed watching her become a fine young lady. The break
between Samantha and me didn't change at all. She continued to build her real estate company after buying out her
partner, who left her then-colonel husband for a plumber
she met while trying to sell him a house. Must have been a
hell of a pipe layer.

On May 31, 1986, I resigned my commission rather
than accept another assignment to the Pentagon. Yes, I
would have received the rest of my stars, but I had been
too far from the flag pole for too long. I could never again
mold myself to fit into the Pentagon's formal structure. I
received many phone calls from people who knew me and
one who didn't, President Ronald Reagan. They all asked
me to reconsider and stay in the service, but I had up my
mind.

I did seriously consider one offer from the CIA director asking if I would like to go to the Baltic area and just
consult on a copy-cat mission of TA-CIRP. I had to think

about that one, but came to the conclusion that I had just had enough. I was tired. I'd been on that treadmill in that pressure cooker long enough. My answer was, "Thank you, but, no thank you."

Leaving Mary Lee was much harder on her than me. I knew she truly loved me, but as much as I liked her and enjoyed her, I never loved her. Mary Lee accepted a sizable promotion and went to Washington to work at the State Department headquarters for the director of all South American Intelligence. I was very happy for her when they married a year later. I headed back to Austin not knowing what I would do next.

Chapter 10
Sobering up

"Nelson, if you're going to get knocked out drunk every night, then I want to rescind my offer for you to stay here with Emma and me," Samantha said as she sat down on a deck chair by the pool. "When I made the offer, you said you had your drinking under control."

It was just about 8:00, the sun was setting, and the shadows were becoming a mosaic moving toward dark. I was already half-kicked in the ass as I'd been sipping scotch since noon. I gave her a big smile and jokingly said, "Hey, you don't wanna push it too hard. You know, since we're still husband and wife, I have half ownership in this mansion. Oh, I'm just joking. I know I have no moral ownership in your beautiful new home. Believe me, it's all yours."

She frowned, shook her head and responded, "I know you're being funny. But I want to be serious for a minute here."

When I had arrived in Austin, I took a suite in a small extended stay motel. Shortly, Samantha invited me to live in her guest house until I found a permanent place. Samantha had just finished having her spectacular new home built. It sat on a low mountain on the west side of Austin. The area was known as the high-dollar area of town and hers was the highest house on the hill. It was very impressive. The house faced east. The view from the front was the downtown Austin skyline about three miles away. The scene was framed between two low mountains. When the sun rose over the city in the morning it was a spectacular sight.

The house had six bedrooms, five bathrooms, a four-car garage and maid quarters. Most of the exterior walls were glass. The plot of land was six acres carved out of the cedar trees and oaks and was surrounded by a federal green belt. The property was landscaped to the max. There was even flood lighting in the high palm trees that were scattered around the property. The rear half of the house had 20-foot ceilings, and the glass walls looked down from the mountain to the Colorado River.

The pool was three times the size of a normal pool with a full outdoor kitchen on the deck beside it. The guesthouse I was occupying was a two-bedroom, two-bath cottage. Adjacent to it was an enclosed cabana the size of a small house and fully loaded with exercise equipment as well as a sauna and separate steam room. The entire place was breathtaking. I figured it must have cost well over $2,000,000. Samantha could afford it. She owned almost 100 real estate offices in Texas and Oklahoma with over 1,000 full-time real estate agents

I continued our conversation by saying, "Well, I'm trying to get it under control, Samantha. It's difficult as hell to select which option I should choose each night; either knocked out drunk or experience the worst of the worst nightmares. The day after the nightmares, I'm so screwed up it's unbelievable. It's so much worse than the hangover from the scotch. I actually function better the day after the scotch than the day after the nightmares. I know this has to come to an end, but I honestly don't know how to end it."

Samantha picked up quick on the opening to push her position on the Veterans Administration supposed help for Vietnam veterans. "Nelson, I'm reading that the VA has professionalbcounselors as well as psychologists available, especially for Vietnam vets."

"Yeah, I know that. I've been in touch with several guys I know who go to these clinics. The problem is, they'll never be given any responsible job assignment again. The Army put them out as disabled and businesses won't touch them for the same reason. After World War One they called it shell shock; World War Two it was battle fatigue or combat fatigue, and now there's a fancy new name—Post Traumatic Stress Disorder."

Samantha got up and came over to me. She bent down, took my hand, raised it to her lips and kissed it lightly. "Nelson, I still love you very much. I just can't ever deal with the drinking. I have to believe that there's something or someone in the VA to help you. Just as you said, it has to end. Please let me make you an appointment to just go and talk to the VA and just see what's there, would you, please?"

"Samantha this is a giant waste of time, but I'll go and talk to them."

I gave in to Samantha's wishes and she had her secretary make an appointment for me to visit a psychiatrist at a nearby veterans hospital. I was surprised to find that the shrink had been in Nam on two different six-month tours. He was a squared-away guy who spent an hour and a half giving me information about PTSD and the close relationship between that and alcoholism.

He wanted to ask me to enter an inpatient treatment program, but I didn't give him the chance. I pulled the trigger by saying that I had another appointment. It was obvious he didn't really believe me, but he allowed me to end our appointment without further comment. He asked if I'd like to make another appointment. I said not at that time because I wanted time to absorb what he had told me. When I left the hospital I was glad to be out of there, but I knew I still had to face Samantha and tell her what had happened.

That night when she finished dinner, she came out to the guesthouse and asked me about my appointment. She and I sat in the kitchen. After she fixed herself a cup of hot tea she said, "Tell me how your visit to the VA went today."

I wanted a drink, but I was able to hold it off. I looked at her and said, "Samantha, I can't do what they want me to. I am not crazy and I don't need to go into a psychiatric ward to take treatment. The doctor explained that the treatment or recovery program is centered on what the VA calls trauma groups. In these groups, the participants open up and talk about the specific traumas each one experienced in the war. This exposure, and the discussion of the experience, is supposed to be cathartic."

I hesitated and Samantha said, "I can understand that. But don't you think this would be good for you? To get it all out and talk about it."

I shook my head, exhaled, and said, "Not just no, but hell no. I don't have any interest in revisiting that shit and I don't have the desire to tell it to other people. I see enough of it in nightmares and flashbacks." I stood up and continued, "I'll plan to leave here tomorrow, if that's what you want."

Samantha was angry. "Damn it, that's not what I want," she said loudly. "I want you to go get well. Can't you understand that? It's possible we could try to have a normal life again if you can just get a handle on this. But, if you aren't even willing to try, then it's best if you just leave."

"I'll be out of here in the morning, or do you want me to go tonight?"

The next minute Samantha stormed out and slammed the door so hard I thought the glass in it was going to break. I immediately jumped into the scotch bottle and proceeded to get very drunk. I still didn't know what I was going to do next, but I damn sure knew what I wasn't going to do. I wasn't going to go to a bunch of head shrinkers and live with a bunch of psychos in a VA hospital.

The next morning it dawned on me what Samantha had said. It was like a rock hitting me in the face. "It's possible we could try to have a normal life again." What was I supposed to do with that? I'd have to deal with it later, but first I had to find a place to live.

I'd bought a fancy new Ford conversion van when I got to Austin, so I decided to drive to Mexico and tour the country. Through the years I had kept in touch with Juan Rodriguez, my partner from jungle survival school. I knew

Juan was the Commander of Forces for the northern third of Mexico. Juan lived in Guadalajara on a large Army post.

It took me five days to drive there. The drive through the Sonoran Desert brought back memories of our previous experiences. I was surprised to see a lot of the desert had been turned into fertile vineyards. They were irrigated from deep wells using a drip irrigation system. When I talked to Juan about it, he said that the vineyards produced some of the finest grapes in North America. He also said that many of the larger fields were used by local wineries and that the wine industry was new to Mexico. Surprising, too, was the fact that about half of the harvest was immediately flown out to European wineries.

During our visit, Juan and I sampled way too much of the local products—wine, beer, and tequila. Unlike me, Juan was a normal social drinker. He could party, drink too much one night, and not have another drink for days. Juan had a lovely wife—when he married her she already had five sons. Three of them were in the Army and two were in college in the U.S. My visit with Juan lasted a couple of weeks and then I was off to the south and headed to Cancun.

I liked Cancun. Similar to most of the Mexican beach resorts, it was the destination for lots of women who were there for S and S—sun and sex. A fresh supply seemed to arrived every day.

The tourist population in Cancun was from many different countries throughout the world, and the fact that I had mastered several languages made meeting and greeting easy for me. The gals almost always traveled in pairs and, because most were there for just a short few days or possibly a week; it wasn't necessary to wine and dine them; just bed them down.

Many times two women would go with one guy, safety in numbers I guess. Most of those gals seemed to be living out the lyrics to the Charlie Rich song, "Behind Closed Doors." I often thought they must not have had any sex since their last vacations. Cancun was my first experience with two on one and once, three on one. I found it very exciting and quite to my satisfaction.

I hung around for a couple of months then decided to leave Cancun and head for the Yucatan going west toward the remote coast of southwest Mexico. I liked traveling alone, and many times I'd camp in the van and spend several days alone on a remote beach.

Most cities of any size had American bookstores, so I always had a supply of good books to read. Scotch was often hard to come by, but tequila, although not my favorite, was cheap and abundant. My Spanish was fluent, thank heaven, and I never once felt uncomfortable.

Juan had provided me with a document that allowed me to use the facilities at any Mexican military installation in the country, including their international phones. A few times while in Mexico I phoned Samantha, mainly to talk to Emma. Most of the calls were brief and Samantha never once mentioned my drinking.

I had been in Mexico almost a year when I worked my way up the west coast. There I took a 24-hour ferry ride west across the Sea of Cortez to Cabo San Lucas. Back then, Cabo was a tiny, remote fishing village of only 600 inhabitants. It sat on the very tip of the Baja Peninsula. The town was about 2,000 miles of dirt road south of San Diego, California. The width of the peninsula was only 60 to 75 miles wide at its widest point.

All of the coast-line was rugged and most of it was completely deserted. There were areas where the rugged lava stone mountains came down to the water. Sometimes there were long and beautiful beaches lined with palm trees and sometimes there was no beach at all. It didn't make any difference as it was all stunningly beautiful.

There was one place along the coast I will never forget, for two reasons. One was because there was a truly magnificent landscape; an underground river poured out of the top of a 2,000-foot mountain. The river came out of the mountain with such force it shot out ten yards from the mountain and arced to the beach below, crashing thunderously on a huge, flat, black rock. The second reason I will always remember Cabo is because that is where I met a man who would influence positively the rest of my life.

Cabo's only accommodation was a tiny 12-room communal hotel, built around a lush central garden near the center of town. The building contained a large kitchen for the guests to use. Anyone could use the refrigerators to store food and then cook it on the two propane ranges. The kitchen got a lot of use since there were very few places to eat in town.

My first afternoon in Cabo I visited the city market and bought supplies. Every Mexican town had a central market where local venders sold any and everything required for existence, no matter what it might be. It was exactly like Juan's hometown where we hung out many years earlier.

One night shortly after I arrived, I met a chef who was from Italy. Several nights a week, he took everyone's food, put it together and cooked up a great smorgasbord for dinner. Everyone was drinking. The drinking choices were local rum, local tequila, or an unbranded local Cabo beer known as Iguana Piss. I chose the tequila since it was the strongest, which meant it was the quickest way to my goal of getting drunk.

The partying always went on until the wee hours. The main topic of conversation was the places we had all visited. I sometimes talked about visiting Guatemala. Of course, I didn't say I had worked there. I didn't ever mention Vietnam, and I never mentioned being a career military officer.

It was my first experience with the vagabond culture of professional, low-budget travelers. I spent a couple of months there and met lots of the most interesting people. Many of those people literally didn't have a permanent place to live. They lived wherever they were traveling.

I also found it interesting to learn that many of the travelers were well-educated. It wasn't unusual to meet doctors, college professors and wealthy people as well as those vagabonds who were quite financially strapped. Their sabbaticals seem to last from a few months to many years. While they usually traveled alone, most of them had great experiences that they were usually anxious to share.

Perhaps the single most interesting person I met at the hotel was Kathy Wayland. Kathy was a seasoned and very weathered traveler who had backpacked all over the world for the last 30 years. She said she was 68 years old, but she looked at least 98. She was a retired school teacher from Calgary, Canada, who supported herself writing travel articles for the Calgary newspaper. She told us it had been over 20 years since she had been back home.

The morning after we met, Kathy and I continued our conversation. We talked most of the day about her travel experiences. I told her little of my background, but she was especially interested to learn I had spent some time in Guatemala. She said she was headed there when she finished traveling in Mexico. I gave her some special things to see and do there and told her about a couple of superb restaurants. As Kathy and I talked, other hotel guests drifted in and out of our conversations. The Italian chef was still working, making a plan to cook a gourmet dinner that night. He said it would cost us about four bucks each. Money, in this type of living, went a long way .

Kathy told me about a retreat just a short way from Cabo that she was planning to visit. Sunshine Inn was about 12 miles north of town. It was owned and run by a German couple who had built it 10 years earlier. Since Kathy didn't have any transportation, I offered to give her a ride thinking I'd stay for awhile myself.

The only access to the place was a curvy, three-mile long sand trail that was so narrow the mesquite trees scraped the sides of my van as we drove in. As we got closer, I become increasingly anxious. I wasn't at all sure I could handle staying there since I'd have to abstain from drinking. Alcohol was not permitted at Sunshine Inn. Not to mention the place was a nudist camp.

The inn was a unique grouping of 15 tiny, one-room-and-bath adobe clay huts with thatched roofs. They were built in a large circle with an open palapa building in the center. Each hut was just large enough to contain a bunk, a small desk, and a wooden chair. The huts didn't have electricity; light was provided by candles. The windows, surprisingly, were glass that opened wide for ventilation. The floors were packed clay that was hard and as slick as concrete.

As we approached the perimeter of the camp, a simple sign tacked on a mesquite tree read: "SILENCE PLEASE." We drove up to the edge of the compound and were met by the owner, Juals, a tall, thin German man who was, of course, completely naked. I judged him to be in his late 50s. He had long, salt and pepper hair worn in a ponytail and a full beard. He adjusted his wire rim glasses as he walked over to the window of the van. Juals welcomed us to the Sunshine Inn and invited us to get out and visit.

Juals said, "Sunshine Inn is a combination nudist camp and silent retreat. You will find this place most interesting. Our guests are from all over the world and over half of them are people who have been here before. If you will come with me, I will introduce you to my wife, Breellen. She will show you where you will be staying."

When we went into their small modest office beside their adobe house, Breellen stood up from her desk, walked around it and put her hand out for a shake. What a piece of eye candy this one was. Old Juals did good. She was tall with short blond hair, a perfect build, brown as a berry and, the nicest part, she couldn't have been a day over 30.

"Hello, and welcome to our home," she said. "I came here nine years ago and Juals and I finished building Sunshine Inn a year later. You're going to love it here. Tell me, have you stayed in a nudist environment before?"

After each handshake she came front on and gave each of us a light hug and a kiss on each cheek. I still had my clothes on and my anxiety was already off the scale. I didn't know if I felt more concern about the fact that it was a nudist camp or that I was embarrassed. Some of both, I'd guess.

Kathy was first to answer and said, "Oh yes, I have, many times over the years."

"This is my first time at a place of silence," I said, hoping to imply that I had stayed in a nudist retreat before. I had not, of course. I had never even been on a nude beach. Later I examined my feelings about the place. For a guy who had been naked with as many women as I had, I just needed to get over my initial nervousness.

Breellen gave each of us a small instruction book and said, "You'll find everything in this book, from our history to our rules. I'll take you to your houses now, we call them homes, and you can store your clothes and freshen up. You'll find linens in the room and you can exchange them as often as you like. There's no maid service, but fresh linens are always available. I'm sure you will always remember to keep a small towel with you to sit on."

"Do you require payment now?" I asked.

"No, don't worry about it now," Juals said. "You can pay when your stay is over."

He sure was a trusting soul. As we went through the center of the inn, I felt very conspicuous and, hell, I hadn't even gotten my clothes off, yet. The other guests were sitting silently in wooden chairs in the palapa, and I felt every eye follow me to my home. Breellen asked us to go back to the office after we washed up. Of course that meant get naked, too. I got my clothes off, hung them in my room, washed my face and hands, brushed my hair and went out to show the world my body. No one had to be concerned with me talking; I was still much too inhibited for that.

Kathy's hut was two doors from mine and she was stepping out as I walked by to go back to the office. She spoke, although I immediately thought she shouldn't have. "This is great, isn't it? Oops, silence, right?"

Her body looked a lot worse than I had envisioned; her wrinkles were deep and they had wrinkles of their own. I sure hoped I'd never have to contend with that when I reached that age.

When we got back to Breellen's desk, she gave each of us a towel and reminded us to always take one with us to sit on. She started her little talk. "You know, we have strict rules here about silence. In fact that's the most important rule we have. Quiet time is 24 hours a day except for a three-hour communal meeting every other afternoon. A tiny bell notifies you when it's time for the meeting. There are no watches or clocks allowed. By the way, if you have any questions as we continue here, please ask; it's okay."

"Breellen, I understand during the communal meeting that talking with the other guests is okay," Kathy said.

"Yes, it is, but only in the palapa. No guests are allowed to visit other guests in their homes even during communal time.

She continued. "We have a very simple menu here— all vegetarian. There's lots of fruit. It's all fresh and the fruit is always available if you wish to have a snack. There are three staff members who also do not speak, but they fix the best meals in the world. You can eat in the palapa with others who are there or you may take the meals to your home."

"Breellen, what are the meal times, please?" I asked.

"They're about seven, noon, and six in the evening," she said. "Don't be concerned, the little bell will tell you when meals are ready. We drink only water and it's always ice cold. Our water is wonderful and it's from our own deep well. One of our staff brings ice every morning. All meals are self-serve from a buffet and you're welcome to go back for seconds. Juals and I are almost always at the communal meetings, and if you have requests for, or about, anything, please voice them at that time. Our guests vary from six to as many as twelve. You'll be amazed at the people who come here from all walks of life. And it's amazing, too, how much information can be exchanged in a three-hour meeting."

"Please excuse my curiosity but you don't have any accent at all. How long have you been out of Germany?" I asked.

"Oh, my father was an Air Force man, and we moved to Tucson, Arizona, when I was two. I was born in Germany, so I have dual citizenship."

So my first experience with being nude in public was, at the very least, unnerving but as time went along, I learned to like it and to feel very comfortable. There's no way to explain that, but it was good. I could see why the Sunshine Inn had a lot of repeat guests.

There were several people I met there who stuck out in my mind. Edward was a very large, 55-year-old, man from South Africa. He was on vacation from his government job. He had been visiting different nudist retreats somewhere in the world for 20 years. Two lesbian ladies in their 30s were barristers in London. One was as ugly as the other was nice looking. They never touched each other, but they were open about their relationship. They talked at great length about how England accepted gays but many other countries did not.

Kathy was very popular with her stories of backpacking around the world for so many years. Of particular interest was the story about when she was held captive for several months by a band of Mongolian gypsies along the northern China border. She said she was treated well by the men, but the women saw her as a threat and would have nothing to do with her. They wouldn't even let her eat regularly or bathe.

Kathy said her greatest concern was that each night the men chose a different woman to sleep with in his wagon or tent, and she was afraid they would select her at some point. "Thankfully, this never came to pass," she said. Eventually, the women of the band forced her release by withholding their love from the men. They refused to sleep with any man until Kathy was released.

There were no schedules, no agendas, and no structure of any kind at our retreat. After the noon meal, we were allowed to take a long siesta. During my stay, the only thing I saw that violated the rules was when guests spoke during quiet time. The first time a guest was cautioned with a wave of a finger and a shake of the head. The guests policed themselves. If you committed a second infraction, you were asked to leave — no exceptions. Twice during my month-long stay a guest was asked to leave.

Since there were no lights in the compound when it got dark we all went to our homes. In the early morning light, when it was cool, I'd take my chair outside my door and enjoy the silence surrounding me. I did miss the morning coffee. I don't know if I missed that or the alcohol more. I think it was the alcohol. I had several monstrous nightmares, but they seemed to occur less frequently.

Each day the camp's owners wrote a simple phrase on a chalkboard to help guide our thinking for that day. There were phrases such as, "What makes me happy?" or "How I can be a better person?" or "My most gratifying activities and thoughts are..." Those instructive phrases were always positive, never negative.

Everyone spent hours and hours just sitting and meditating with their eyes closed or just staring into the distance. A strange energy seemed to come to the group after sitting on the ground in a circle holding hands with our eyes closed. We did that every morning after breakfast for long periods of time.

People could leave the circle at any time or they could stay until the tiny bell rang to signify the end of the session. Often a large part of our next talk time was taken up discussing our individual feelings and reactions to those sessions.

During my stay at the Sunshine Inn, I participated in 29 of those sessions and always felt refreshed at the end of each one. During the individual silent times, I was able to look deep inside myself. Trying to examine my life and how I had lived it was a very difficult task indeed. My mind wanted to wander away to more pleasant thoughts, but often it was to more intrusive thoughts of Vietnam. Those intrusive thoughts came at will and with no warning. Sometimes I'd sit for long periods before I became conscious of what I called off-center thinking, and I'd have to force myself back to the task at hand.

There were two major areas I had to capture and get a fix on. First my drinking. I spent a good deal of time trying to deal with that. It was very obvious my drinking was progressing, similar to a slow-moving cancer. It was demanding more time and extracting more of my energy. For years, most of my nights had been spent in black-out drunks and most of my mornings had been made more difficult because of the hangovers. The last year or so, I had been having a couple of drinks in the morning to get me going and I was also drinking at lunch as often as possible.

If I didn't drink, I could look forward to a totally sleepless night or if I did let myself go to sleep, a nightmare would come like a violent storm in the night. Whether the demons came or not, the threat and fear of them was always there. Later, I learned from the VA psychiatrists that people who suffered from chronic PTSD and had nightmares subconsciously trained themselves not to go to sleep. It was normal for me to stay awake until I was so fatigued I was punchy or silly, but if I closed my eyes I became wide awake and hyper-vigilant.

Thank God, the lack of a drink got a little easier as the days went along. After a couple of weeks, I realized how much better I felt. There were some days during which I'd hardly thought about a drink. The slow pace was definitely helping my problem. How unfortunate that I hardly realized it then.

Second, I had to decide what I was going to do with the rest of my life, and where I was going to do it. My impulse was a bad one — relocate to someplace where I could just be alone with the alcohol and drink as much as I could every day. I knew that was a disastrous thought; it was major insanity thinking. I had to find a new career, identify what it was going to be, plan how I was going to do it, and then establish when I would start.

Once during my trip I had called Samantha, I had been away about six months then. She told me that John Mills was looking for me. He told her he wanted to speak with me and left word for me to call him ASAP. I called John from the Mexican Army base where I was staying. When he came on the phone, he said he had a job for me with a four-year contract that he would like me to consider.

Before he could say any more I said, "John, I am not interested. But thank you for thinking of me."

John replied just as if he hadn't heard me. "Come on, good buddy, listen to this. Will you accept a White House position as Latin America Advisor to the President?"

I quickly decided to screw with him. "John, can you give me a week to think it over?"

"Sure, not a problem. We both know you're the most qualified person in the world for this job. Take a week and call me back."

"Okay," I said. "I'll be in touch in one week."

Six days later I probably made a mistake, but I called him at all. "John, I have tremendous respect for Reagan, but I'll not come back to Washington even for him and this plum job. Please respect my decision and don't pursue it further."

He didn't pursue it further; we visited a little about his family and we hung up.

Late in my stay at the Sunshine Inn, I was pretty sure I noticed a lessening in the frequency of my nightmares. They were still just as violent as ever, but they seemed to come a little farther apart. During my very last week, I was sure they had lightened up.

When Kathy and I were just a week or so from ending our stay at the inn, an elderly gentleman arrived and joined our group. He was a healing shaman from Columbia, South America.

Juan Batos was in his seventies and was almost like a spirit creature. It was his third visit to the Sunshine Inn. He was there to renew himself, although he was planning to stay only two weeks. He was the seventh son of a seventh son of a Venezuelan father and a Spanish mother. His parents were wealthy ranchers in the northern part of Venezuela.

Juan had been educated in boarding schools in India and Tibet. He was a Rhodes Scholar and also a graduate of Cambridge Medical School in England. Juan and I immediately had a bonding chemistry I couldn't explain.

During communal time, he quickly told us he was on his annual sabbatical and would be returning to his teaching assignment at the university in Bogotá. He also had a private practice in mind healing at the university.

I was fascinated with the man and after the end of a week, I asked him if he'd see me professionally in Cabo after he left the retreat. He agreed. My stay ended before his and when Juan arrived back at the Hotel Cabo, it was full. I felt very happy when he accepted my offer to room with me. I had been anxious to talk with him more. During the days leading up to his arrival, I was very pleased that I still hadn't started to drink. I realized I was over a month sober and that was by far the longest I had been without a drink since before Vietnam.

Kathy decided to stay at Sunshine Inn for another month and before she came back to Cabo, I had already left. I'm sure she continued traveling the world; I hope so, anyway.

Juan stayed with me at Cabo for a couple of weeks and we spent every waking hour talking. He instructed me as if I were his student. I learned many things during that two weeks.

Juan's philosophy for a happy life was along the lines of Buddhist belief that a simple life was a happy life. The more in control a person felt of their environment, the happier they were. Conversely the less control, the more emotional discomfort one felt.

Sometimes we'd go all night until well into the next day before we would eat or sleep. Several very key things in my life came out of those days and nights.

Juan helped me realize the devastation my abuse of whiskey was causing me and the emotional toll it was taking. Additionally, he displayed the depth of his wisdom when he said my life situation would continue to deteriorate as long as I continued to abuse mind-altering substances.

I came to realize that if I was going to accomplish anything worthwhile again in my life, I had to quit using alcohol for good. His solution to that problem was simple and direct. He said, "If something is not good for you, then it is most likely bad for you, and when you identify something that is bad, then cease it."

Juan taught me to try and make friends with my nightmares. Talking with him, it became obvious that my simple and slow-paced lifestyle in Baja produced fewer nightmares than normal. I agreed to work on trying not to obsess about expecting the nightmares to return. I also wouldn't expect them to be as intense when they did come back.

Juan Batos was full of old proverbs and when I brought up the tragedy of losing Samantha and Emma he simply said, "Time is a strong medicine. Give it time and never put pressure on a relationship you desire."

One of Juan's best sayings was: "When one who is expected to do something does not meet expectations, then the one who expected it often feels the most disappointment. Don't expect too much of others."

There were a hundred more bits of new knowledge, all significant spiritual life tools that I learned from Juan.

What a fascinating experience it was for me to learn from him. I felt like I was sitting at the feet of the master. I gained more useable knowledge from him than I had in all of my schooling put together.

The morning Juan caught the ferry to leave, we had breakfast alone. I told him about the promise I had made to my father many years earlier. I then put out my hand, looked Juan in the eye and said, "Juan, I am not going to drink again." Then I left to drive the 2,000-mile dirt road back to the States.

Chapter 11
Screw It, I'll Just Get Rich

"I don't fucking believe you," Samantha screamed as she slammed the front door. "How dare you arrive in this condition! How drunk are you, you son of a bitch!"

It was 10:30 at night, and I looked pretty cruddy after four days traveling from Mexico with no rest or showers.

I found myself screaming back through the door. "You can go to hell, too. I told you that I would never have another drink and I haven't. Now, goddamn it, if you want to talk about it, then open the goddamn door."

I knew that Samantha was standing right inside the door, and I knew that she was waiting to continue her attack on me. I regained my composure and spoke just loud enough for her to hear me through the door. "Samantha, I haven't had a drink for over six weeks and I never intend to have another drop of alcohol. I've been on the road for almost four days without any rest. Now, if you will open the door, I want to tell you how I was able to quit. Please, open the damn door."

After a long minute she cracked the door with the security chain still attached. "You swear you haven't had a drink in two months?"

"Yes, I swear it. Not quite two months, but I'm finally done with it, Samantha. I know, I've said it a million times and I know you have no reason to trust me now. But if you'll let me in, I'd like to tell you how I've done it and why I don't think I'll ever have the problem in the future. If you'll let me in, I'll explain how, then I'll leave you alone and won't bother you again."

"No, I'm not going to let you in. I'll talk to you at the pool. If you want to come around there, I'll be there in a few minutes."

I turned and humbly said, "Okay, okay. I'll wait for you at the pool." I went back through the driveway to the deck and sat down at a patio table. The lights came on, and as I looked around, it seemed as if the landscape had matured and all the deck furniture was new. There were new flower beds at the edge of the deck. The blooms were full and as symmetrical as if they had been sculpted.

In just a moment, Samantha came out the back door of the sunroom, and as she approached, I could see she was as stunning as ever. She was wearing taupe-colored linen slacks and a white silk blouse, and I felt a little twinge in my groin as a flash of our previous sex life crossed my mind. I said, "Samantha, you look great! If anything, you look better than the last time I saw you."

"Just stow that and get on with what you have to say," she responded.

I spent the next hour telling Samantha about my experiences at Cabo and my stay at the Sunshine Inn. She asked lots of questions. It was obvious she was very interested, but she still handled the conversation like it was a hot potato. When I started telling her about Juan Batos, it seemed she was starting to believe me. Then she asked, "Do you plan to stay in Austin now? John Mills said he offered you a fantastic job in Washington. Why didn't you take that?"

"Because I don't want to go back to Washington. I could never live under the flag pole again. I hated the Pentagon duty and being in the White House would be double worse. I can't even imagine the politics in a job like that. Actually, I'd have some concern about being up there and living on the cocktail circuit. I'd be expected to attend every administration function. Not very conducive to sobriety."

"Well, it just seems a shame to miss that kind of a position," she said. "I can picture it being so exciting to be in on everything that goes on in the world."

I said. "It's over Samantha, for sure. I damn well don't want to be in on everything that goes on in the world. I don't want the job and it's gone by now anyway. It's gone, period. To answer your question I'm going to get a place here in Austin, find a job and try to get back into life."

"Do you have any idea what you'll do?"

"I don't have the foggiest idea at this moment, but what the hell. I'm smart, educated to the max, healthy and handsome, too. I'll come up with something."

We laughed a little and Samantha said, "Oh shit, I know. How about becoming a greeter at Walmart?" Then we had a big laugh. Samantha continued, "I have a friend who's in Alcoholics Anonymous. Would you like me to introduce you to him?"

"Yes, I think so. I'm ready to do whatever it takes to stay off the whiskey."

"Okay, when you get settled, I'll arrange for you to meet him," she said. "Understand how I feel about everything you've told me and I have heard it all before. God knows, I wish you all the success in the world. I love you very much, but at this time I can't see that I'll ever being able to trust you again. There have been just too many lies, too many disappointments, and too many failed attempts. I didn't stop trusting you quickly and it will take a long, long time for me to start trusting you again, if I ever do. Just go do what you have to do and show me."

Then Samantha put a sword straight through my heart. "I think, no, I believe, this time we are done. What I think you should do is just go and try to live your life as best you can. Good luck." She stared at me a moment and I could see her contempt and anger boiling. She was trying to contain it. She continued. "You shouldn't ever have another thought about us healing this relationship. It's never going to happen." She turned and went inside. I left.

Several weeks later I talked with Samantha's friend from AA. Woody Linwood was a pillar in the AA community in Austin. He was in his 40s and had been an AA member for 10 years. That same week, I phoned the Austin veteran's clinic and requested an appointment with a psych doctor. I had to make sobriety work this time. I had no other choices.

I found a very nice, furnished apartment. It was on the northwest side of the city and was within walking distance of a 24-hour AA club. The club had meetings every four hours, around the clock. With Woody's encouragement, I attended two meetings a day, every day. I liked AA and found comfort there. I immersed myself in the program and the literature. The AA Big Book was 164 pages long and the more I read it, the better I understood my alcoholism.

I realized there were a lot of very happy people at those meetings and some that were not so happy. Many had been mandated there by a judge. AA members are from every kind of background: rich and poor, educated and ignorant, ex-cons and every type in between. Many of the folks had lost their driving licenses — some for as long as 10 years, and a few for life. I met one individual who had 13 drunk driving offenses for which he had spent 7 years in jail and lost his driving privileges for life.

There was one common thread among all the people I met in AA — every one of them had the desire to stay sober. I soon learned to develop a trust for those in the AA program, realizing they were totally honest when they said the only thing they wanted from me, and for me, was for me to stay sober. Just one day at a time.

Soon the VA clinic called to tell me I had an appointment for an intake interview with one of the psychiatrists, Dr. Kamilla Saborra. Kamilla was the director of the Combat Post Traumatic Stress Syndrome Recovery Program at the VA hospital in Temple, Texas. She was very attractive — a tall, flat-chested blond, who was very fair skinned. She didn't look like she was from the Slovakian countries of Europe. At 51 she had been working with PTSD patients for over 10 years.

"Hello, may I call you Nelson? And I hope you will call me Kamilla," she said.

"It's certainly okay to call me Nelson, but I prefer to call you Doc, if you don't mind?"

"Yes, that's fine."

During the appointment, I told Doc about the night-mares and intrusive thoughts that plagued me. I admitted they were very destructive, and that it was not unusual for me to stay up for 24 hours or more. I told her that when I lay down at night to try to sleep, I immediately became hyper-vigilant, that I frequently took sleeping pills and how much I hated this. It seemed very demeaning to open up all my weaknesses to her. She started to rattle off some questions. "Do you startle easily? Do you relive the events of your combat, both in nightmares and intrusive thoughts? You told me you have intrusive thoughts, do you re-live your combat in them? Do you have a tendency to want to isolate?"

"Yes to all. The startle response is uncontrollable. I can watch someone make a loud noise and almost go into shock. Sometimes it takes me several seconds to come out of it and realize where I am again. As far as the nightmares and the flashbacks, they're horrible. The day after a bad nightmare I'm almost worthless for at least half the day."

"All you vets with combat related PTSD have the same symptoms. Unfortunately, no person, regardless of how well they know you, can even start to comprehend the hell you guys live in your heads. We can't cure you, but we can help you," she said. "We can teach you some good coping techniques, and there are some very good medications that will improve your quality of life."

I didn't tell Kamilla about how bad my alcohol abuse was. I think she knew. Nor did I tell her that I had taken antidepressants on and off for several years. I never took them regularly, but over the years in the service, I did get them from several civilian doctors.

On my second appointment, the Doc convinced me to go into a six-week inpatient program at the VA hospital in Temple, Texas. I reluctantly agreed. I knew it was on a psych ward, but I also knew that it was a locked ward and I wouldn't have any outside contact.

When I did go into the hospital I was impressed with all the doctors and nurses there. Kamilla's entire staff was well trained and highly-motivated and most of all, they were dedicated to helping vets. Many of them were Vietnam veterans. There were 29 other vets in the program and every one of them manifested the same symptoms I did. Every one of them used alcohol or drugs to medicate themselves into oblivion to suppress their illness.

Our daily routine left very little private time. I found that very difficult, and on several occasions I gave serious thought to leaving. The daily activities included two one-hour trauma group therapy sessions. I never came close to spilling my guts as most of the other patients did. I couldn't see how talking about it could make me feel better.

There were a few malingerers in the group, but they were easy to spot — they were the bullshit artists who talked about how their experiences in Nam had screwed them up so they couldn't function in society. What these guys wanted was full disability. Then they would get a monthly check for life. Those of us who had actually experienced severe trauma and actually looked death in the eye had great disdain for those disability compensation chasers.

It seemed to take forever, but I stayed and finished out the six weeks, although I never developed enough trust to talk about my death experience in Nam. I left the hospital with handfuls of medication and instructions to stop and breathe deeply when I woke up from a nightmare or had an intrusive thought. Big fucking deal.

When my treatment team gave me my discharge briefing, I was stupefied when I was handed a full disability diagnosis form. As I read it, I heard Doc Kamilla say, "We, as a team, have concluded that you deserve a 100% disability for your Post Traumatic Stress Disorder illness. You can sign this form then I'll sign it certifying your condition and that's it."

I realized they were telling me I was mentally ill. I never hesitated a split second. I stood up, pushed my chair back, picked up the form and tour it into four pieces. "No, thank you." I turned and left the room.

For several months, I thought about what Samantha had said at our last meeting. And although I wasn't sure it was the right thing to do, I phoned her office to ask if I could meet her for lunch. It was the first time I had spoken to her since the night I arrived back in Austin. I spoke with her secretary who told me Samantha and Emma were attending a real estate convention in San Francisco. She assured me she'd give Samantha the message when she called in later that day.

Early the next morning the phone rang. It was Emma. She greeted me the same way she had greeted me since she had grown up. "Hi, Dad. How the hell are you? I hear you quit drinking again. I'm proud of you for that. Do you think you can last?"

"Yes, honey, I think I have it beat this time."

Samantha picked up an extension in the living room of their suite. She was cool. "To what do I owe the pleasure?" she asked.

The call ended with Samantha's somewhat reluctant promise to meet me for lunch when she got back. Emma said she'd call me in a couple of weeks and invite me over for a swim and a visit.

I was fighting for some kind of normalcy in my life, but it wasn't easy. The nightmares were coming several times a week. The day-mares and flashbacks were there, of course, and sleep was at most, impossible. I couldn't tell that the hospital stay had helped me. I kept waiting for the antidepressants to kick in; they never did. And every day I was struggling not to take that first drink. I spent a lot of very uncomfortable days and nights. I also developed a strange anxiety that seemed to intensify as my lunch date with Samantha got closer.

The day finally arrived. It was a Wednesday and we were meeting at the Four Seasons Hotel. The Four Seasons was, by far, the nicest hotel in Austin. It was set majestically above the Colorado River which ran through the middle of the city.

At an early morning AA meeting the day of my appointment with Samantha, I took the opportunity to voice my anxiety. Several people told me to just stay cool. They said Samantha was suffering the same anxiety that I was. Not likely, I thought.

I left my apartment an hour early for our lunch. When I entered the hotel I was, as always, struck by the beauty of the place. There were fresh flowers everywhere; the floral arrangements were almost over the top. The lobby was very large and spacious and offered a view of the landscape and the river below. I took a seat in a ridiculously overstuffed, tan leather chair being careful to position myself so I could see the front entrance as well as the river.

At that hour, there were not a lot of people in the lobby. Very quickly, a cocktail hostess arrived and asked if I would like a drink. That was the first drink I'd been offered in 180 days. I thought about that as I replied, "No thanks, just a black coffee, please, and would you help me arrange for a nice table by the window for lunch? I'm expecting a special guest."

The hostess replied, "Certainly, sir. I know the perfect table for you. I'm sure your guest will love it. I can also get you a red rose for your guest, if you like."

My mind raced back to the first time I sent Samantha flowers, and how I finally convinced her to date me. I wanted to give her a dozen, but knew that wasn't the thing to do.

"One would be nice. Thank you very much."

Before she could return with the flower, I had relived the turbulence in my life since I had sent those first roses. It was like reliving the movie, "The Good, The Bad, and The Ugly." Pictures raced across my mind like a hyper-fast movie reel. I felt great remorse for the way I had let whiskey take over and totally screw up my life.

If someone had told me there was much, much more, as well as much worse to come, I would have said they had to be crazy.

Without realizing it, my thoughts turned to Vietnam. I don't know how long I stayed with those thoughts, but I was returned to consciousness when the hostess came back with the rose and a fresh cup of coffee. The rose was beautiful; it was wrapped in green tissue paper and had a yellow ribbon and bow.

She said, "Please tell me about the special person you're expecting."

Again my mind covered vast territory before I replied, "Oh, just a very good and dear old friend. Thank you for asking."

"Well, I'm sure it must be someone very special."

She placed the rose on the low, glass-top table in front of my chair and left. I looked around and noticed the lunch crowd had almost filled the lobby. There were many well-dressed folks having cocktails or coffee before lunch. Looking at my watch, I couldn't believe it was 12:20 already. Being late was not one of the things Samantha was known for. I figured something very important must have come up that caused her to be delayed. Of course, I also thought about the negative bullshit, too—maybe she wasn't coming; maybe she was going to punish me. God knew I deserved to be punished. I continued to wait and watch as people in the lobby moved into the dining room.

"Okay," I said to myself. "She'll be here, just calm down and get a grip. Try that deep breathing."

At five to one the hostesses appeared, holding a phone. She handed it to me and said, "It's a call for you, sir."

I took the phone; it was Samantha's assistant who told me a very important client had unexpectedly shown up and Samantha wouldn't be able to meet me for lunch. She sent her regrets and said she would phone me to reschedule in a few days.

I disconnected the handset and laid it on the glass table. A horrible feeling descended over me. It was like devastation, defeat, and disappointment all wrapped up in anger. A drink would help. Just one drink. I fought to regain my composure. After several minutes, I heard the hostess speaking to me.

"Are you okay, sire? Could I get you more coffee or a glass of wine, perhaps?"

I didn't miss a beat. "Yes, how about bringing me a double scotch on ice, with a splash of soda."

My mind was really twisting. I felt like someone had put me in a vice. Before the hostess returned with my drink of poison, I realized I must have felt like Samantha felt all those times I swore to her I'd never touch another drop of alcohol. Suddenly I was very tired and realized I was shaking my head.

The hostess quietly set the drink down on the table, smiled, turned and left without saying a word. I looked at the glass of scotch for a long time. My thoughts were all over the place. I picked up the glass and, as I moved it to my lips, I rationalized that I could certainly justify a drink after that disappointment. I would have just one and let it calm my nerves.

I savored the aroma for a long moment. As I moved the glass back and forth under my nose, my head filled with the smell of the whiskey. I remembered hearing several times in AA meetings that for the alcoholic, one drink was too many and 1,000 drinks were not enough. Should I do this?

It had been six months since my last drink, but I knew just how good it was going to taste going down. I could feel the warmth of the scotch. Again I inhaled deeply, letting the aroma of the scotch almost burn my nostrils. I placed the glass back on the table, picked up the rose, placed two $20 bills beside the glass and left the hotel.

On the drive back to my apartment, I decided that I should get to an AA meeting as quickly as possible realiz-

ing that I had way too much time with way too little to do.
I had to get my ass to work.

I decided to place a call to an old military buddy who
worked for me in Guatemala. Don Dale Demboski had
retired several years before I did and went to work in DC
for the Federal Emergency Management Agency. He was
hired on as a regional director and moved up rapidly. He
was now the number-three man in FEMA. Don Dale had
always told me that when I got out of the Army he'd give
me a job.

His direct line rang twice. "Hello, this is Don Dale.
Can I help you?"

I said, "Sure you can, you renegade bastard. I need a
job."

"Is this Nelson? The good-for-nothing drunk who
lied and cheated his way through an Army career? The
chicken-shit fellow who flew Mohawks in Nam? The same
one who married way over his head to the most beautiful
woman in the world?"

"Yeah, yeah, Don Dale. How the hell are you?"

"I'm doing just fine, Nelson. How are you liking civilian life? How's Samantha and how you doing with your
sobriety? I heard you quit drinking."

"Well, civilian life is okay. I think I'm going to like it;
it's sure a low pressure way to live. After being responsible
for 12,000 troops all over Latin America, this should be
a piece of cake. I'm doing okay, except for trying to stay
sober, that is. Samantha's fine. I haven't talked to her but
twice since I got back to Austin. She looked great and her
business is still growing like crazy. She's riding this real estate boom and still opening new offices. Thanks for asking.
I still haven't had a drink. I'm active in Alcoholics Anonymous, working very hard to stay sober."

"That's great, Nelson. You think you and Samantha
will ever put it back together?"

"Hell, I don't think so, Don Dale. She's still 100%
pissed off at me, although she says she still loves me.

There's no way she can trust me to stay off the hooch."

Even as we were talking, my mind ran away with the thought of getting back together with Samantha. I returned to the conversation and said, "I need to get a job Don Dale. I know you've said for years that when I got out you'd put me to work. There's nothing holding me in Austin and I feel that I'm strong enough now to keep the hooch at bay, so I'm ready."

"That's great, old buddy. When can you come to DC so we can talk about it? You can stay with Sarah and me, and I'll tell you about something I've been thinking about for a long time. Maybe we can help each other make some real money."

The next week I flew to DC. Don Dale had hatched a plan for us to go into business together. During the next two weeks he took some time off and we worked nonstop day and night on a plan for our future. I would start a new construction company and that company would use Don Dale's contacts at FEMA to capture contracts to rebuild properties devastated by disasters.

Our new company was soon incorporated in Austin, Texas. I was Chief Executive Officer and President and Don Dale Demboski was Executive Vice President. I rented some very nice offices and, much to Sarah's distress, Don Dale resigned his position with FEMA and moved his family to Austin.

By the time Don Dale got to Austin I had hired two top-notch construction superintendents, a secretary, a bookkeeper and several other staff people. Our first contract was for a respectable $3.2 million. The job was to rebuild three large houses in northeastern Oklahoma that had been flooded by a river during heavy rains.

Before we were halfway through the job, Don Dale brought in another contract for $17 million to rebuild a shopping center in Alabama that had been mostly destroyed by a tornado. Don Dale flew back to DC frequently to visit and lobby his buddies at FEMA.

It was a good thing those contracts were extremely profitable because Don Dale was running up big expenses wining and dining his FEMA buddies. I didn't care about his extravagant dinners, expensive wines and whatever, since he kept producing sweet contracts.

I was instantly busy and, although my attendance at AA meetings had slacked off, I still made it to several each week. Many days, I was totally ragged from lack of sleep and trying to shake off a raging nightmare from the night before. In spite of that, I just kept pushing the bar of success higher and higher. In a short time, I had several hundred thousand in the bank and decided it was time to buy a place of my own.

Samantha's company managed the sales of a new luxury condo project in downtown Austin, and I bought a beautiful large penthouse unit from her firm. Almost before I could move in, I got a long-awaited call from Samantha. "One of my gals tells me you bought a new penthouse, congratulations. And by the way, thank you for the business. You were smart to select the unit you did. That wraparound panoramic view of the city, with both the capitol and the river in sight, will ensure you get maximum appreciation on your money."

"Yeah, thanks. I think I'm going to like it very much."

"I hear your business is doing great," she said. "Hell, my builders tell me you're hiring up all the good construction people in town."

I wanted to be courteous, but still a bit standoffish. "Yes, Don Dale and I are doing very well, growing almost too fast."

Finally Samantha got around to the real reason she called. "I never called you back after the missed lunch. I got so busy, I just couldn't find time and then, after awhile, I was embarrassed to call. Think you can forgive me for that?"

I warmed up a bit and said, "Sure, it's forgotten. I do miss you, Samantha and would love to see you. I hear

Emma is working for you in the real estate business, and that she's built a big new house of her own. By the way, just so you know, I'm two years sober last week."

"Nelson, that's wonderful." But then Samantha quickly got back to business. "You know if you continue to build a big company as it seems like you will, and I have a large profitable one, the fact that we're still married could be a real complication. If something happened to either of us, it all could end up in some giant mess," she said. "Why don't we meet for dinner and talk about it?"

"I'd love to meet you for dinner, but I've got a question about your earlier comment. Did you decide all this about our assets or did your attorneys come up with it?"

"Some of both, I guess," she said. "Would you like to come over to the house Friday night for dinner, say around sevenish? That will give us a chance to relax before dinner. I'll have Rose fix something special."

Rose was Samantha's longtime live-in maid. Samantha had sent Rose to enough gourmet cooking schools that she could have been a chief at the White House. We talked a while more about Emma and her success. When I hung up, I wondered if I'd done the right thing by accepting Samantha's invitation. Oh, what the hell, I'd have a nice evening and some great food, too.

There was no question I badly wanted to see Samantha. I used a life lesson I'd learned from Juan Batos about decision making. In order for me to make a good decision I must have my head, my heart, and my gut aligned on the matter. If any one of those was not in agreement with the others, the decision would likely be wrong.

That Friday night dinner was the first of several over the next few months. Soon those dinners led to the bedroom. In the bedroom, the original passion returned and we were both enjoying the sex as much as we ever did.

Samantha was as good a lay as I have ever had and the passion she regularly displayed was just fantastic. She was able to bring out my best and regularly made great demands on my endurance. Samantha was quite open about how much she was enjoying our sex life.

About a year later, I was staying overnight at her house so frequently that we decided to return to living as man and wife. I soon sold my condo and, as Samantha had predicted, it sold quickly and for a very large profit. The quality of my life was great again.

I was sober, although I was attending fewer and fewer AA meetings. I was making enormous money, had an extremely successful business, and Don Dale and I had become best of friends.

During the next few years I seemed to be doing everything right. The only exception was that I was sleeping with some other women from time to time when I was traveling on business, but never in Austin. I was always careful. I never saw any of them more than once; although there were a few I would sure have liked to. Some of these gals were top-notch pros. I rationalized this infidelity as my reward for not drinking.

Every month Don Dale and I had a standing meeting. These meetings usually lasted for two or three days, and we always had them out of town to insure minimal interruptions. The agenda was to catch up on the status of our contracts, the company's financial status and to take a close look at our upcoming contracts.

Month after month Don Dale was producing more and more work, and we were getting richer and richer. It was obvious, though, that the good life of wine, woman, and song was taking a toll on him, but he never complained. Although, from time to time he would say the partying was getting old.

When I suggested he hire somebody to party with the FEMA guys, he rejected the idea totally. He said that things were going too good to take any chances. Besides, we all knew that the way we were bringing in those contracts and the prices we were charging the government were way beyond the bounds of legitimate. Everyone was winning except Uncle Sam. Were our actions unlawful? No. Unethical, perhaps, but I don't think they were unlawful. Don Dale and I justified it all as paying back the government for the way it treated us over Vietnam.

We had grown rapidly to over 600 employees and had more than a 140,000,000 dollars annually in revenue over several years. Our work stretched from Texas to the Carolinas and south through Florida. At one time, we were working in seven states at once.

Our business model was to hire great managers. Many of them were prior military officers, and even though they weren't construction people, they were excellent managers. We paid them much more money than they could make anywhere else. For that matter, every person in the company made at least one and a half times the going rate for their skill levels.

Those managers all had substantial cash slush funds to pay graft to any inspector who gave them problems. I knew all about payoffs, having spent so many years operating in Central and South America where graft was the only way to get anything done. This company structure assured me that there would be minimal problems in the field.

Even so, there were considerable requirements on my time. I had to travel constantly. Most of my key people who lived in Austin were working away from home and living apart from their families. That meant they were traveling back and forth to their homes on a frequent basis.

I decided to buy a business jet and soon bought a second one. Although I was well-qualified to fly them, I hired pilots. The larger Gulfstream jet carried 12 passengers and a crew of two. I also hired a full-time flight attendant for that airplane.

Nellie had fair skin, a beautiful head of red hair and magnificent green eyes. She was easily a ten on a scale of one to ten and she knew that. On our trips with the FEMA

executives, Nellie always wore her best and most reveal-
ing outfits. Her low-cut blouses would stop a man in his
tracks. Every time I looked at those breasts I thought about
Moss. On the other trips, she wore a conservative uniform.
Nellie was off limits to my managers and she and they
knew that.

While I was getting rich, so was Samantha. By that
time, we had accumulated a net worth of just over $14
million dollars and $3 million of that was cash in the bank.
Each time we got money ahead, I would build another
project for our own personal portfolio. I was building
apartments, low-rise shopping centers and a few nursing
homes. Samantha managed the rentals and together we
were a winning combination.

I heard about some Austin movers and shakers who
were starting a new bank. They invited me into the deal
and I became a director of the First Cash Bank of Austin
Texas. The building program, the investments and the
businesses seemed to ensure our long-term security. No
matter how secure, I felt there was a big storm approaching.

I stopped attending AA meetings and justified my
decision by telling myself that I had been sober for years. I
told Samantha that I no longer felt alcohol was a threat.

I was a skilled manager and a champion at delegation
as well as being highly motivated. Even though the business and it's demands grew, I continued to seek out exceptional people to work for us and each one was given the
authority to go with his or her responsibility. That made
our company hum. Production was always at a peak and
problems were kept at a minimum. I empowered my staff
to settle almost any situation as quickly as it arose. As a
result, I was able to take a good deal of time off whenever I
wanted.

Samantha and I became world travelers. We soon
decided to buy a beach home on the Algarve in Portu-
gal. That meant we needed another jet, one with a wide

enough range to allow for flights to Europe. That jet was a little smaller than the others and only had seating capacity for eight. The cabin was incredibly luxurious with maroon carpeting and light gray leather seats. With a price tag of about $3 million, it was also faster than the other jets we owned and could easily cross the ocean to Europe. I borrowed the money from my bank at a preferential rate, of course. We also had a limo and full-time driver.

Next came a mountain home in Aspen, Colorado and a million-dollar penthouse condo on Seven Mile Beach on Grand Cayman Island in the Caribbean. We both were certified scuba divers and spent many hours diving on the Great Wall there as well as Cayman Brac and Little Cayman Island. For weekend use, we also built a beach house in Corpus Christie, Texas.

As our company continued to expand and prosper, we realized the key to its success was still the senior staff at FEMA. They were virtually our sole source of business. Don Dale was a fantastic partner; he owned 40% of the company and he never objected to anything I wanted to do. He took all the shit I didn't want to do and handled it. That left me to manage and plan. The combination turned out to be magic. But it was all too good to last.

Don Dale started to unravel. The pace he was keeping, the partying, and the daily business responsibilities were just more than he could handle. He was drinking way too much and was openly whoring. Sarah left him and moved to Memphis, Tennessee near her family to raise their kids. That little divorce cost Don Dale several million dollars. No matter how hard I tried to get him to throttle back, he just steamrolled ahead. He started to drink more and more and gained a huge amount of weight.

I did everything possible to stay as far away from Don Dale's partying trips as I could. While I felt safe about not drinking I was not secure enough to test it very often with wine, women, and gambling in Vegas. There were times when I just couldn't get out of going along. One trip in particular was a real pisser.

We were entertaining two of the very top FEMA executives and a U.S. Congressman. Congressmen were not usually regulars on our trips to Las Vegas; they liked out of the country trips better. I guess they figured there was too much chance of being recognized with a strange honey on their arms in Vegas. There was a lot less chance of detection in some foreign country.

That particular trip was the first one I had taken with Don Dale in almost a year. Our first night in Sin City, I saw just how out of control he was. By the time we landed at McCarran International Airport, Don Dale was already pretty well in the sauce. We arrived at the Sands Hotel where we had reserved our regular wing of suites and he insisted that we order up a couple of prostitutes for our own use. It wasn't too difficult to convince me. He said he'd take care of placing our order. His couple turned out to be four. For a few hundred dollars a trip, the bell captain usually had plenty of girls ready for our guests.

I was kind of looking forward to it all since most Vegas gals were top-talent and well worth the money they charged. A quality pro could cost a thousand bucks for a couple of hours and up to five or six grand for the entire night. As always, Don Dale and I shared a suite. It had a beautiful entryway that opened into a huge center room with a three-story, full-glass wall looking over the strip, two giant bedroom suites that opened off either side of the living room. The open kitchen bar was 25 feet long and, of course, it stayed fully stocked with everything imaginable.

Our regular concierge, who was a beautiful, young woman herself, always took excellent care of us. She always had everything ready for our arrival. All our guests knew that all they had to do was pick up the phone and she would provide anything they wanted.

Tired after the flight, I left Don Dale on the phone and went to my suite to shower and change out of my suit and tie. I made a few calls in my room then went to take a long, hot shower. To my delight, the shower room was 12-feet square with shower heads on the ceiling and three walls. That damn shower also had it's own sound system and psychedelic lighting.

I hardly got wet before I was joined by what Don Dale called a "special present" to show his appreciation for me. Don Dale entered the shower with all four spectacular gals, and of course everyone was as naked as I was. One of the girls had a tray of martinis, which I declined.

The party continued all night and finally ended with me sleeping in my huge round bed with three of those lovelies in the nude with me. It was by no means my first orgy, but it was sure the best one I'd ever attended. The total bill for that night including the caviar, lobster, wine, and gals came to almost $20,000. Don Dale told me the next morning he'd been wanting to do that for a couple of years. His way of showing appreciation for me bringing him into the company and, as he said, making him "real goddamn rich."

Flying back to Austin the next day, I felt a slight tinge of guilt. I remembered when I started living with Samantha again that the only promise I made was not to drink, but there was no promise about being faithful. Of course, I used that to rationalize that screwing around on her was permitted at these great distances.

Don Dale was also very much into me staying sober. He, too, didn't see anything wrong with a strange lay when it came along. I smiled to myself thinking about Samuel's rule to never miss a piece of ass. I did remember the threat Samantha made in the topless bar in Arizona, when she said if she ever caught me fooling around she'd leave me. But she had threatened to leave a lot of times.

Shortly after that Vegas excursion, I was on a business trip to Jacksonville, Florida, when I received an urgent call from Samantha. She told me Don Dale was in the hospital in DC. He had collapsed in a restaurant while having lunch with some FEMA executives. She didn't know any particulars except that he was in critical condition. I rushed to the airport and had my pilots fly me to Washington National Airport. A limo was waiting to take me to Georgetown Medical Center. I made a phone call to a Congressman friend who arranged a police escort and we were at the hospital in short order.

It was early evening when I arrived at the hospital and Don Dale was still in the operating room. Information was sketchy, but I soon learned he had had an aneurism in his brain and had been admitted in critical condition. He was on the operating table for more than six hours.

Samantha had taken our other airplane and flown to Knoxville to pick up Sarah. They arrived at the waiting room just moments before the two operating surgeons came out to tell us the results of the operation. I was struck dumb when we were informed that there was severe brain damage and Don Dale would likely never regain consciousness. We were all so shocked no one spoke. Sarah and Samantha burst into uncontrollable sobs. I felt tears streaming down my face as I asked the doctors if there was any chance they were wrong and if there was any hope for a recovery. The answer was an emphatic no. Not even a slight chance.

One of the doctors took me aside in the hallway and said, "Honestly, the best thing that could happen to your friend and everyone involved would be if he passed right here in the hospital tonight."

I went nuts when I heard that. I grabbed the doctor by the collar and pulled him to my face. "If you say that to another human being in this room, I will terminate your life with my own hands," I said. I could feel the blood vessels in my neck throbbing.

I pushed him backwards and he and the other doctor left quickly left without saying another word.

Don Dale never regained consciousness. He lived on life support for almost eight years during which time Sarah moved him to a private care facility in Memphis. I borrowed a ton of money to buy Don Dale's stock ensuring that Sarah would have whatever money she needed to take care of him, the girls and herself forever. I was actually putting the entire company in deep debt.

It was well over a year after Don Dale died that I found out he was dead. It didn't make much difference because I was broke, drunk, and in federal prison when I learned of his death.

Many years later, when I was growing old, the most wonderful person I had ever met took me to put flowers on Don Dale's grave. After she helped me place the bouquet, she held me in her arms while I cried. I told Don Dale how very sorry I was. I felt that I had let him kill himself trying to prove himself to me. I didn't go to see Sarah; I just wasn't strong enough.

Life started turning to shit soon after Don Dale became ill. Almost immediately, the contracts started to slow down and it was apparent that the FEMA guys wanted out of the trap we all had created. The preferential treatment they were giving my company was coming to a quick end.

When I was forced to start laying people off, I decided to pay a visit to Jerry Delong, FEMA's top man in Washington. I phoned Jerry on his direct line. "Jerry, this is Nelson in Austin, Texas."

"Hi, Nelson, what can I do for you?"

His tone was all business. He spoke as if he had never met me before. That was bullshit. Hell, I'd been supplying this guy and his cronies with Vegas trips including all the amenities for years. Now he was talking to me like I was a stranger.

I fought for composure and said, "Jerry, I'm going to be in DC next week for a few days and thought you might be available to have lunch with me." I continued in a more formal tone myself. "How about Tuesday at Four Seasons? Around noon okay with you?"

I knew he didn't want to face me or talk about cutting our work back. I also knew I didn't give him a chance to say no. With no small talk at all, we agreed to meet at my hotel the following week.

When the day arrived, we met in the lobby of the Mayflower Hotel. As Jerry approached, I realized he had never looked like a typical government bureaucrat. He was always a rag bag. That day he was wearing scuffed shoes, wrinkled pants that were too long, and a sport coat that didn't match. His tie had enough food spots on it that he could've had it for lunch.

I was wearing a $3,000, perfectly tailored, handmade suit from an exclusive tailor on Rodeo Drive, a hand-stitched white shirt, power tie and $500 dollar shoes. I couldn't believe a man who looked the way he did could have the power to hand out or to deny me multimillion dollar contracts. Unfortunately, he did have that power, and there was not one damn thing I could do about it.

I knew full well what the problem was. Those FEMA guys had been sucking on our tits for so long, they were all scared shitless someone was going to find out and get the entire bunch of them fired or put in jail. What they wanted was for me and my company to go away. They each had a sudden attack of ethics. We greeted each other, shook hands and went into the dining room to talk. Just as I thought, he and the rest of his senior staff were afraid for their jobs. What I didn't know, until that moment, was that FEMA had been put under congressional oversight. That meant that auditors were looking at every contract to ensure it was properly bid and that there was no preferential treatment given to any one contractor. That meant my company was a casualty. As much as I hated it, there was nothing I could do about the situation. It was over, the goose was dead, no more golden eggs.

That afternoon I left the hotel to meet my pilots at the airport. I'd told them to fly up from Austin and I'd be ready to leave by 5:00. They were, as always, on time. Nellie had snacks onboard. We got caught in a weather delay that made us almost an hour late getting off the ground. I had a briefcase full of work so the time passed quickly.

Minutes after we finally lifted off, Nellie came over and asked if I'd like anything to drink or maybe a snack. I asked for a club soda and, for some reason, I thought about how it would taste with scotch in it. When she brought my soda she asked, "Do you mind if I have a glass of wine since we don't have any passengers?"

"No problem, go right ahead."

Nellie got her glass of wine, came back and sat across from me. She pulled her legs up under her when she sat down, and I had a great shot of her pink panties. I clearly remember thinking just how beautiful she was. Then I ruined that thought when I realized Nellie was only one year older than Emma.

An hour later, somewhere over Tennessee at 22,000 feet, I made a conscious decision to have just one drink. It had been over ten years since I had had my last drink and I was sure I could handle just one. I couldn't.

Two hours later when we landed in Austin, Nellie and I were both very drunk. We had made love once or twice, I'm not sure which it was. I was almost too drunk to stand up. My chief pilot had called ahead and the driver helped Nellie and me into the limo. My pilot told him to drive me home first and then take Nellie home. By the time we got to my house I decided that Nellie should come in for a night cap. It was late and I knew Samantha was in bed.

I figured I shouldn't let Nellie stay in the house all night, so we went to the guest house. On the way to the guest house, Nellie decided she wanted to take a swim, so we took off our clothes and went in the pool. Later, we had a few more drinks and we both passed out. Sometime during the early morning hours, Samantha appeared in the guest house. That was a bad scene.

I don't remember all of what happened during the next couple of years. What I do know was that Samantha and I were granted an uncontested divorce. She kept the house, her cars, and her business. Samantha soon sold her company for a large amount of money and went on with her life. Obviously, I proved she was right when she said she could never trust me again.

I did the hardest thing I ever did in my life, but it was possibly the most correct thing. When we came out of the divorce court, I asked her to stop on the sidewalk a moment and let the lawyers go on ahead. I looked at her and said, "Samantha, you are a fine woman, and I know you have wasted your love and your life on me for all these years. Please know this—I have never felt anything but the deepest true love for you. I would give my life here on this spot if I could take back all the hurt I've caused you."

I touched her hand and as I turned and walked away. I heard her doing the same thing I was doing. Crying.

The shutting down of the FEMA money spigot, finishing up the last of the construction jobs, and letting the remaining few employees go was tough for me. Some of those guys had been serving with me from the inception of my company. Some even before that in the military. I knew they loved me and I loved each of them.

If all that wasn't enough to deal with, the economy was turning to hell. Banks and savings and loans were being taken over by the Federal Deposit Insurance Corporation. FDIC was closing banks and calling loans. Foreclosures were everywhere.

It took just over a year for me to lose the rest of the investment property. I was drinking hard by then and it was showing on me. When I looked in the mirror, my eyes were glassy, my hair was graying, and my face was red and puffy. I had long since stopped taking my medication and the nightmares were raging. I just tried to drink it all away. At that point, I just wanted to drink myself to death.

In addition to foreclosing on all the investment property; the FDIC filed a $7,000,000 lawsuit against me. I filed bankruptcy because of that and, a few million more, including the unpaid balances on the airplanes and cars that I had given back to the bank and finance company. The executives at First Cash Bank asked me to resign as bank director just before the FDIC closed it down.

The judge at my bankruptcy hearing was so pissed off at me that he threatened to put me in jail. He was angry because my last official act was to raid my company of it's last $110,000. I distributed it equally to my seven key people when I let them go.

The judge asked me for the Rolex I was wearing. I was about drunk and made some dumb remark to him. "Just don't fine me, Judge," I said. "I'm fresh out of cash right now."

He rolled his eyes, shook his head and said, "Please leave my courtroom."

When I left the federal courthouse in Austin, all I had to my name were the six $100 bills I had hidden in my wallet. I went directly to the closest bar. The next morning I woke up in the city jail. I had no idea how I got there.

That was my first experience with jail and the Austin police, but it certainly would not be my last. Later that day, the magistrate let me out after lecturing me about how I needed to get some professional help for my drinking problem.

Had I been sober enough to take my inventory, I would have realized that in less than four years I had gone from mega-wealth to totally broke, all because of just one drink of scotch.

Once outside the jail, I could only find $20 in my pocket. My first impulse was to find the nearest bar. Hell, I couldn't get very drunk on $20, so I walked to the nearest bus stop and caught a bus to the AA club. The same one I started out in years earlier.

I slept and ate in that AA club's flop house for several days. I had a bad case of the shakes, but I attended every meeting that was held around the clock. I saw an old friend in one of those meetings. Ed Valentine had been in the AA program for 20 years. Ed was a successful home-builder in Austin. His company was small, but it was very profitable. Soon Ed offered to let me live in a furnished apartment that he owned and he give me a job. The agreement was that I would go to at least one AA meeting every day and I had to return to the VA for medication and therapy.

God had seen fit to give me another chance and I was determined not to screw it up this time. In just a few months I was starting to feel human again. By then, Ed had given me full responsibility for a 25-home subdivision and I had a very capable superintendent to run the job. After driving one of Ed's company trucks for a while, I bought a car and financed it on the used car lot where I bought it. The car had a high interest and I paid way too much for it, but I had one. Reminded me of my first car.

I found that my days were very pleasant and I was glad to be sober. I was able to make more money than I needed to live and was actually saving some money. Next came my own rented apartment and then some pretty good used furniture.

Step 9 of AA's 12-step recovery program tells members to make amends to people we had hurt with our drinking. I wanted so much to apologize to Samantha and Emma and tell them just how remorseful I was. I was so very ashamed, but was helpless to make that happen. Although it tore my heart apart, I knew I should never see her again. She would be much better off if I didn't.

When I had 90 days of sobriety, I arranged with Ed to take enough time off to attend another inpatient PTSD recovery program at the VA hospital in Temple. The doctors who ran that particular group were a roaming group from the VA hospital in Washington state. They were all very good and everyone in the group agreed it was superb. I did the best I could with it, but was still unable to talk about the trauma of my death experience.

Dr. Saborra, who was now the director of psychological services at the hospital in Temple, took an active role in leading the trauma group sessions. One afternoon near the end of the program, I had a meeting with Kamilla in her office. She opened the conversation by saying, "I understand you've gotten a divorce. Tell me, how has that worked out?"

"Well, Doc, it's worked out about as well as it could work out. I love my wife very much, my ex-wife, that is. She also loves me very much. I got back on the whiskey and she asked me to leave immediately. I wasn't surprised. When she took me back after I got out of the Army and sobered up, she said that if I ever had another drink the marriage would end. Simply stated, I did, and she did."

"Do you think there's any chance for reconciliation in the future?"

I turned in my chair and looked her directly in the eyes. "I don't want reconciliation. I don't think I can trust myself to stay off the whiskey. God knows I want to almost more than I want life itself, but when things get too good for me or they get too tough, it always ends in a bottle." I continued, "Each time I start back on the booze it's as if I never quit. The need to drink has increased just as if I'd been drinking all that time. It gets harder and harder to stop each time, too. The bottom line here, Doc, is I am afraid I can't stay stopped. I seem to be able to stop drinking, but apparently I can't quit drinking."

"Before you leave this time, we're going to make a list of things you must do to stay sober," she said. "Nelson, you know that as long as you drink, your PTSD will not be manageable. Your life will not be manageable and you will continue to spiral down."

"I'm sure of that, Doc. When I drink to black out, I forget all the war shit. Why, hell, that's the only reason I drink. If I don't drink, the nightmares return the moment I stop the medicine."

"I know that, Nelson, but by continuing to drink you'll never get to any kind of emotionally comfortable life. You'll just continue to live in turmoil, from one life crisis to another."

A little later, Doc and I spent time designing a plan for

my aftercare when I left the hospital. It consisted of things like get lots of rest, get on a good exercise program, don't work too much, don't get too hungry, and on and on. Of course attending AA meetings was a must-do. Take my psych meds and don't forget what happens when I don't. As I said I knew all this, but doing it was the problem.

I had very little faith in myself at that point; in fact, I had no faith at all. The only chance I had was to follow the plan and try not to have that first drink. I said a prayer begging for God's help. I promised myself and I promised my daddy that I'd try hard to pull it off. I had to do it the AA way and just stay sober one day at a time.

After a five-week hospital stay I returned to Austin. When I got back, Ed asked me if I'd go down to South Padre Island, Texas and run a job there. He was having trouble finishing a 17-story, high-rise condominium. I didn't want to go, but he said his ass was really hung out on that thing and he couldn't get it on track. Hell, he had been so good to me I just couldn't say no. When I arrived in South Padre, I found my predecessor was not a very proficient builder and even less of a manager.

After years of working with the best of the best in my own company, I was totally qualified. I fired the guy and two of his buddies left with him. This was a small project compared to the many we had done at my construction company. It took me a month to get the work going again and programmed out properly so we wouldn't have any more downtime. The subcontractors were changed to in-centive contracts with strict performance clauses in them. I lived in a mobile home on the site and we worked twelve-hour days, six days a week. Once I got the work and the subs lined up and on a good schedule, the project moved rapidly to completion. The whole thing took just over a year.

Ed flew down for the grand opening of the build-ing. When he came over from the airport, he had a lovely young blond gal with him. Her name was Trace McGill.

She looked just like a Trace McGill should look. Trace had long, blond hair; she was almost six feet tall with fair skin, bright blue eyes, and a perfect figure. Stunning was the word for her. I had met her several months earlier in Ed's office.

Trace had a real estate license, and had been selling new homes in one of Ed's subdivisions. Ed had told me earlier that Trace was going to move into one of the model condos and manage the sales office on the property.

The grand opening gala was a big hit. There was great food and two open bars. Ed and I both avoided them, of course. Most of the "who's who" in the area was in attendance as were several Texas moguls. Even the governor was there, but she didn't stay long. A lot of those folks had way too much to drink. I knew that if I had even one drink, I'd be doomed. I did okay drinking only Coke, and I spent most of the evening talking with Trace. She was half my age, and she was truly lovely. Trace had traveled extensively and I found her articulate, interesting, and very much a free spirit. I liked her charisma and found her classy beyond her age.

The party broke up late and Ed and Trace were staying in furnished model condos. We talked about how well the party had come off, and then Ed said. "Nelson, I have a little something for you before we go to bed."

He reached into his inside coat pocket, removed an envelope and handed it to me.

"You know how bad this project was when you took it over; it was way behind schedule and way over budget," he said. "You turned it around, finished it early and ended over a hundred grand below the budget estimate. I know you've worked your ass off down here and I want you to have this, along with my thanks."

I took the envelope, but I had no idea what was in it. "Thank you, Ed, but I was just doing my job." I hesitated a moment, then opened the envelope.

There were two first-class airline tickets to the island

of St. Kitts in the Caribbean. There was also a bank check for $50,000 made payable to me, and a brochure of a beautiful resort. I took a deep breath and started shaking my head. "Ed, this is too much, man. I can't accept this. No, man, no way."

"Do you know what the overrun costs would have been on this project if it had gone over time and over budget? Hell, we could have easily lost half or even possibly a million dollars here. You did all the work and you deserve all the credit. There'll be nothing more said about it. Please accept it graciously and with my thanks," he said. "You have your butt on that American Airlines flight from Austin day after tomorrow and enjoy your week in Kitts. Oh, yes, the other ticket is for Trace; she needs a vacation, too, and I'm sure you don't mind if she goes along." He took one of the tickets from me and handed it to Trace.

I looked at Trace. "Trace, you knew about this, didn't you?"

"Nelson, I can't tell a lie. Yes, I knew about it," she said, smiling. "I'm excited about going to St. Kitts." She rolled her eyes up to the left and said, "I think we're going to have a great time. I've never been to St. Kitts, but a travel agent friend of mine said it was terrific."

And it was terrific. Our accommodations were spectacular. We stayed in a cute little, brightly painted Caribbean cottage sitting up on pilings a couple of feet above a beautiful blue lagoon. When we first arrived, we walked out a long dock to our front porch. When we entered the cottage, there was cold champagne waiting for us. I had a decision to make and it very well could have been a matter of life or death.

"Oh, isn't this wonderful? It's just perfect. Let's have some champagne and take a swim," Trace said.

I walked over to the table where the champagne was, picked it up and started to open it. "Trace, I'm an alcoholic. I don't drink anymore, but I'll pour you a glass and I'll toast you with my Coke."

"I've never known an alcoholic, does it make you sick?"

"No, it just makes me drunk." We laughed. "When I start drinking, I don't know when to stop."

I opened the champagne, popped the cork with flair and poured a goblet about half full. I handed the glass to Trace, took a Coke from the refrigerator, and proposed a toast. "To Trace and Nelson, a week of relaxation, sun, fun, swimming, great food, and good wine – oh, and Coke, too."

"To us," she said.

Trace changed into her suit, which was so tiny she could have carried it in a thimble. It was white and she was tan; all in all, it was a wow! She left me in the room to change into mine.

As she went out the door she said, "Meet you on the beach."

We swam, played in the water like a couple of kids – one of us was a kid – and laid in the oversize lounge chairs. I couldn't help but think about Emma. What the hell, just enjoy it while you can, boy. It ain't like you're gonna marry her.

By late afternoon, Trace had consumed more than enough piña coladas and was extremely happy and a little stupid. We went back to our cottage and she quickly came out of her suit. She came over, kissed me, and said, "Let's take a shower and make love."

"I think I can go for that program." I dropped my suit and we headed for the shower. We fell on the bed, wet from the shower and made love. We were both passionate about it and was apparent that it had been a good while since Trace had had sex, too.

Our last night we had dinner brought to our cottage. We dined on the porch, watching a huge orange sunset over the ocean which was magnificent. It was a magical moment made all the better for me since I had stayed with the Coke all evening. But was I going to be able to hold on?

Chapter 12
A Tragic Price for Peace of Mind

I remember falling over the coffee table with the glass top crashing into a million pieces when it hit the marble tile floor. I had gone back into the cottage for a refill on a second bottle of scotch. Trace was asleep and when the glass crashed she sat bolt up in the bed. The moon was bright enough through the window so she could see clearly what was going on. She screamed at me and told me to get the hell out of the cottage and not to come back. I made it back to the porch and passed out on a chair.

When I came to the next morning, Trace was gone. She had caught our scheduled flight back to Austin. I decided to stay another day on the island after Trace left. I knew I had to sober up before going home. Next day I went to the airport sober. Waiting for the American Airlines flight to Austin to be called, I took ten milligrams of Valium and had a couple of quick double scotches. I took another ten milligrams of Valium on the plane before we got to Austin, and then chased them down with who knows how many scotches. I don't remember changing planes in Dallas for Austin, but obviously I did.

I woke up lying on a stretcher on the floor in the Austin airport with a lot of people in uniforms looking down at me. My first thought was, Oh, shit. There were pilots, flight attendants, emergency medical folks and, of course, the trusty Austin cops. I was pretty crazy from the concoction of drugs and alcohol and when they began asking questions, I started giving them a ration of shit which, of course, they didn't appreciate. So they strapped me to a gurney and took me to a local hospital. Later that afternoon they moved me to the VA hospital in Temple, where I was quickly put back on the locked door psychiatric ward and started, once again, on a diet of psych meds and psychotherapy.

Ten days in the hospital rendered me fit for duty. The last hour before I was released, Dr. Kamilla Saborra visited with me. She again cautioned me. "Combat veterans with PTSD follow a pattern of behavior as surely as if it were a circle of life they were on. First they exhibit the symptoms of their illness: nightmares, day-mares, intrusive thoughts, isolation, and drink or drugs to self medicate. These actions most often lead to a stay in a psychiatric hospital or jail. Once in the hospital, they start medication again, attend psychotherapy groups and one-on-one sessions with the psychiatrists, then stabilization followed by release from the hospital. That feeling of wellness and security is achieved, but most often short lived. Next, a wrong decision is made that medication and psychotherapy is no longer needed. After quitting medication the vicious cycle begins again and again and again."

Doc ended by making a profound statement. "Nelson, you are going on 60 years old and if you don't make it this time, I very seriously doubt whether you will ever make it. This may very well be your last try at having a life."

I stood and simply said, "Thank you. I have a handle on it this time. I won't be back."

I left the hospital and went to my apartment. That night I attended an open AA meeting, I said, "I really don't want to drink anymore." Tears were streaming down my face. I described and confessed my actions of the last few weeks and reaffirmed my commitment not to drink again. As always, there was lots of support in the meeting. Several people gave me their phone numbers and each encouraged me to call them if I even thought I was going to have a drink.

As much as I dreaded it, the next morning I called Ed. He was calm and collected as ever. He didn't give me any indication that he was displeased about anything and warmly invited me to his office that afternoon. What I took from that phone call was nothing like what I found when I got to Ed's office.

Before I left my apartment, I sat at my desk and did an assessment of it all. That inventory that had served me so well in my life. I had the $50,000 Ed had given me. My checking and savings accounts combined were another $27,000 dollars. When I went to work for Ed after my bankruptcy, I didn't have any problem getting credit cards. I didn't owe more than $2,000 and had $18,000 available credit left on my cards. I only owed two payments on my car loan. I totaled everything up and gave myself a huge atta-boy when I realized I had cash and available credit equal to almost a $100,000 dollars. In my past life I'd had many millions in the bank, untold cash and credit, but that was then and this was now. If I'd had a million dollars in cash at that moment, I would have bet every penny that I would never have another drink of alcohol.

For a few minutes I was ecstatic as the happy feelings washed over me. I had a good job, I wasn't going to drink any more — ever — and I had plenty of cash. Add to that I was fresh out of the VA hospital and on proper psych medication. Life was good.

What I didn't know was that the biggest train wreck of my life was about to happen. All the bad experiences were not even close to what I was about to do.

I parked in the parking lot at Ed's office. As I got out of the car, I saw Ed come out of his office and start walking toward me. As he came close I put out my hand to shake his and said, "Hey buddy, I'm..." I was going to say, "so sorry for this screw up," but I never got the rest of the sentence out.

Ed hit me in the face with a roundhouse punch that came with all his might. The punch stunned me and I went down hard, hitting my head on the car and then on down to the gravel. I was almost unconscious. Ed bent over me, grabbed me by the hair, jerked my head back and then kicked me in the chest. The breath went out of me and I thought I was never going to have another centimeter of oxygen in my body. I fell over helplessly onto the gravel. I was having trouble opening my eyes. Ed's face was inches from mine and he was screaming.

"You worthless piece of shit. You good-for-nothing son of a bitch. I took you in when nobody would touch you. I gave you a chance at a new life. I gave you money and I gave you transportation. You ate and lived off me until you could support yourself. This is how you say thank you, you good-for-nothing piece of shit."

He screamed even louder. "I even set you up with Trace, somebody I think the world of. You sure fucked that up. I want you to listen and listen good to what I'm saying here. You betrayed me. You betrayed the trust I put in you and you embarrassed me so bad I damn sure never want to see you again. You leave here; don't come around me ever again. If you see me on the street, you fucking better cross to the other side. If you ever go to another AA meeting, you better be damn sure it's never at the club where I go."

He finished his tirade by saying, "So long, loser." Then he walked away.

I raised myself up on one elbow and looked at Ed's back as he walked to his front door. "I'm so sorry." Barely whispering, I said again, "I'm so sorry, Ed." I lay back down and thought just how fucked up I was. goddamn, it wasn't two hours earlier I was gloating and telling myself how great I was.

One of Ed's secretaries eventually came out of the office headed for her car and walked by me as if I wasn't even there. I don't know how long I laid there, but I was sure a mess when I got up. Blood was running down from the corner of one eye and my nose. It had dripped on my white polo shirt. Both my elbows were scratched up from the gravel. I crept over to my car and headed home. When I stopped at the liquor store near my apartment, the clerk looked at me pretty hard as I set two half gallons of Johnny Walker on the counter.

That night all I could do was drink it as fast as I could. I woke up some time in the early morning and did it again.

I didn't have to leave the apartment for two days, when the whiskey ran out. When I got up off the sofa to head back to the liquor store for another supply, I realized I still had on the bloody white shirt. I hated waiting because I wanted another drink, but I took a shower and put on clean clothes before returning to the liquor store. This time I bought a case of nine half gallons. I put them into the car and pulled around behind the store to have a drink. I thought about stopping at the grocery store to stock up so I wouldn't have to go back out later. I passed on that idea, deciding to order restaurant delivery instead.

I passed the next days, weeks and months in an alcoholic fog. I sometimes sobered up a little, but when I thought about my predicament, the sober didn't last long. During the short periods of sobriety, I decided to face all the remorse and sadness I felt about my present and past life. That's when I realized just how much anger and rage I felt. I had suppressed and held anger in for so long it was rotting my soul. I knew it, but still I couldn't let it go. I felt the government had double crossed me in Vietnam and it almost cost me my life. I often thought of Jerry. It made me cry. I came to realize just how much I hated and mistrusted the government. I hated any authority. I also knew I would never get over this until I let go of this anger, but I wasn't about to do that.

Sitting in front of my television, drunk, during a television news program about the outcome of an election, I threw an empty scotch bottle through the television screen. The cleaning ladies who had been coming to my apartment every week for over a year stopped coming after that. The place became a garbage heap of empty food containers, boxes and piles of empty scotch bottles. The only time I left the apartment was to get whiskey. I started going to different liquor stores so the clerks wouldn't think I was a drunk.

Some months into this binge, I was driving drunk to the liquor store when I pulled through a stop sign and another car hit me. The police took me to jail for drunk driving. I was in really bad shape by then and they didn't keep me very long before taking me to the hospital in Temple. It was a short stay in the hospital because I demanded to be released. I wanted to get on with my drinking. When I got out, first thing I did was go find my car. I found it had been a total loss so I bought another one and paid cash for it. I was paying no attention to spending my money.

I had a couple of drunken run-ins with my neighbors. Both ended with them calling the police and me going to jail for being belligerent. Sometimes the police jailed me until I sobered up; sometimes they'd take me straight to Temple. By then I had learned exactly what I had to tell the hospital staff in order to get out quickly.

Once I returned to my apartment and found myself locked out. There was an eviction notice on the door and I was padlocked out. I couldn't even get in for my clothes; no matter. I just left, went to the Four Seasons and got a room. For almost a year it was like that. I lived the life of a total drunken recluse. During that period I was becoming more and more insane and my actions were more and more bizarre. By then, each time I left the psych hospital, I threw away my meds and picked up another bottle.

I went to the bank, closed my accounts and took all my money in cash. I don't remember how much it was, but it had been substantially depleted by then. I was paying several thousand dollars a week for a room and room service. One of the maids there at the hotel was very nice to me and she'd even bring me whiskey on occasion when I didn't want to go out. While cleaning my room once she started to cry. She told me that her little daughter had to have an operation; I don't remember what for. I gave her $5,000 dollars in cash. It was the only time I'd felt good about something in a long time.

Finally my insanity led me to decide the scotch wasn't enough and I needed to get some Valium. I don't know why since I had never bothered with drugs. That was a very bad decision, but I was in too much of a stupor to even start to think about it.

I knew I could buy Valium in Mexico over the counter, without a prescription. I sobered up enough to drive there and crossed the border at Laredo. While I was there, I also bought a car full of scotch as it was very inexpensive. I parked the car on the street with the scotch and about a million, ten-milligram Valium pills in it. After asking a couple of kids to watch the car and giving them some cash, I walked to a bar to have a few before I crossed back over the border. My Spanish was very good, of course, and I laughed and joked with the locals in the bar. I became popular when I bought a couple of rounds for them as well as a lot rounds for myself. After a few slow dances with one of the working girls there, I tried to get a blow job in a back room. I couldn't even get an erection. It would ordinarily have cost $20, but I gave her four $100 bills. That was more cash than this gal had ever seen at one time. She offered to repeat the try for me. I wanted to get back to drinking so I passed on her offer.

Next thing I knew, I woke up and the bar was closed. I was sitting on the sidewalk with several drunk Mexicans with my back against the wall. I went back to where I'd parked my car and it was gone. I decided to deal with that later and found a taxi to take me to the border. I walked across the bridge and through the check-point without immigration questioning me. On the U.S. side, I negotiated a fee with a taxi driver to take me to a local liquor store and then drive me all the way back the 135 miles to Austin. It was expensive, but I don't remember how much. I paid him and I gave him a generous tip.

I never got around to going back to try and find the car and in just a few days, I could no longer pay my bill at the Four Seasons. When the night manager told me he wouldn't extend me any more credit and that my last credit card had been refused, of course I became belligerent. The police showed up and back to jail I went.

Next day it was off to the hospital at Temple. That time when I was committed, I was so mentally and physically trashed, it was four months before the hospital would release me.

During that hospital stay, I realized I didn't have any more money, no transportation, no credit cards left to use, and no place to live. Once again everything I owned was gone. I didn't even have a toothbrush left.

That time, like all the many other times, I thought about trying to stay sober again. Just maybe I could try and get some kind of life back. The reality was, I was so far gone that I gave little serious consideration to that line of thinking. Deep down I knew I was ready to give my life to alcohol. I made a conscious decision that I would drink myself to death.

That decision made me very sad on the one hand; however, on the other hand, it provided calm. I felt the pressure lift and knew I would never have to attend another AA meeting.

No alcoholic wants to be an alcoholic. What we do want is to be able to drink like normal people who are not addicted. We dream of having a drink or a few, getting a little buzz, relaxing, then quitting, going home, getting up the next morning, and going to work like other normal people. We can't do it, though—one drink and we're off to the races.

There was no cure. Only total abstinence could hold our addiction, our disease in remission. I'd been told that in AA for years, and the doctors at the VA preached it constantly. Hell, I personally knew all this to be fact as I was a living example. My craving and my total obsession to get alcohol into my body was the insanity of the disease manifesting itself. I was a perfect case study alcoholic. The VA had classified me as chronic and I had no defenses to argue with that. I knew, like all alcoholics, I would end up in one of three places: jail, hospital, or an early grave. Even knowing that, I was helpless to quit.

Each time the VA hospital released me, I received clean clothes, $5, and a bus ticket to wherever I lived. Those were the things that every psych patient got.

The afternoon I was released, Alvin, who was also from Austin, and I left the hospital together. As always, a hospital van gave us a ride to the Greyhound bus station in Temple. It was three hours before our bus was scheduled to leave for Austin.

Alvin wanted to have a cigarette so we went outside. In just a few minutes a fancy dressed black man walked up to us and offered to trade us each a bottle of vodka for our bus tickets. It didn't take Alvin and me but a split second to take that deal. I didn't have a clue what the guy did with those bus tickets, but it appeared that it was a regular gig for him.

There was a 7-Eleven convenience store across the street from the bus station where Alvin and I both spent our $5 on vodka and beer. We went behind the store to drink. Sometime the next morning, as we were digging in the dumpster looking for beer cans that weren't totally empty or some food, the Temple cops rousted us, loaded us in the back of a patrol car, and took us to a truck stop at the edge of town. They let us out of the car and said if they ever saw us in Temple again they'd put us in jail.

We soon bummed a ride to Austin in the back of a delivery truck headed south to San Antonio. I was very hung over from mixing the beer and vodka, and all I could think of during the two-hour ride was how I was going to get another drink. When we got out of the truck in Austin, Alvin said he knew where there was a homeless camp that we could stay at.

Funny, the camp turned out to be just a few blocks from the Four Seasons Hotel where I had been evicted just a few months earlier. The camp was located under the bridge where Interstate 35 crossed the Colorado River near downtown Austin. The camp was occupied by homeless veterans, some of whom had lived there for years. My new home was appropriately named Camp Home and residency was restricted to veterans.

The trees, shrubs and bushes had entirely enclosed the camp. The only access was a narrow winding path near the river. It was so hidden that even someone standing a few feet away would never know it was there. The shrubs and bushes also provided protection from the elements. There were two privies and even electricity. At some earlier time, an industrious Camp Home resident had wired an electric line from a street light on the bridge above the camp.

Austin had always been known as a liberal town. It was a place where street vets, as we were called, could live without hassle from the public or the police. In fact, I never saw the police come to Camp Home during the three years I lived there — until they came there to arrest me.

Alvin and I had arrived during the afternoon of the day before Christmas Eve. The temperature had dropped and it was quite cool. There was a large fire burning in a fire ring in the center of the camp. Some residents lived in tents, others had some type of lean-tos and others just slept in sleeping bags or blankets open on the ground.

Alvin immediately met an old friend who had enough money to lend us enough for a bottle. He also had an almost full gallon-bottle of wine. Alvin and I had a couple of big drinks from the bottle. There was a strict code among street vets — share what you have and never touch anything that isn't yours. Don't steal anything, anywhere, any time. A person could go away and leave anything he had, including food and even whiskey, and it would still be there when he returned. If someone was arrested, his property would be neatly stacked awaiting his return. It was hard to believe, but some residents' property had been stacked and covered for several years awaiting his return.

I was still sick from mixing the vodka and beer the previous night, but I knew the wine would make me feel better. Alvin gave me the money and I walked the few blocks to the nearest liquor store. Alvin stayed at the camp, borrowed blankets, and located the best spot for us to bed down.

That night we got drunk on the cheap vodka and slept close to the fire as the temperature continued to drop. When we woke up on Christmas Eve, it was freezing. There were probably ten residents at Camp Home when I first arrived.

During the summer the number of residents grew, but when the weather cooled, several had left to go further south. A few had done some petty crime in order to spend the winter in jail. Those guys knew exactly what they had to do to draw winter sentences. The number of veterans living at the camp varied from six or seven to fifteen or even twenty during the almost three years I made it my home.

On Christmas Day, the many churches in the area, as well as the Salvation Army, fed the homeless who wanted to eat. I didn't leave camp. I decided to drink instead of going to eat. During my three years at Camp Home, I pursued my commitment to drink myself to death. In fact, death would have been a blessing. As I completely gave my life to alcohol, I lost days in an alcoholic fog. Much of the time I was deranged. Sometimes I'd go for long periods of time living in Vietnam in my mind, never really knowing if I was in Vietnam or Austin. I earned my money for whiskey by panhandling on street corners. Many days I ate out of dumpsters behind restaurants and grocery stores.

For anyone who wanted it, there was always a hot breakfast at the Salvation Army on Fifth Street. It was usually only oatmeal or thin soup, but you could eat all you wanted. Many times, though, I was too hung over or still too drunk to get up early enough to go.

I had joined the ranks of the derelicts. My clothes came from the Salvation Army, much of my food from dumpsters and my alcohol from anywhere I could get it. I'd drain empty cans and bottles, beg from other homeless guys, and buy the cheapest liquor I could find with the money I made panhandling.

When I panhandled, I'd go to different corners with my cardboard sign that had the words, "Homeless Veteran" written on it. I didn't want to look like a regular at any one corner. There were days I'd get ten or twelve bucks and there were rainy days when I'd get almost nothing. I never knew how much I could make in a day because as soon as I had enough for a bottle I'd go get one.

While walking by the emergency room entrance of an Austin Hospital one day, I came up with a great idea to raise money. I walked into the hospital and rolled out a wheelchair. I took it to a busy intersection and set in the median at a traffic light. That time I wrote "Disabled Veteran" on the sign and people gave me dollar bills, fives and even tens instead of dimes and quarters. It was a great gig until several of the other street people who were not vets figured it out. Vets would never infringe on another vets' gig. Pretty soon it made all the newspapers and television news and the gig was over.

During the nights I wouldn't make it back to camp, I'd pass out on the street or on a park bench. I had no idea how many times I was locked up for public drunkenness, but it must have been well over 30. Many arrests led to a hospital stay of just a few days. Other times it was a week, or a month, or more.

I lost 70 pounds, and my skin was pasty white. I looked like a dead man with uncombed hair and a scraggly beard. I only had the clothes on my back and they were often dirty. A couple of times a week, the Salvation Army let me stay after breakfast and take a shower. Occasionally, they gave me clean clothes. Sometimes they fit, sometimes they didn't. There were times I didn't even accept the invitation to clean up as I just didn't have the motivation to do it.

Austin had an annual art street fair downtown where Samantha and I used to spend several thousand dollars every year since the profits went to local charities. It was street fair time now and I was on a corner near by. I

watched two ladies crossing the street coming toward me
and I realized one of them was Samantha. She was walking directly toward me. I turned quickly and walked to the
corner of a building. I hunched over and she passed inches
from me, but thank God she didn't recognize me.

After a couple of years at Camp Home, life had become routine. I had long passed the days of worrying
about whether I'd be able to get enough money to buy my
next drink. There were weeks I only had to work a few
days to get enough money to sustain my drinking.

My longest running gig involved selling flowers
I found in a dumpster behind a local flower shop. The
owner often discarded her older stock of cut flowers, even
if there was life left in them. I dug out the best of them and
took them to a large office building downtown. I stood
outside the doorway when the building was emptying
in the afternoon. My sign read, "Please have one." There
were hundreds of people coming and going and I accepted
any donation for a flower. I developed many regular customers. There weren't always flowers in the dumpster, but
when there were, I knew I'd make some good money that
day.

Eventually the owner of the shop figured out I was
taking the flowers and I assumed she knew I was selling
them. Sometimes when she saw me, she smiled and nodded. A good feeling came over me. I felt respected. There
were days when it looked like she discarded her better
stock just so I could have some flowers.

Once I opened the dumpster and sitting next to the
flowers was a brown shopping bag with fresh ham sandwiches and cookies in it. There was also a small envelope
with a note that said, "God blesses you," and a $20 bill.
When I turned around I saw her standing outside the back
door just a few feet from me. She smiled and went back
inside. I don't know why, but I never went back there
again—some insane pride, perhaps.

Before I knew it, the holidays rolled around again. It was a perfect fall day, the Tuesday before Thanksgiving. Everyone at Camp Home knew that panhandling on the corners the two days before Thanksgiving and again just before Christmas produced some damn good income. The few camp residents who had more or less regular jobs even took those days off because they knew they could make more on the street corners. I drank hard the night before and I was late going out to work that Tuesday.

I went to a corner I hadn't worked for some time and held up my sign. The very first car that pulled over was an old blue Buick with a dented front fender. An elderly man and his wife were in the front seat. He made eye contact, smiled and handed me some folded $5 bills. He told me he and his wife had lost their son in Vietnam. Then he smiled again and pulled away. I felt very sad and sniffled to fight back the tears. I threw down the sign and walked away.

I stepped back from the curb, put down my sign, and counted the money. There were ten $5 bills. That was the most money I'd ever been given, and the most I'd had at one time in a long time. I left the street, went to the liquor store, and bought a half gallon of Johnny Walker Red and headed to the park across the river from the Four Seasons and let the scotch work its magic.

Just as there were good days and good memories, there were some very bad ones, too. The greatest threat to the street vets were young, high school age boys who got liquored up at night, then went out looking for some homeless bum to beat up. I was lucky enough to only have this happen to me once, and that time the boys were interrupted by a patrol car that was approaching. They jumped back in their car and sped away. The patrol car eased by me and continued down the street without stopping.

Late one afternoon, I was sitting on my usual park bench nursing a bottle of vodka. That day I was trying not to think about what my life used to be like. Often, until I got good and liquored up, and frustrating as they were, those thoughts crept into my consciousness. In other words, feeling sorry for myself.

I was having one of my bad days, couldn't keep my past off my mind, and when I did get rid of those thoughts the intrusive thoughts of Nam came. Suddenly, I was startled by a fellow walking up on me. I quickly realized he was one of us. Although he was clean and his hair was combed, it was obvious he lived on the street. I don't know how, but one of us could always identify another who lived on the street. We talked a moment and I gave him a pull off my bottle.

He told me he didn't have a place to stay. He was actually passing through town from Tulsa, Oklahoma, headed south for the winter. He had worked the summer in Tulsa for an oil company and still had his last pay check in his pocket. I told him about Camp Home and invited him to stay the night there. He asked if there was any place he could cash his pay check. I told him I didn't have a lot of practice cashing checks lately, but we could try. We had another drink and headed downtown. I just happened to have had a shower that morning at the Salvation Army and I looked half presentable, at least I was clean. We tried several places with no luck and the one check cashing store in the area was closed by the time we got there.

On the way back to the camp, we passed a Kinko's print and copy store that had just opened in the area. Seeing the copy store reminded me of a intelligence class I had taken somewhere in the Army on duplicating and changing documents. We went into the Kinko's store and when we left, we had two checks; the original one for 269, and another for $2,690.

I had made a perfect replica just by cutting, pasting, and copying. I was really quite proud of myself. The next day the guy came back bragging that he had actually cashed the check at a bank without difficulty. He gave me $250; I was rich. I shared my wealth with many of the vets at Camp Home. We sent guys out for pizza, BBQ, and fried chicken. We had a party including lots of whiskey, wine, and beer. I had plenty left to sustain me for a long couple of weeks.

It wasn't long until the word got out and I was altering checks for several other vets. When they cashed them, I got 10%. There was only one time that a guy stiffed me out of my cut. Over the next couple of months I probably changed 10, 15, maybe 20 checks. I sure didn't have the kind of money I had 15 years earlier, but I had plenty for myself and my friends.

So, at 59 years old, I had life easy again and was considering getting myself an apartment and some nice furniture. It didn't quite work out the way I planned. I did get to move out of Camp Home; in fact, several of my friends left the same night. On that fateful night when it all came to a sudden end, we were all asleep, passed out, or a combination of both.

What seemed like an army of federal marshals raided Camp Home and took me, and I don't know how many others, to jail. I awoke suddenly when one of them hit me across my calves with a short bat. The pain was excruciating. Another one of the marshals almost tore my arms off cuffing me behind my back. A floodlight that looked the size of a truck was held close to my face and they were yelling like crazy men.

I was soon shackled and folded into the back of a sedan and taken to a federal holding jail in San Antonio. We were all separated and no one knew who else had been apprehended. That old jail had been built in the 1920s and I'm sure it had never been renovated. The cell I was put into was filthy — in fact, the entire jail was filthy. As enraged as I was, I found it humorous that I should be complaining about accommodations. I chuckled to myself as I looked at the commode and sink. Hell, at least I had indoor plumbing.

That holding jail, like many others around the country,

was staffed with guards who worked for a private security company. I later came to believe that the entire staff of several hundred didn't have enough combined brain power to blow their nose. They were all total imbeciles.

During the next week or so, I suffered some serious misery as my system started to live without its constant infusion of alcohol. I went through a very difficult physical and emotional sobering up. The DTs weren't the word for it. The snakes were eating me, the worms were eating me. I was so spaced out a lot of the time I didn't know who or where I was and as I'd slip in and out of consciousness. I only saw my guards. I wasn't questioned or even arraigned during that time. My food was shoved through the bars, god-awful as it was. It didn't matter because I was too sick to eat it, anyway.

Within a couple of weeks, I became so enraged I screamed at the guards and cursed them every time I saw one. I know my rage was the result of suppressed anger about anyone having authority over me. In jail, authority is absolute and I had no options. I wasn't allowed to come out of that cell for three weeks. I had a prison uniform, pants and shirt, no underwear, no socks, not even a toothbrush. Of course, I couldn't even take a shower and the only bathing I could do was in the tiny sink. So I just kept on verbally abusing the guards. Finally a federal marshal came to my cell along with a Secret Service agent.

I soon learned that the Secret Service was responsible for investigating federal bank and currency violations and those two guys wanted to question me. No matter what they said, I answered them belligerently. I reminded them I had not seen a lawyer and my rights hadn't been read to me. I also told them things they already knew, about how important I once was in the military, and how much money I once made in civilian life. It was obvious they didn't give a shit. They just kept asking me how many checks I had altered and how much money I had stolen doing it. I gave them nothing but grief. That was a major mistake.

In the early hours of the morning, I don't know which day, I awoke to a loud clanking noise. Guards were hitting the cell bars with their night sticks. The cell door swung open and six marshals all in riot gear and carrying long night sticks rushed into the cell. The damn cell was so small there was standing room only. They jerked me off my cot, rolled me onto the floor, and beat me. I'd had a couple of beatings in my life, but that one was profession-ally administered. I screamed at them and screamed at the pain they were inflicting. They just laughed at me.

One of them said, "This son of a bitch is gonna get his attitude adjusted or get killed." They didn't seem to care which. One of them had a cattle prod. It was so big, it must have held ten or more batteries.

The marshal in charge kept asking me over and over, "You gonna be nice?" I kept telling him to go to hell and calling him a fucking pig. The ordeal ended with three strategically placed blows: one broke three fingers on my left hand, one my nose, and the third hit me in the mouth and broke several teeth. I was just about out—conscious, but barely. They backed out of the cell, one at a time, as if I was going to get up and accost one of them. The last man out, the one with the prod, pushed the tip of it against my arm. It shocked me so bad I was shunted into unconscious-ness for a few seconds.

The next day a medic came to the outside of my cell. I was on my bunk, so black and blue and in so much pain I couldn't get up. He told me life would be easier if I just calmed down and cooperated. I asked for gauze for my mouth and he took some from his bag, pushed it through the bars and dropped it on the floor. He said again, "Man, if you'll just cooperate, they'll leave you alone. I replied by saying, "A giant fuck you, shithead."

I was eventually notified that I was going to be ar-raigned; the date was almost a month away. I'm sure the marshals wanted to give me all the time necessary to heal before taking me before a judge. By the day of my arraignment, I had been locked in that solitary cell for five months and I hadn't even seen a lawyer. I never saw any of the other residents of Camp Home, either.

The day of my arraignment finally arrived. The San Antonio federal holding jail was some two miles from the federal courthouse. The prisoners were transported to court by bus. Each prisoner was shackled and chained to the others for the ride to the courthouse. The guard put a steel chain around my waist and then handcuffed my hands to that chain. Then he put larger cuffs connected by a 12-inch steel chain on both ankles.

I couldn't really walk with the ankle chains, all I could do was shuffle along. After each of us was shackled and cuffed, we were chained to the man in front of us and the man behind us with two-foot chains. All the chains were padlocked for security. There were usually six men on a chain and there could be as many as ten groups of men chained together on a bus.

There was a massive thunderstorm passing through when it was time for the guards to load us onto the bus that day. But once those guys started moving us out to the bus, they didn't slow down. The guards, who were mostly federal marshals, had on rain gear. They were armed with nightsticks, shotguns, side arms, and those trusty cattle prods. They called the cattle prods adjustment sticks.

Since we didn't have rain slickers, we looked like drowned rats by the time we got on the bus. Each of us got into a seat. Then the guards locked us onto that seat. When we arrived at the courthouse, the rain had slowed but it was still coming down. I was the fourth man on the second chain to get off the bus. A very fat Mexican guy in front of me slipped as he stepped into a puddle of water directly at the bottom of the steps. He fell and when he did, he pulled me down, too. Then the two guys behind me tumbled on top of us.

The guards were going crazy. They thought we staged all this on purpose. The big Mexican guy started cursing the guards and the rest of us followed suit. The guards started poking us with the cattle prods. My wet clothes combined with lying in water, and my weakened condition were just too much for my system. I passed out and woke up back in my cell. I didn't get arraigned that day or any other day in the near future. That night I overheard two guards talking about what had happened that day. They said everyone thought for sure we had all done it on purpose. They had a big laugh talking about the electrical stimulation given to us that day.

Shortly after that incident, two federal marshals came to the outside of my cell and told me they had decided to give me some badly needed therapy. I was belligerent and said, "Just go and piss up a rope. I don't want therapy. I want a fucking lawyer."

They looked at each other. Then one said, "A couple of months of attitude therapy will help this bastard get his mind right."

"Yeah, we'll start tomorrow morning," the other one replied. "I think we can help him get over that anger."

Next morning I was introduced to the Federal Bureau of Prisons method of bringing unruly prisoners in line. "Diesel Therapy" was known throughout the bureau as the most effective method of changing a prisoner's bad behavior to good behavior.

Here's how it worked: The Bureau of Prisons had a fleet of specially-equipped diesel buses that constantly traveled the country transporting prisoners to and from various facilities. Prisoners were moved for a number of reasons including suppressing gang formation and allowing easier family visitation. Then there were those special people like me who were put on buses because they just needed attitude adjustments.

From the outside, these buses looked like any other except they were black and had no markings on them. Dark windows prevented anyone from seeing inside the bus and inside the same covering prevented anyone from seeing out. There was no light from the outside except the little that was filtering in from the front. Most were equipped with wooden bench seats that had big bolts protruding through the seats to secure the handcuffs. Only one of our hands was locked down so we could use the other to eat with and to pass the piss bucket around.

There was no schedule and no one except the guards knew where we were headed each day. Each morning we boarded the bus and were on the highway before dawn. We stopped for the night usually after dark. We were then unloaded into a county or city jail drunk tank, given a blanket, and bedded down on the concrete floor.

We would have breakfast in the jail where we slept and sometimes we got dinner when we arrived at our next destination. If we got dinner, it was an extra meal because after getting on the road each morning, the guards would hand out three brown sacks, each containing three sandwiches. There was always a piece of fruit. Sandwiches were the same every day, made from peanut butter or bologna. You could eat the sandwiches any time during the day you wanted to but, when they were gone, that was it.

I was in that bus therapy for almost three months. It was a horrible experience, but I have to admit, it did get my mind right. After that I never once gave a guard any shit.

Once the bus stopped in Olympia, Washington, and because of a maintenance problem, we were there four days. I had traveled all over the country from corner to corner. The day before we resumed our movement, a U.S. Marshal and a transfer guard came and took me out of the communal cell and moved me to a single, maximum security cell.

A marshal, an older compassionate type, stood outside my cell and said, "Sir, I spent 27 years in the Marine Corps. I served a tour in Korea and two in Vietnam. There I was shot up bad on a long range patrol out of PlayKu. I know what PTSD is and I have seen a good bit of your service record. I retired and five years ago became a Federal Marshal. Now all of that should earn me enough respect for you to listen to me. I want you to hear this good. If you feel like you're ready to treat our staff and guards with some respect, we're ready to end this bullshit traveling you've been doing. It's been over two months now, you should be getting the idea. This can go on for a long, long time. You can't win this battle, please try to change your attitude no matter how much you don't want to. Just stop this behavior."

I was ready to acquiesce and anything they wanted by that time. I was so trashed from riding that bus and eating peanut butter and bologna that I was ready to accept any offer to end it. "I'm ready, Sergeant." That's all I said. After that moment, I never gave another guard anything less than total respect.

It took another two weeks for the bus to make its circuit back to San Antonio, and the holding jail. Soon after returning to San Antonio, I was transported to the federal courthouse to be arraigned. As I was being taken down a hallway to the courtroom, a man approached me and said he was my attorney. He was the public defender assigned to my case. Less than five minutes later he walked into the courtroom with me, and I was arraigned on multiple charges of bank fraud. After the arraignment I was returned to the holding jail to await trial.

It was almost a year later that I was again taken to the courthouse and held in a small cell outside the courtroom. A different attorney met me there. He said, "I'm your new attorney. We got a great deal on a plea bargain offered from the prosecutor. They're offering you time served and no restitution or repayment of the million bucks you stole."

"Hey, man, I didn't steal a million bucks. It couldn't have even been a tenth of that. The biggest check I ever changed was under three grand."

"Okay, I'll get that straightened out," he said. "You have to sign this form and then we can go to court; we'll explain it all to the judge."

I took his pen and signed where he told me to. We entered the courtroom together. I stood in front of the judge and told him my name when he asked me to state it. On December 13, 2000, 25 months after I had been arrested, I stood before the judge as he spoke these words. "It's a shame a man like you, who is intelligent, educated, and with your background of service to this country has turned out the way I see you here today. I realize that you are probably very sick and I believe you need help. Maybe it's time we did something to help you."

"Yes, sir," I said in a low voice. I felt like a whipped dog.

The judge continued, "I'm going to sentence you to 13 months in the Federal Medical Psychiatric Hospital in Fort Worth, Texas. I further sentence you to repay the government 50% of the million dollars you stole. Restitution will be $500,000 even."

He then said, "Good luck."

When I turned to leave, my lawyer was already walking out of the courtroom. I had seen a lawyer for less then ten minutes in the entire 39 months I was incarcerated.

While I was at the FMPH, as it was referred to, I had twice monthly visits from psych interns. All things considered, it wasn't bad compared to the jails that I'd been hanging out in. The facility consisted of a large dormitory style building that housed 1,500 inmates. The guards inside didn't carry guns, and they were called counselors. The grounds were nicely kept—the inmates kept the whole place sparkling and clean. The food was good and plentiful. The inmates walked to a dining facility; the food wasn't pushed through the bars of their cells.

My very first week there, I was approached by a giant of a man who happened to be black. "What you want, boy? What you need?" he asked.

"Man, there ain't nothing I want," I responded. "I just want to do my time and get along."

He broke into a big smile and said, "I'm the supply

man. I can get you anything you want, bro. You want
whiskey? You want a woman? How 'bout some dope? I get
you some good weed."

I knew his offer was real—anything was available in
prison if an inmate had the money to buy it. The procedure
was that some family member or friend would mail money
to a post office box somewhere, and the inmate could
then purchase anything he wanted. There were hundreds
of guards coming and going every day at those facilities,
although only a small percentage were corrupt. There was
always someone who'd bring in contraband. I heard about
one group of guards in a Tennessee prison who ran a large,
well-stocked storeroom inside the jail. Inmates could actually take a push cart and shop the aisles.

"Man, I just wanna do my time and get outta here," I
said. "I ain't got no money and I ain't got nobody on the
outside to send me any." That was completely truthful, I
had burned off every relationship I ever had.

I knew that I could get whiskey if I wanted it, but
I was into my third year of being sober. I asked God to
help me resist drinking just one day at a time. I must have
prayed that prayer a hundred times a day.

Eventually, I was allowed to attend meetings at an AA
group. There were some very spiritual people involved
in that group who accepted me and as well as helped me.
There was one particular person whom I will never forget.
His name was Shorty. Shorty was 51 years old and was
serving a life sentence without parole. He lived his life sitting in a cradle in his wheelchair. His lower body had been
mangled and his legs amputated at his hips after a gun
battle, when he was 34.

Shorty was born in the hardcore crime area of East St.
Louis, Missouri. He was arrested for the first time when he
was nine and sent to a Missouri juvenile detention center.
Released at age 17, he lasted only one year on the street
until he was arrested again and sentenced to 15 years in
prison for armed robbery.

Three weeks after he was released from that sentence, Shorty, along with several other gang members, were caught in a gun battle during a drug deal gone bad. Shorty had been incarcerated for 40 of his 51 years.

Shorty was a spiritual inspiration for many people there; he had a genuine sincerity about him that made every person he touched feel as if they were the most important person on earth. During his years in prison he had earned over 300 college credit hours in theology. He spoke eloquently of God's grace. When another inmate was totally stressed out, Shorty's council was both calming and effective. I believed Shorty was doing God's work. Shorty always closed every conversation we had with this most profound statement: "You get on up out of here and you do right."

Once when he and I were visiting about my background, I told him about the military service, the education, the businesses, and wealth. He looked deep into my eyes and I felt as if he was looking into my soul. After a long silence he smiled and said, "Nelson, you been standing alone fighting the world all your life before now. Never let anything concern you again. Just let go and God will take care of all of it."

Then he let out a giant laugh and said, "I know. I know. You think God's a woman because, when you went to heaven that night in Vietnam, it was a woman who spoke to you. You think she could have been an angel of God?"

"I know now with great certainty that when those marshals took me from under the bridge that night it could only have been God's work," I said. "If that had not happened, I would have drunk myself to death long ago."

Finally, my 13 months was coming to an end. I still had no idea where I was going or what I was going to do when I was released. Even with much reassurance from my AA friends and, particularly from Shorty, I was very apprehensive about going back to living on the street.

At my last meeting there, I was expected to stand and say goodbye in front of the group. When a member asked me if I'd promise them I would never drink again I replied, "No, I have never been successful with making that promise. What I will promise, though, is that I will do my very best, one day at a time, not to."

Three days before my scheduled release, I was instructed to report to my case counselor's office. She told me I was being released to the custody of my youngest son, Earl. I didn't even know where he was living. I hadn't seen or spoken to him for over 10 years.

"Your friendly Bureau of Prisons is going to give you a first-class bus ticket to Brick, New Jersey," she said. "This fun excursion will take you five days. When you arrive in Newark next Wednesday, your son Earl will be there to pick you up. He's agreed to have you released into his supervision. I spoke with him this morning and he's arranging a place for you to live until you get settled. We're going to call him in 15 minutes. He's waiting at his office for our call."

The next few minutes were the most uncomfortable minutes that I'd spent in many days. The counselor had me wait outside her door in the hallway until it was time to make the call. Those 15 minutes seemed like hours. Finally, she summoned me back into her office and handed me the phone. My voice was broken and weak, higher than normal, when I said, "Hello, this is Nelson."

So on Jan. 13, 2003 with $50 and a bus ticket in my pocket, I was dropped off at the Greyhound bus terminal in Fort Worth, Texas by an unmarked federal transport van. The day was appropriately special for my release.

God had made every possible thing perfect for that day. The temperature was about 75 and warming. The sun was a round orange globe rising on the sky. I stepped down to the ground, held out my hands, and the guard removed the handcuffs. As I started to move toward the terminal door, I said "thank you, Edith, for this beautiful day."

When he heard me, he said, "Who's Edith?"

Edith is my God, God's a woman you know." He shook his head and headed out.

I left prison, wearing a t-shirt, shorts, and used sneakers. The 2,000-mile trip across the country took five days. The $50 lasted the entire trip because I passed on the gourmet meals and opted for hot dogs and hamburgers instead. I didn't complain because that bus trip was a hell of a whole lot better than the last bus trip I had taken.

I arrived in Newark at 3:00 in the morning. My son, Earl, was due to pick me up at noon. During the trip, I had spent my time sleeping in bus stations while I waited to board my next bus. But when I arrived at my destination in Newark, I sure as hell wasn't going to close my eyes. I soon learned that the local folks in Newark were not the take-a-stranger-home-to-dinner type of people. Of all the places I had ever been in my life, including prison, Newark was the scariest.

By noon, when Earl hadn't arrived, my anxiety level was off the scale. Would I recognize him? Would he recognize me? I'd ventured outside several times that morning, but I didn't stay out very long. The temperature in Newark was a bit different from that of Fort Worth; it was 22 degrees and snowing.

Soon it was 1:15, and I was wondering if it had all been a mistake. No, he'd be along. I just had to get hold of myself. By 3:00, I was a basket case. I had lost all track of reality and was starting to make plans for how I was going to get through my new mess. I tried to remember what Shorty had told me. "You haven't found God. God has found you; now let him handle it."

Just then a tall, good looking, well-dressed guy walked up to me. I thought, what does this guy want. He said, "Hi, Pop. Sorry I'm so late, but the parkway was a parking lot with the snow and all. I think half the traffic in New Jersey is out there playing bumper cars in the snow. Wrecks everywhere. You ready to go?"

A feeling of pride flooded over me as I looked over this great looking man. I was glad he recognized me as I never would have recognized him. "Yes, I'm ready. And I want to thank you for your help. I'll try to be as little trouble to you as possible," I replied.

"No trouble. You don't know how long I've waited for this moment. Let's get out of here. We have 60 miles to go. It may take us all night to get home. I just hope they don't close the highway on us."

I didn't care if it took all of two nights, I just wanted to learn about his life and that ride gave me the time to do it. He told me he had rented me a little apartment on a bus route, just a few blocks from a shopping center with a large grocery store. Earl had come to New Jersey while he was in the Air Force. When his enlistment ended, he became a professional financial planner. It was obvious he was quite successful.

I also learned that I was a grandfather as he had an eleven-year-old son. Earl told me that Nathan, his older brother, was a bad alcoholic. Nate, who was deaf, had recently come to live with Earl after his wife had divorced him and taken their two children. Earl had helped him get sober. The plan was to help him get a job and become self supporting again.

By the time we arrived at my new apartment, it was 7:00 and the snow had let up. We were pretty well talked out by then and I could tell Earl wanted to get home. He insisted I take some money. He told me where the grocery store was and offered to drive me there. He had purchased warm clothes, a coat, and high top boots for me. "I'll walk," I said. "I need to clear my head." I changed into the warm clothes he'd purchased for me.

As I approached the shopping center, I realized just how cold the air was. I was impressed that the parking lot had been plowed and the walkways were shoveled clean of snow. I noticed that next door to the grocery store was a liquor store. As I recognized it and came close, my heart started to race. I had to pass it to get to the grocery store.

My first thought was that I'd been sober for over three years. My second was that I could get a bottle of vodka and no one would ever know the difference. I stood in front of that liquor store and watched the people inside. It wasn't fair that normal people could drink normally. It wasn't fair that I couldn't. Or could I? All that time in prison I hadn't even tried again to see if I could have some liquor and then stop. I walked on past the grocery store and to the end of the shopping center. I was cold and I knew a drink or two would warm me and that was a good reason to buy a bottle.

I slowly walked back, opened the door and went into the store. The shelves were full. There was a lady checking out with her bottle of bourbon. I went down the aisle to the vodka. I stood there, waited for a couple seconds, and then lifted a bottle of vodka off the shelf. I turned and walked to the front of the store. By now there were three people in line to check out. I thought about what I was getting ready to do.

Like any good alcoholic, I was convinced that I could have just one or even a few and then stop. Suppose I couldn't? What would happen the next day, and the next day, and the next day? Would I be back on the street? How would I explain to Earl that I bought a bottle and tried to have just a few but I couldn't stop?

At that point I thought to myself. "This would be my last bottle. Finish this one and I'll never buy another one. I decided to walk next door to the grocery store first. There were just a few people shopping. I was only going to get some sandwich meat, bread and mustard. I didn't know why I had taken a shopping cart. I looked at my three items in the cart and thought about how glad I was that I had put the vodka back on the shelf until after I bought the groceries.

I walked every aisle in that grocery store, trying to stall the inevitable. I just couldn't stop thinking about how that first drink would taste, how warm it would feel going down. My plan was that after I checked out of the grocery store, I'd go next door, get my bottle and go back to the apartment. I'd control it this time.

When I got to the front of the store there was only one man in the quick checkout line. That was good. I wanted to hurry and get that drink. I wouldn't wait until I got back to the apartment, I'd have one on the side of the store. The one guy in front of me was in no hurry. He was talking to the checker and loading his groceries on the counter. They obviously knew each other.

"How goes it in this cold?" the checker asked him.

His reply caught me totally unprepared. "Man, I'm about to freeze. I'm just trying to stay warm and take it one day at a time."

"One day at a time's the only way," the checker said, as he looked past his customer and made eye contact with me.

I looked at him for a moment, then at the other guy and I dropped my eyes to the floor. When I looked up again they were both looking at me. I felt a tear slide down my cheek as the fellow checking said, "You're in the AA program, aren't you?"

Tears immediately started streaming down my face and I started crying uncontrollably. "God, I want to be, so bad." Then I did something very unlike me; I confessed. "I'm about to have a drink," I said.

"Don't do it, man, just don't have that first one," the checker said. "Go with my buddy, here. I get off in 30 minutes. We'll go to a meeting."

In an hour I was sitting in an AA meeting. I stood up and heard myself saying, "My name is Nelson and I'm an alcoholic."

Epilogue

It is 2010, I'm quite old now, and I live in New Jersey with that lady who took me to Don Dale's grave. She is the finest person I ever met on the face of the earth. She is also my best friend. She has been a psych nurse and has worked with PTSD veterans on locked wards for many years. Even in spite of all my horrible past, she cares for me like I am the only person in her life. She gives me all that any human being could ask of another, total unconditional love.

My first thought every single morning when I awake is to honor my relationship with her. She is truly my soulmate.

My son, Earl, and I have become very close and we are able to meet frequently and have great conversations; there is much laughter between us.

I have been without a drink for nine years and still have to work at sobriety every day, one day at a time. Since I was released from prison in January 2004, I have completed another 28-day inpatient alcohol recovery program and a 45-day PTSD recovery program at the VA hospital in New Jersey. This time I finally accepted that I have PTSD. I told of my death experience in Nam. I still meet with the VA psychiatrist every month and take medication as prescribed to help me cope with the PTSD. The demons still come, but not so frequently.

I work to keep my life simple. I attend several AA meetings each week and work with new people who are coming into the AA program, trying to get and stay sober. I have had many failures as many of these people go back to their drinking. I have also had some miraculous recoveries.

Several times during each day I stop and say the prayer that keeps me centered. I first prayed this prayer in the Republic of South Vietnam. I've been praying it now for over 45 years.

MY DAILY PRAYER

Thank you, God, for this beautiful day.

You have made it for me and provided it to me; I may do with this day anything that I wish, I can be happy or sad. Please help me be happy.

Please help me to think light.

To learn by listening.

Remind me to give a compliment.

Help me maintain my discipline.

Help me maintain my perspective.

And most of all Lord keep me from judgment of any thing or person.

AMEN

I HAVE FINALLY FOUND PEACE OF MIND.

Profits from the sale of this book are used to reach out to those who are psychologically wounded, but will not seek help.

If you are that someone or you know someone who just wants to talk about it, please contact me. Remain anonymous if you wish.

Nelson is available for speaking engagements and will joint venture with interested organizations.

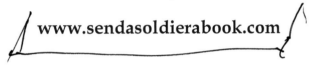

www.sendasoldierabook.com

Made in the USA
Charleston, SC
17 June 2013